Crime, Culture and the Media

Crime, Culture and
the Media

Eamonn Carrabine

polity

First published in 2008 by Polity Press
Reprinted 2009, 2011

Polity Press
65 Bridge Street
Cambridge CB2 1UR, UK

Polity Press
350 Main Street
Malden, MA 02148, USA

ISBN-13: 978-0-7456-3465-4
ISBN-13: 978-0-7456-3466-1(pb)

A catalogue record for this book is available from the British Library.

Typeset in 10.5 on 12 pt Plantin
by Servis Filmsetting Ltd, Stockport, Cheshire
Printed and bound in Great Britain by the MPG Books Group

For further information on Polity, visit our website: www.politybooks.com

Contents

		page
Acknowledgements		vi
Introduction		1
Part I	Audiences	17
1	Media Effects	19
2	Fearing Crime	39
3	Making Meaning	57
Part II	Representations	77
4	The Print Revolution	79
5	Entertaining the Nation	99
6	Telling Stories	119
Part III	Industries	139
7	Producing the News	141
8	Revisiting Moral Panics	161
Conclusion		181
Notes		189
References		197
Index		225

Acknowledgements

As always, a large number of people have helped in the writing of this book. Rachel Kerr initially invited me to contribute to the new 'Crime and Society' series, then Emma Longstaff and Jonathan Skerrett at Polity have waited patiently for the manuscript and guided it through to completion. Part of the book was written during a four-month period of study leave financed by the Research Promotion Fund administered at the University of Essex, for which I am grateful. I would also like to thank my colleagues in the Department of Sociology who took on extra duties during this period, providing support and generous help. An early version of chapter 8 was presented at the Department's inaugural research conference and a later version was presented at the Centre of Criminology, University of Oxford, in November 2007; comments from colleagues at both these events helped improve the ideas appearing here.

Over the years students taking my courses on the *Criminological Imagination* and *Crime, Media, and Culture* have all contributed to the work by challenging, enthusing and thinking through the material to provide fresh insights. Chrissie Rogers kindly read the manuscript and has continually offered encouragement, making the book a better one in the process. Thanks are also due to Polity's anonymous reviewers for providing constructive criticism and thoughtful advice on the initial proposal and final text. The staff at the Albert Sloman Library, University of Essex, and Colchester Library helped in accessing a number of the sources used in the book. Finally, on a personal note I would like to thank Chrissie and Sherrie for continuing to make life exciting and fun.

Introduction

The relationships between crime and the media are many and complex. Indeed the topic has been central to a range of disciplines: criminology, psychology, sociology, cultural and media studies have each contributed distinctive perspectives on how we should understand the issues at stake. Initially attention centred on cinema, radio and television, before turning to computer games and music videos as these later technologies took hold, while the Internet is now attracting much commentary for the ways in which it facilitates new kinds of criminal activity (like hacking, spamming, malicious software and spyware) as well as enabling many old crimes (such as fraud, stalking, smuggling, money laundering and certain kinds of pornography) to flourish.

In criminology at least three distinctive approaches have developed. One assesses whether the media through violent depictions of crime contagiously cause criminal conduct in real life – through imitation, suggestion and identification, as in 'copy cat' crime, or more subtly through sensitization (by shaping expectations of how to act in certain situations). A second examines how the news media create moral panics (Cohen, 1972; Hall *et al.*, 1978) thereby provoking public fear of crime. The third and more recent development attends to a broader consideration of how crime and punishment have been consumed (Carrabine *et al.*, 2002), imagined (Young, 1996) and represented (Sparks, 1992) in popular culture. Each of these approaches tackles important issues and will be covered in what follows. However, the tendency in criminology has been to focus on individual media and their specific impacts on particular emotional states (whether this is increased aggression or fear). Instead, this book offers an account of crime stories in the media that is more interested in their social character: the ways they are produced, circulated and read.

Investigating the ways in which the press and broadcast news report crime is now an established field in criminology and owes much to the pioneering work of figures like Stan Cohen, Stuart Hall and Jock Young who have been concerned with how the media ideologically distort the reality of crime. Robert Reiner (2007:303–15) has provided an extensive review of the vast literature analysing media content and it is clear that crime stories are, and always have been, prominent in all parts of the media. Moreover, the pattern of crime in the news tends to concentrate overwhelmingly on violent and especially sex crimes. A major claim of these studies is that the media tend to exaggerate the likelihood that one might be a victim of crime. For instance, Williams and Dickinson (1993:40) found that in one month in 1989, 65 per cent of British newspaper stories dealt with personal violent crime, which they compare to the British Crime Survey's (Mayhew, 1989) finding that only 6 per cent of crime involves violence. Studies of the provincial press indicate similar forms of exaggeration – Smith (1984:290) observed that offences such as robbery and assault accounted for less than 6 per cent of known crimes in Birmingham, but occupied 52.7 per cent of the space devoted to crime stories in the local press. Similarly a content analysis of Scottish newspapers over a one-month period found that 'crimes involving violence and crimes involving sex together constituted 2.4 per cent of real incidence yet 45.8 per cent of newspaper coverage' (Ditton and Duffy, 1983:164).

There is little doubt that the mass media are selective over the kinds of crimes, criminals and circumstances they report, but Richard Ericson (1991) not only wonders why this should come as a surprise to these researchers but also queries why anyone would expect the cultural products of the mass media to reflect the social reality of crime. He is thus critical of studies that compare media representations of crime with officially recorded statistics. As he explains, police statistics do not mirror the reality of crime but are themselves 'cultural, legal and social constructs produced by the police for organizational purposes' so that what is presented is one symbolically constructed reality compared to another (Ericson, 1991:220). His crucial question then is why do media organizations focus on particular events and privilege particular classifications and interpretations of these events over others? Answering this calls for an understanding of how institutions make the news and interact with events that occur in an uncertain world.

One of the earliest and most influential books making this point is Stan Cohen and Jock Young's (1973) edited collection, *The*

Manufacture of News: Deviance, Social Problems and the Mass Media, which draws together a number of essays on the dynamics of news production processes and has set the parameters of much subsequent debate. Here they identify two polarized traditions in media research. One they define as a 'Mass Manipulative model' which regards the public as 'an atomized mass, passive receptacles of messages originating from a monolithic and powerful source' (Cohen and Young, 1973b:10). Adherents of the political Left argue that the media serve the powerful, stifle dissent and reinforce dominant views, whereas Conservatives condemn the role of the media in glamorizing wrongdoing, undermining morality and encouraging permissiveness. In either case the media are understood to be all-powerful and harmful.

The contrasting 'Commercial Laissez-Faire model' developed largely as a critique of the manipulative picture and its conspiratorial implications – unsurprisingly it is the view most often held by those who work in the industry itself (editors, journalists and sources) and they point to the diversity of opinions found in the media to challenge charges of manipulation. In this more pluralistic perspective the effects of the media 'are seen as less awesome than in the Manipulative model: people's opinions might be reinforced, but rarely changed in an opposite direction and moreover the primal source of attitude formation and change is personal experience and face-to-face contact' (Cohen and Young, 1973b:11). I draw attention to their distinction in these opening remarks because they go on to describe their fleeting involvement in the landmark *Oz* obscenity trial held in 1972 over the countercultural magazine, so as to demonstrate some of the complexities behind these standard approaches to media power, and then describe some of the subsequent debates surrounding pornography to introduce some of the central issues covered in the book.

At the *Oz* trial the different sides took position:

Here the one side was arguing that the contents of the particular edition of the magazine would corrupt its younger readers. Advertisements for homosexual contacts, features presenting a tolerant attitude towards certain forms of drug use, cartoons depicting school authority in an obscene and derogatory way, articles and advertisements drawing attention to sexual deviation – all would have a harmful effect on values and behaviour. The opposed position drew attention to the selective nature of the audience (not everyone would buy the magazine) and the unlikelihood that the objectionable messages would actually have any effect on individuals not already committed toward the particular line of thought. (Cohen and Young, 1973b:339)

Indeed, Cohen and Taylor were approached as potential witnesses for the defence. They had impeccable radical credential themselves and would easily have found fault with the prosecution's case.

But doubts soon surfaced following an initial briefing with the defence lawyers. As they go on to explain:

> We were being asked to support an extreme laissez-faire model which we knew in this case to be patently absurd. Clearly the publishers and editors of *Oz had* intended to change people's values and opinions, otherwise why produce the magazine at all? (ibid., emphasis in original)

Once the defence lawyers saw they were unable to overcome their misgivings, Cohen and Taylor soon found themselves dropped from the courtroom line-up. Their concerns remain important, for while the trial has now passed into history the issues posed by media effects, state censorship and liberal tolerance continue to structure much debate – as the controversies surrounding pornography exemplify.

The Politics of Pornography

From the 1970s onwards there has been much debate within and beyond feminism over the question of pornography. Of course, the production of sexually explicit imagery is as old as human history and the Victorian era, which is often thought to have had a particularly repressive attitude towards sexuality, actually witnessed a thriving industry around pornography (Sigel, 2002). The permissiveness of the twentieth century can be traced from the early silent 'stag' cinema through to magazines like *Playboy*, *Mayfair* and *Penthouse* and now the Internet, where one recent estimate has calculated that there are around 4.2 million pornographic websites (12 per cent of all sites), with over 372 million pornographic pages (Yar, 2006:107). Up until the 1970s the main objection to pornography focused on its power to deprave and corrupt decent moral and aesthetic standards that were enshrined in obscenity legislation (and had brought about the *Oz* trial, among other things). But the emergence of a strong feminist movement at this time and its uneasy alliance with the conservative moral critique of pornography provided a new radical political condemnation, this one emphasizing how it harmed women.

The slogan 'pornography is the theory and rape is the practice' (Morgan, 1980) caught the mood of the new feminist radicalism. By exposing how pornography is central to women's oppression the conventional lines drawn between the 'decent' and 'indecent', 'family viewing' and the 'obscene', 'clean' and 'smutty' images were all challenged. At the same time campaigns were launched opposing 'the irrelevant use of women's bodies in advertising, and against the cultural stereotypes which insisted that women must always be young, slender, blonde and white if they were to be considered beautiful' (Wilson, 1992:16–17). The leading representatives of this feminist radicalism included Andrea Dworkin, Susan Griffin and Catherine MacKinnon, who argued that pornography is, in itself, violence and circulates in a broader cultural climate where 'acts of sexual hostility directed against women are not only tolerated but ideologically encouraged' (Brownmiller, 1976:395).

The argument is that men have colonized female sexuality to gain power and use this power to maintain domination through a rule of terror. The connection drawn between sex and violence is that male power works through the depersonalization, objectification and degradation of women. Their apocalyptic critique is not so much in terms of there being a direct causal connection between media representations and violent behaviour, but that pornography helps to sustain a culture where the violent and sexual exploitation of women is the norm. Nevertheless, the kind of pornography they allude to is of the highly extreme kind that depicts violence against women and children – which most people would find wholly abhorrent – and described as 'Dachau brought into the bedroom and celebrated' (cited in Segal, 1992:7). Even where pornography does not directly involve representations of violence (and much of it does not), the argument is that women are still objectified and reduced to sex objects for the gratification of men while placing women in relations of inferiority – existing purely to service male desires.

This strand of radical feminism has proven to be highly influential and has entered into controversial alliances with neo-conservatives to denounce pornography by generating a new form of 'legal moralism'. This has been particularly successful in the United States, where campaigners like Andrea Dworkin have proposed legislation censoring anything deemed to be 'offensive' as a violation of women's civil rights (Watney, 1997:62). Other feminists have pointed to the problems and contradictions inherent to the anti-pornography position. Elizabeth Wilson (1992) has accused the movement of fundamentalism: intolerance, denial, preacher-style harangues, living life through repressive rules, and above all else a profound suspicion of sexuality. Moreover, it has been argued that anti-pornography feminism was based on an unhelpful distinction between male sexuality as violent and lustful and female sexuality as gentle and tender, which upholds the 'notion that women are victims of sex and that sex is degrading to women but not to men' (Turley, 1986:89). The author Angela Carter (1979a:37) was one of the earliest to put 'pornography in the service of women' while others have sought to show how the guilty pleasures derived from 'bawdy traditions may embody a masculine view of the world, but they may also mock and undermine it' (Attwood, 2002:94).

One of the problems facing the feminist left is the question of how far to take censorship while preserving democratic freedoms, since anti-pornography campaigns have attracted strong criticism from gay and lesbian groups because such legal regulation can easily be extended into other areas of social life. Of course, today much public concern is focused on the Internet where the problems of children viewing obscene imagery and the harms posed by child pornography itself dominate attention. Criminologists recognize that there are many difficult moral questions surrounding pornography, but would emphasize that there are different kinds of content found on websites and its varying legal status:

> The majority of internet based pornography is adult consensual pornography, whether it is soft-core sexual imagery or even hard-core imagery depicting penetration and other sexual acts. Although subject to moral strictures, its consensual nature leaves it largely non-contentious within most western jurisdictions, and with some caveats, within the boundaries of law. Even 'extreme' pornographic materials depicting acts on the borders of consensuality are unlikely to be prosecuted so long as the acts are consensual . . . It is only where there is clear evidence of violence against one or more parties by the other that an investigation may take place, and then usually only after a formal complaint has been made to the police. (Wall, 2007:107–8)

However, it is the fear that children will be unwittingly exposed to such material that causes much alarm and has led to the growth of Internet filtering software that is at best only partially effective in blocking access to explicit content – suggesting that there are no easy technological or legislative remedies here given the supply of and demand for illicit material.

When considering the problems posed by on-line child pornography it is important to recognize that the abuse is not new and there is a long history of commercial production (O'Toole, 1998), but that the Internet has transformed the ways it is produced, distributed and consumed (O'Donnell and Milner, 2007). It also forces criminologists to rethink the ways social problems are constructed, as the following admission from one of the leading studies on the subject makes clear:

> Despite activists' claims to the contrary, child porn is extremely difficult to obtain through non-electronic means and has been so for twenty years, so I believed it was equally rare on the Web. I was wrong. It is a substantial presence, and much of the material out there is worse than most of us can imagine, in terms of the types of activity depicted and the ages of the children portrayed. This is not just a case of soft-core pictures of precociously seductive fifteen-year-olds. Having spent a decade arguing that various social menaces were vastly overblown – that serial killers and molestors did not lurk behind every tree, nor pedophile priests in every rectory – I now found myself in the disconcerting position of seeking to *raise* public concern about a quite authentic problem that has been neglected. (Jenkins, 2002:9, emphasis in original)

Philip Jenkins's overall position has been one that draws attention to the socially constructed nature of reality – how problems become defined and created by assorted claims makers (victims, politicians, professionals, social movements and the media) each attempting to develop frames of understanding that categorize troubling events. As he explains, there are many versions of social constructionism. The 'strict' constructionist is not especially interested in the truth or accuracy of a problem, but instead concentrates on the collective work involved in claims making (with sociology being one further voice pressing definitional claims on the world). In contrast, the 'contextual' constructionist adopts a more moderate line and is not simply concerned with debunking but recognizes that there is a real, plausible problem out there. The questions then are why some issues become perceived as social problems in certain times and places (but not others) and what methods are used to establish claims (Jenkins, 1998:5). Examining the changing frames in which a problem is understood can capture how issues are stirred up through the mass media as well as showing why some issues are not taken seriously enough. These are issues explored in some detail over the following chapters.

Crime, Entertainment and Representation

In this book I also explore why wrongdoing becomes an occasion for storytelling. Narratives that claim to describe, respond to or displace crises in the moral order are always structured by social conflict (between heroes and villains, good and evil, self and other, fate and

choice, home and abroad among others). Crime stories, even when
they are explicitly and obviously intended to uphold the authority of
the law, can appeal to forbidden desires as political warnings are
played out in uneven fields of cultural struggle. Moreover, the narrative structure itself is often devoted to the task of unmasking facades
and resolving mystery. The reader of detective fiction soon learns that
appearances are not what they seem and downmarket newspaper
editors are well aware of how sex sells – from the sexualization of
mundane events, through the detailing of celebrity sex scandals, to the
salacious reporting of violent sexual crime.

It has been argued that crime stories are universally popular as they
address the universal problem of human mortality:

> Millions are fascinated daily by reports about crime and by crime
> stories. They flock to films whose two main themes are crime and mis-
> fortune. This interest and this fascination are not merely the expression
> of bad taste and a craving for scandal, but correspond to a deep yearn-
> ing for the dramatization of the ultimate thing in human life, namely life
> and death, through crime and punishment, struggle between man and
> nature. (Fromm, cited in Mandel, 1984:9)

The point here is that rather than dismiss the enduring popular fascination with crime and punishment we must seek to understand it.

Even though their task may well be clarifying and sharpening the
normal boundaries of daily life, stories of transgression are absolutely
central to every society's imaginary origins. For instance, in Greek
mythology Prometheus stole from the gods the gift of fire and in retribution Zeus created the first woman, Pandora, to seduce and harm
mankind. A more familiar account of the 'Fall of Man' is to be found
in Genesis which tells how the first man and woman, Adam and Eve,
succumb to temptation and are expelled from paradise. The birth of
the novel in the eighteenth century is utterly dependent on the individual deviance of key protagonists. One example is *Moll Flanders*
(1722), which is widely regarded as one of the first English novels. It
vividly describes 'midnight' Moll's outlaw adventures and struggles to
escape the constraints of identity before ultimately repenting in
Newgate prison to begin a new life as a reformed penitent. Indeed,
the developing literary form is so rich in wayward figures that it has
been claimed that 'the whole project of the novel, its very theoretical
and structural assumptions, were in some sense criminal in nature'
(Davis, 1983:123). Since the plots include deeds which breach conventional codes of normality the novels were castigated for morally

corrupting readers. These concerns echoed earlier attacks by the great and the good on the corpse-strewn stages of Elizabethan playhouses, which were condemned for inciting the unruly passions of audiences.

Consequently, it is important to recognize that worries over the harmful effects of popular culture has been a recurring theme since at least the sixteenth century and continues in the current anxieties surrounding video nasties, computer games and Internet pornography. Each development in media technology has been accompanied by much alarm over the dire consequences of exposure to this or that medium. From the earliest days of the printing press to cyberspace chat rooms there have been persistent concerns raised over the criminogenic effects of the media. Yet at the same time the media are fascinated with crime. This takes many diverse forms, whether as 'entertainment' in such staples as cop shows, crime novels, 'true crime' stories and films or as 'news' in television documentaries, newspaper articles and broadcast bulletins, while the rapid growth in 'reality TV' over the last decade has further blurred the boundaries between fact, fiction and entertainment. Under this kind of postmodern 'hyperreality' it has been argued that the boundary separating reality from its representation has 'imploded', leaving images with no real-world referents (Baudrillard, 1988). However, the boundaries between fact and fiction have always been fairly fluid. For instance, during the sixteenth and seventeenth centuries both novels and news reports were seen as neither entirely factual nor clearly fictional (Davis, 1980, 1983). We will see in chapter 6 that for what we now regard as a news story to appear in the press during the eighteenth century it would frequently have to be cast in the form of fiction. Some would say little has changed!

It should be clear from these opening remarks that this book will argue that history matters. In the most obvious sense, current representations of crime in the media bear traces of earlier codes and practices. Recognizing this past enables a more sophisticated understanding of the present – especially since many current controversies have much longer histories than is usually acknowledged. This is not to suggest a long line of steady continuity stretching back from the earliest forms of oral, face-to-face storytelling to the latest mediated technology that encompasses the lives of millions around the world. Instead, the argument is that understanding changing forms of representation requires an attention to how developments in communication media are themselves integral to the formation of modern societies. As John Thompson (1995:4) puts it, once 'individuals use communication media, they enter into forms of interaction which differ in certain respects from the type of face-to-face interaction

which characterizes most encounters of daily life'. These processes
have had important consequences, which I now briefly introduce.

Media, Spectacle and Amusement

It is often said that we live in a media-saturated world. In attempting
to grasp the profundity of this now familiar observation characterizations like information age, information society or even information
revolution (to draw parallels with the earlier seismic consequences of
the industrial revolution) have been used to describe this apparently
recent transformation. Yet information is only part of the story.
Likewise, the tendency to refer to 'the media' in the singular obscures
the diversity of media forms (film, television, magazines, newspapers,
the Internet, books and so on) that surround us. The word media
is the plural of medium, which was initially used to refer to the materials used for communication (Briggs and Burke, 2005:5). From the
papyrus, clay and stone of the ancient world to the plastic, metal and
wire of modern media it is clear that the technologies of communication have an immense influence, ranging from the most inner dimensions of personal experience to the organization of power, political
practice and social control.

Although the current extent of media saturation is quite unprecedented it is something with which many of us are very familiar and
find commonplace. Todd Gitlin describes this phenomenon well:

> The flow of images and sounds through the households of the rich
> world, and the richer parts of the poor world, seems unremarkable
> today. Only a visitor from an earlier century or an impoverished country
> could be startled by the fact that life is now played out against a shim-
> mering multitude of images and sounds, emanating from television,
> videotapes, videodiscs, video games, VCRs, computer screens, digital
> displays of all sorts, always in flux, chosen partly at will, partly by whim,
> supplemented by words, numbers, symbols, phrases, fragments, all
> passing through screens that in a single minute can display more pic-
> tures than a prosperous seventeenth-century Dutch household con-
> tained over several lifetimes, portraying in one day more individuals
> than the Dutch burgher would have beheld in the course of years, and
> in one week more bits of what we have come to call 'information' than
> all the books in all the households in Vermeer's Delft. (Gitlin, 2002:14)

Indeed, one of the themes running through this book is that the media
form part of the fabric of everyday life in ways that are both routinely

ordinary and exceptionally complex. In certain respects it is the taken-for-granted and habitual character of much media consumption that is one of the most striking features of contemporary experience. It is this 'media drenching of ordinary life' that is one of the core processes driving social change (Longhurst, 2007a:102) and will be explored in what follows.

At the same time the media contribute to the 'society of the spectacle' (Debord, 1967/77), organized around the immense consumption of images, relentless array of commodities and dizzying profusion of sensations in crucial ways. Guy Debord's critical understanding of the spectacle as a subjugating force that entrances human subjects is one that is part of a long tradition. It maintains that the mass media are a powerful force producing conformity and passivity among undiscriminating audiences. As an argument this takes many different guises. For example, Neil Postman (1986) contends that we are *Amusing Ourselves to Death* through tranquillizing entertainment forms that trivialize issues of importance. Postman's (1986) target is television, which he compares unfavourably with the medium of print. The contrast is based on the view that the linear sequencing of printed words encourages rational habits of mind, which is firmly rooted in traditions of political debate, rhetorical devices and oratory performances that shaped the public sphere from antiquity to well into the nineteenth century. For Postman, television is not simply an idle source of amusement but a harmful medium that is destroying democracy by transforming all on it into show business, turning the banal into the serious and promoting incoherence over informed debate.

This nostalgic privileging of some forms of communication over others is a persistent theme in many of the critical positions on the media, while the tendency to reduce the message to the medium is ultimately a sophisticated form of technological determinism. The problem with such determinism is that each medium is held to mould our senses so completely that certain social outcomes become inevitable and this thereby oversimplifies complex processes. Nevertheless, the most important point to be made here is that we must be alert to the specificity of media – how there are key differences between oral, print, radio and television technologies that encourage distinctive social practices. For instance, television is primarily a domestic medium and the programming largely addresses a family audience, whereas the cinema is designed to be a public event and continues to be a kind of theatre offering a single, complete performance (Ellis, 1982). It must be emphasized that this is not an argument for isolating the study of different types of media. Instead, this book will advocate an approach that integrates the diverse media forms and situates them in the cultural contexts in which they have emerged, evolved and transformed social life.

Conceptual Framework

As will become clear the conceptual approach used in the book develops Stuart Hall's (1980b/2003) arguments on 'Encoding/Decoding', which were originally published in 1973. Hall emphasized that the production and consumption of media messages are structurally determined by a range of powerful influences (including the medium used, discursive conventions and institutional constraints), and highlighted the cultural struggle over meaning among audiences (which he defines as 'preferred', 'negotiated' and 'oppositional' positions that viewers can adopt in relation to a media text). This approach has been extended over the last couple of decades into a 'production-text-consumption' framework and versions of it can be found in studies of television (Abercrombie, 1996), music (Longhurst, 2007b), film (Turner, 2001) and media research methodologies (Bertrand and Hughes, 2005). Likewise this book is divided into three parts: audiences, representations and industries. The strength of this way of organizing the argument is that it demonstrates how media texts are forms of representation that are commercially produced commodities, which circulate as culturally meaningful objects and are actively interpreted by audiences in diverse settings. Its main weakness is that it tends to keep the analyses of producer, text and consumer artificially distinct from each other when in fact the three domains are interrelated in a multi-faceted 'circuit of culture' (du Gay *et al.*, 1997). However, much of the textbook commentary implies that the various approaches can be simply added together to form a satisfactory resolution of the problem. Yet as this book will reveal, there are some fundamental differences over how the same domain ought to be approached – undermining any crude synthesis of incompatible positions.

A further difficulty is that many of the studies restrict themselves to a specific medium rather than covering the mediation of social relations as a whole and consequently they ignore the diversity of media forms themselves. In contrast, this book examines different types of media (including print, television, film and the Internet) and process (producing, regulating, viewing, interacting and so on) to explore connections across issues that are often isolated and treated separately.

Of course, the focus here is on stories of crime and punishment, which remain a strong current among many in the flow of media narratives circulating around the world. Crime has been found to be more frequent than any other category of news item for every medium at all market levels (Cumberbatch *et al.*, 1995:7). This is not even counting the fictional dramatizations that fill television schedules, cinema screens and bookshop shelves. Having said a little about the overall approach adopted in the book I now outline the specific chapter contents to make the logic clearer.

The book begins with the audience and the debates surrounding media 'effects'. Many of the studies, particularly in the United States, were informed by the empiricist assumptions of behavioural psychology and used quantitative research methods (of the large-scale survey or laboratory experiment) to produce decidedly mixed, if not contradictory, results. Although more sophisticated approaches have developed, this mass communications tradition remains allied to a linear model of communication, which will be contrasted with more semiotic understandings of meaning exchange (between readers, texts and institutions) that had their origins in European cultural theory. At the same time a much more critical criminology developed among Anglo-American scholars that was profoundly influenced by Marxism and a more sceptical sociology of deviance that sought to expose how crime is socially constructed. In doing so critical criminology gave birth to that much-used and -abused concept of moral panic that we will encounter many times in this book. The arguments outlined in the next chapter are the formative positions that continue to shape contemporary disputes.

One response to these developments was the turn to fear of crime, which is now a significant sub-discipline in criminology and is covered in chapter 2. Problems soon surfaced though and commentators complained that the conventional approaches could not grasp the emotional complexity of fear nor situate these experiences in broader social context. Feminists were early critics and argued that the conceptual thinking and methodological preferences of orthodox criminology failed to comprehend women's encounters with sexual danger (Stanko, 1988) while advocating more nuanced understandings of fear, reason and emotion (Walklate, 1998). But fear is only part of the story and chapter 3 addresses processes of desire at work in media audiences, much neglected in criminological treatments of the area. Characterizations of a passive, easily manipulated mass audience were challenged from two directions. One was influenced by psychoanalytic film theory and Marxist understandings of ideological structures, which came to be associated with extreme forms of textual determinism, but nevertheless pointed to hidden desires in the spectator. In contrast, ethnographic studies of television audiences attempted to convey the active, conscious ways in which viewers interpret the medium in domestic settings. The tensions between these two approaches are not easily resolved and in key respects echo the problems identified above with the 'Mass Manipulation model' and more pluralistic 'Laissez-Faire model' of the media effects debate reappearing in this later work.

The second part of the book turns to the texts themselves and chapter 4 describes the impact of the print revolution on representations of crime from 1500 to 1800. Here the intention is to provide a sense of the rich diversity of criminal narratives found in the early modern period. It is important to recognize the complexity of the cultural mix here, where oral, literate and visual forms of communication intermingle and co-exist, while also charting the rise of the public sphere and Enlightenment thinking. Chapter 5 takes the story up to the present day and the emergence in the nineteenth century of what was then described as the 'new journalism', which was defined through its attention to crime, sexual violence and human interest stories and thus laid the foundation for modern news reporting. The chapter also traces the origins of detective fiction from the Gothic up to contemporary representations in film, television and popular literature. Chapter 6 is the final chapter in this part of the book and looks in more detail at textual analysis and the social work storytelling performs for human societies. Here I cover influential analyses of narrative and genre to suggest that contemporary crime stories, much like ancient mythic tales, follow familiar patterns and chew over the core dilemmas confronting society as well as providing imaginative ways of living with them.

Texts do not write themselves and the last part of the book examines the industries involved in making the news. In chapter 7, four different approaches to the issue of how the media select, shape and present the news from the chaotic mess of events that happen out there in the world at large are outlined. Each of these approaches tends to foreground economic, political, social or cultural forces operating either separately or in tandem to structure the field of media production. These range from understanding how micro-level, face-to-face interactions between journalists, editors and sources are structured by bureaucratic routines, organizational cultures and corporate strategies which are themselves situated in broader political and economic contexts that are at once global in reach and local in character.

For the remainder of the chapter the focus turns to what has been called the sexualization of the media and focuses on the representation of sex crime in the news. In a way chapter 8 returns us almost to the beginning as it revisits the concept of moral panic in an effort to grasp contemporary media spectacles. As we will see, the concept has received much criticism over the years and I revisit it here as there is much still to be learnt from how the media make sense of disorder, danger and the unexpected. Rather than close the book with settled conclusions the final chapter reviews the arguments presented in the book and suggests some directions for future research.

PART I

Audiences

1

Media Effects

Audiences pose problems. They are cultural phenomena created through human interactions with others, while taking many forms in different settings. The proliferation of mass communication technologies like film, radio and television from the 1920s onwards, which addressed a mass of people simultaneously, was accompanied by a surge of academic research on the possible harmful effects of media content. The research questions echoed, on the one hand, widespread public concerns over gratuitous sex and violence on screen morally corrupting vulnerable young viewers; while on the other, critical commentators pointed to the ways mindless media audiences are politically manipulated, ideologically controlled and culturally degraded by the power of media industries. Underpinning both positions is the assumption that audiences passively consume media experiences. In its crudest form, it relies on a 'hypodermic model' of causation whereby the media are likened to a narcotic drug injecting messages into a mass audience with direct, immediate and measurable effects. Although the problems with this simple effects model have become well known it remains the dominant form of 'common-sense' explanation in everyday conversations, political debates and significantly in the popular press – where an irony-free media blame other sections of the media for creating social ills.

In the UK the horrific murder in 1993 of Liverpool toddler James Bulger by two ten-year-olds, who were famously alleged to have watched 'video nasties', led to misinformed tightening of the Video Recordings Act in 1994 (Barker, 1997). Similarly, in the US after the Columbine High School killings of 1999 by two teenage boys there was widespread press conjecture on media effects. Their consumption of violent media content, especially computer games, Internet sites and Gothic music were found by the news media to be guilty of causing the massacre. Immediately after the shootings the government launched a Federal Trade Commission and Department of Justice investigation into the marketing practices of the entertainment industries to children. Although no legislative changes followed, because of First Amendment concerns over direct state intervention in the industries (Carter and Weaver, 2003:135), the core belief remains in the enormous power of the media and the intrinsic vulnerability of children. This chapter will begin by situating the media 'effects' debate in social context before describing the enormous effort that has been expended on the topic and then will describe developments in cultural theory and critical criminology that offer a more nuanced way into understanding the effects of media power.

Situating Effects

The common-sense assumption that depictions of violence incite violent behaviour among audiences has a long history. But all too often the debate is polarized, simplified and displaced. As David Buckingham (2003:165) puts it, genuine 'often deep-seated anxieties about what are perceived as undesirable moral or social changes lead to a search for a single causal explanation'. Blaming certain media, like television or computer games, deflects attention away from other complex issues – that may well be uncomfortably 'closer to home' (Connell, 1985). Likewise, questioning who is supposed to be at risk from the supposed harmful effects of the media is revealing: it is not 'the "educated" and "cultured" middle classes, who either don't watch such rubbish, or else are fully able to deal with it if they do so'; instead 'those who are most "affected" are the young, especially the working-class young' (Barker and Petley, 1997:5). The 'history of respectable fears' (Pearson, 1983) demonstrates how popular anxieties in the present often rely on idealized images of the past and are driven as much by generational fear as class antagonism in the creation of moral panics over social problems.

None of these critics denies that the media have 'effects', as the point of the media is to communicate, but they assert that the problem is assuming that the relationship is simple and straightforward while misunderstanding the ways violent imagery and wrongdoing are a prominent feature of storytelling. Nevertheless, in public opinion the overwhelming view is that there is a direct causal link between media violence and real violence, and it is this 'common-sense' assumption that drives the dominant research tradition rather than challenging the question itself. All too often the debate polarizes into either accepting a powerful media effects model or arguing that the media have little or no influence over audiences. Neither position is advocated in this book. Yet it is not enough to arrogantly dismiss popular anxieties surrounding the possible harmful effects of media violence, without recognizing the ways in which everyday representations of violence in the media help to normalize and legitimize certain kinds of violence in society. One of the key problems with both the powerful and the no-effects positions is the tendency to isolate specific textual content from social and cultural processes. Furthermore, few 'attempts are made to examine the meaning systems surrounding portrayals of violence, such as whether it is portrayed as "legitimate" or "enjoyable"; nor are they able to deal with questions of fantasy in fictional formats' (Miller and Philo, 1999:23).

Many of the academic studies are informed by the philosophical assumptions of positivism and have used modern scientific methods to quantify the 'effects' of the media. Yet long before the emergence of science the literary analysis of texts used the hermeneutic methods of medieval biblical scholars to uncover the relationships between meaning and existence in the scriptures, while, stretching even further back into antiquity, philosophers studied how oratory, rhetoric and poetics are constructed to achieve certain effects. These approaches differ in important respects, yet they understand the audience as passive in ways that are not too dissimilar from modern effects studies by privileging the power of the textual performance (Jensen and Rosengren, 1990). For instance, the Greek philosopher Plato expressed his paternalistic worries over the consequences of storytelling in the following fashion:

> Then shall we simply allow our children to listen to any stories that anyone happens to make up, and so to receive into their minds ideas often the very opposite of those we shall think they ought to have when they grow up?
> No certainly not.
> It seems, then, our first business will be to supervise the making of fables and legends, rejecting all which are unsatisfactory; and we shall induce nurses and mothers to tell their children only those which we have approved, and to think more of the mouldering of their souls. (Plato, cited in Ruddock, 2001:25)

Plato's concerns clearly resonate with contemporary anxieties about children and the media. This preoccupation with the supposed harmful effects of popular culture on public morality has been a recurring theme in social commentary.

Theatre-going, now regarded as a form of high culture, came in for fierce criticism in Shakespeare's day. The Lord Mayor of London condemned plays, actors and audiences, proclaiming that 'they are the ordinary places for vagrant persons, Masterless men, thieves, horse stealers, whoremongers, Coozeners, Coneycatchers, contrivers of treason and other idle and dangerous persons to meet together' (cited in Fiske and Hartley, 1978:13–14). If it had been within his power the Lord Mayor would have closed down all the playhouses in Elizabethan London (Picard, 2003:248). Similar anxieties were raised much later in 1751 when the famous author and then magistrate Henry Fielding wrote, in response to a widely reported crime wave, his *Enquiry into the Causes of the Late Increase in Robbers*. In this account of rising crime and social crisis he argued that the 'too frequent and expensive Diversions among the lower kinds of People . . . hath almost totally changed the Manners, Customs and Habits of the People, more especially of the lower sort' (cited in Pearson, 1983:186–7). Debates over the harmful effects of the media continue to be driven by this same compelling combination of class resentment, generational fear and social change. In the nineteenth century the music hall and lurid stories in 'penny dreadfuls' were blamed for inciting hooliganism, while from its beginnings cinema has been accused of encouraging 'copy cat' crime (Barker and Petley, 1997:5).

Nevertheless, a key difference between then and now is that storytelling has become infused with the imagery of sex and violence. Of course, sex and violence feature prominently in Greek epics, biblical stories, fairy tales, Elizabethan tragedies and nineteenth-century novels but crucially this action could not happen before the eyes of an audience. It would have been regarded as 'obscene', 'literally something which must take place, from the Latin "*ob scena*", "off stage"' (Booker, 2004:455). As Christopher Booker (2004:456) points out, in the later decades of the twentieth century 'all that subterranean realm of imagery previously hidden away as "obscene" now came to be regarded as acceptable'. But not without some considerable controversies over censorship that are not easily resolved, as we have seen in the previous chapter, and like the audience research that I now outline a complex dynamic of fear and desire animates much of the debates. Certainly it is the 'fear' school of thought that regards the media as harmful, while the 'desire' school points to the liberating potential and libidinal qualities of media experiences – this distinction is also manifest in the contrasting literary and social scientific approaches adopted in audience research (Hartley, 1999:134).

Mass Communications Approaches

The question of whether media representations of violence have damaging effects upon audiences is one of the most researched issues in the social sciences. Moreover, it remains the most influential form of explanation in public opinion and thereby fuels a research industry that attracts considerable funding and publicity. The continuing legacy of effects studies is that they perpetuate the 'common-sense' view of the audience as defenceless before the destructive power of the media. The overwhelming majority of effects studies have been concerned with aggression, or more precisely with the hypothesis that watching violence on the television screen causes people (young people especially) to behave in similar ways.

Over the last seventy years it has been estimated that there have been more than 10,000 research studies analysing the relationships between viewing violence and subsequent aggressive tendencies (Carter and Weaver, 2003:6). Yet, despite the amount of time and money spent on the topic, no clear evidence for or against such behavioural claims has yet been produced (Livingstone, 1996). Given that thousands of studies have failed to reach convincing conclusions, then it is reasonable to suppose not only that 'the wrong question is being asked' (Brown, 2003:108) but that the agnostic verdicts expose the limits of 'empirical social science' (Reiner, 2002:396). The effects tradition is drenched in the positivist tenets of empiricism, which assumes that there is a world of objective facts waiting to be found by the researcher, favours quantitative research methods and insists on behavioural explanations of human activity. Behaviourism theorizes a 'causal connection between a Stimulus (S) and a Response (R): S can be a media message, R can be an attitude or a form of behaviour' and thereby 'aims to establish predictive rules: that S will always generate R, given certain determining conditions' (Bertrand and Hughes, 2005:97).

One of the earliest pioneers of behaviourism was John Watson (1924), who had been working on his version of it from 1903 and sought to reject Freudian psychoanalysis in order to ground psychology as a true 'science' by concentrating solely on observed behaviour. Watson 'insisted that the relations between stimulus and response were immediate and direct' which crucially meant they were 'eminently suitable for investigation by laboratory experimentation' (Murdock, 1997:80). Behaviourism dominated psychological and sociological approaches to mass communication in the 1930s and 1940s in the United States. For instance, laboratory techniques were used in the Payne Fund studies in the 1930s to deduce the effects of film on young people (Charters, 1933) while Paul Lazarsfeld *et al.* (1948) influentially discerned four kinds of measurable media effect: 'immediate response, short-term effects, long-term effects and institutional change'.

The most famous example of laboratory research examining behavioural changes following exposure to violent imagery is the series of experiments conducted by Albert Bandura and his colleagues in the 1960s (Bandura, Ross and Ross, 1961; Bandura, Ross and Ross, 1963; and Bandura, 1965). These studies were funded by the United States government because it was concerned over the mass media's ability to provoke anti-social behaviour. The experiments exposed children to film footage of an adult attacking a large plastic 'Bobo' doll (an inflatable toy with a weighted base, which wobbles but remains standing when hit). Up to 88 per cent of the children instantly imitated the aggression in the laboratory. These findings were widely reported and lent a lot of support to the arguments that screen violence is both infectious and desensitizing. However, critics have since pointed out that the artificiality of such experiments fatally compromises them (Surette, 1998:122–3), while pointing to the spurious 'psycho-logic' in the studies as they rely on 'mechanistic fairy-tales about how audiences process messages' (Vine, 1997:125). Moreover, behavioural effects researchers have been found guilty of inconsistency, firstly by ignoring other laboratory studies that did not find violent effects and secondly by not recognizing how aggression can be caused by many factors aside from watching violence (Gauntlett, 1995; Freedman, 2002).

In important respects these effects studies were already intellectually passé. Many of the early studies on political campaigns and mass persuasion used market research methods and seemed to show that the media had little or no impact on changing attitudes. 'Paradoxically campaign propaganda exerted one major effect – by producing no overt effect on voting behaviour at all – if by the latter "effect" we naively mean a change in vote' wrote Lazarsfeld in 1944 (cited in Seaton, 2003:330). His findings revealed that media propaganda confirmed, mobilized and reinforced opinions that people already held. Along with Robert Merton, Herta Herzog and others at Columbia University, Lazarsfeld pioneered 'content and response' analysis. Merton, for instance, had a longstanding interest in anomie (the alienation experienced by many who could not attain the American Dream of 'money-success') and how the media make life bearable in a highly competitive, status-orientated, mass society. He sought to explain the 'affiliative dimensions of media use as a functionally meaningful and rewarding activity' in which the 'goal had been to explain when propaganda and persuasion work, and when they don't' (Ross and Nightingale, 2003:24). Jean Seaton (2003) describes the impact of the findings well:

> small town American gossip came to the rescue of democracy. Survey findings seemed to prove that people were not the atomized automatons suggested by mass society theory. Thus the inhabitants of places which sounded like the locations for John Ford movies – Eerie County, Decatur, Elimira, and Rovere – appeared oblivious to, rather than hypnotized by, the blandishments of media propaganda. Far more important influences were provided by friends, neighbours, and drinking companions – whether people were deciding which presidential candidate to vote for or what brand of cornflakes to have for breakfast. It was personal contact, not media persuasiveness, that counted. (Seaton, 2003:329)

These studies did not show that the media had no effect (even though this was precisely the conclusion drawn at the time) but that the audience was not a homogeneous, undifferentiated mass and moreover that personal interaction matters. For instance, Katz and Lazarsfield's (1955/2003) study of 'movie leaders' shows how people with low status could be important opinion leaders mediating the social significance of a film. They demonstrated how those with special interests in film were considered experts and their opinions were actively sought out by their friends before deciding to see a movie. Thus the emphasis was on the social work the media were performing in facilitating bonds between people and, crucially for the pluralist conception of power underpinning these studies, opinion leaders were not drawn from a narrow elite for 'when it comes to consulting a movie "expert", people of all ages turn to the girls' (Katz and Lazarsfield, 1955/2003:27).

Consequently sociological functionalism had replaced the crude psychological behaviourism of media audiences in mass communication studies by the 1950s. The 'uses and gratifications' approach, as it came to be called, shifted attention away from the effects of the media on audiences altogether, and instead focused on what audiences did with the media. Rather than seeing the typical audience member as a passive dupe, the new approach treated the audience as motivated by individual needs and wants. The viewer was understood as an active subject in possession of certain needs, which the media satisfy. A defining theme in these studies concerned the functionalist role the media played in facilitating social consensus and personal integration. The implication is that audience members actively choose media that interest them to meet psychological needs. Armed with quantitative surveys and statistical analysis researchers studied 'how viewers used news to maintain surveillance on society; how they used television-watching as escape or diversion; how they used comedy to maintain personal equilibrium' (Hartley, 1999:131). The emphasis shifted from message to medium in order to explain how the media helped 'people to relax, unwind, exorcise tensions that might otherwise cause aggressive behaviour and keep in touch with the world' (Ruddock, 2001:69)

Although the 'uses and gratifications' approach was ground-breaking in its day and seemed to offer a powerful challenge to the 'effects' tradition it does share a number of behaviourist assumptions with that earlier research. These joint problems will be discussed below. Initially though critics complained that the uses and grati-fications approach gave the audience too much freedom and too little recognition of textual meaning (Abercrombie, 1996:142). Nevertheless, it did move attention away from the immediate and short-term effects of media messages onto the overall importance of the media in securing social cohesion and stability. In doing so it paved the way for 'cultivation analysis', a third approach to the ques-tion of media representations of violence developed by George Gerbner and his colleagues at the University of Pennsylvania under the Cultural Indicators programme from 1967. The focus is on the long-term consequences of cumulative exposure to television viewing. One definition has it that 'cultivation analysis . . . inquires into the assumption television cultivates about the facts, norms and values of society' (Gerbner and Gross, 1976:182). Using 'violence profiles' Gerbner and his associates have annually subjected one week of US prime-time television to detailed quantitative content analysis.

From the start the aim has been to find out how much violence is on television, who are the victims, who are the perpetrators, and what value judgements and social relationships are portrayed in the pro-gramming. In one early study, he found, for example, that 80 per cent of drama contained violence, 50 per cent of leading characters com-mitted violence, while 60 per cent were victims of it, with the average week containing 400 casualties (Gerbner, 1970). Using this kind of research President Clinton claimed in a speech after the Columbine High School massacre that by the time they reach eighteen, most Americans would have seen 40,000 dramatized murders (Boyle, 2005:22). It is important to emphasize that Gerbner is critical of the view that violent media representations cause real-life violence – he has calculated that at most they account for 5 per cent. But in contrast he and his associates have argued that heavy television viewing 'cultivates' a misleading and exaggerated understanding of violence in the real world – the so-called 'mean world syndrome' (Gerbner et al., 1980). Consequently, heavy viewers are more likely than light viewers to distrust other people and possess a 'scary' perception of the outside world (Gerber et al., 1994). As the research has developed its adherents have identified a significant 'mainstreaming' effect, where 'heavy viewing may absorb or override differences in perspectives and behaviour that ordinarily stem from other factors and influences' (Morgan and Signorelli, 1990:22). The political implication is that television viewing reduces social differences and leads the audience in a conservative direction to support an authoritarian consensus for tougher responses to crime and disorder.

The merits of cultivation analysis have been intensely debated. Critics have questioned the way its conclusions have been drawn. They are contentious as the method involves 'simply correlating television exposure with particular attitudes, and presuming that the former causes the latter' (Gauntlett, 1995:100). The implication is that viewers unproblematically soak up media content as 'no evidence is presented to show whether or not "messages" identified through content analysis are actually perceived and learned by viewers' (Gunter, 1985:33). As the conclusions are based on content analysis and the assumption that television viewing is largely habitual rather than selective (people tend to watch in blocks of time rather than by programme is the claim) no distinction is made between the types of programme where violence appears or its context.[1] For instance, violence in children's cartoons is 'often equated with violence in realist drama and horror movies' (Carter and Weaver, 2003:11). In other words, violence takes on different meanings in different contexts. For example, a slap in the face can be shocking in a soap opera (when a story line is dealing with domestic violence), while the same action might prompt laughter in slapstick comedies (like Carry On films or Laurel and Hardy movies).

Others have argued that differing levels of fear and television use are closely related to social location (age, class, ethnicity, gender and so forth) as well as geographical place. It has been claimed that those who live in high crime areas are more fearful and likely to stay at home watching television (Doob and MacDonald, 1979). Richard Sparks (1992:93) goes on to suggest that there may well be 'equally good grounds for supposing that television cultivates security as fear and that this is any case contingent on the motivations people have for using media in the ways they do'. The regular viewing of fairly similar narratives that play on fears can end up alleviating anxieties and reassuring audiences when order is restored at the end of the programme. In any case, unless how audiences make sense of the media and interact with other sources of meaning in their lives (such as daily gossip, local newspapers, radio stations and so forth) are explored, the cultivation analysis strategy of isolating television viewing as the singular causal factor provoking fear is deeply flawed. The next chapter will return to these themes in more detail.

These are some of the specific criticisms of cultivation analysis, which marked an important advance over earlier approaches as it directs attention to the longer-term consequences of television viewing. However, it is worth emphasizing the common ground shared by the 'effects' tradition, 'uses and gratifications' approach and 'cultivation analysis'. It is significant that they each have originated in the USA and pioneered 'mass communication' studies as the social scientific approach to the mass media. The key word here is 'mass', which denotes a preoccupation with 'the people' as a worryingly unknowable multitude susceptible to the exploitative power of the new broadcasting technologies. A defining characteristic of this 'mass society' thesis was that the rise of modern, industrialized culture generated a uniformity of needs, thought and behaviour among an easily manipulated, isolated and homogenized population. Yet it is not surprising that the twentieth-century experiences of totalitarian governments, atomic bombs and ethnic extermination prompted the earliest social research into the use of fascist propaganda, political campaigns and opinion leaders to mobilize the masses. It is in the context of wartime insecurity and subsequent Cold War paranoia that mass society theorists (Reisman, 1953; Kornhauser, 1959) pointed to the role of the media in uniting disparate, alienated individuals. Shorn of the traditional, pre-industrial ties that bonded people to social groups, the atomized mass audience was held to be particularly vulnerable to the influence of media messages.

Similar concerns were also raised by the influential Frankfurt School for Social Research. The Institute for Social Research was founded at the University of Frankfurt in 1923 as a centre for socialist scholarship. Among the many prominent intellectuals associated with the Institute are Theodor Adorno, Walter Benjamin, Max Horkheimer and Herbert Marcuse. The Nazi seizure of power in the 1930s forced the School into exile and to set up loose connections with Columbia University in the United States in the early 1940s. Adorno and Horkheimer returned to Germany in the late 1940s to continue the work of the Institute at Frankfurt University. Thus under the shadows of fascist Germany and American monopoly capitalism were the Frankfurt School's damning analyses of the mass media written.

Adorno and Horkheimer's (1947/73) *Dialectic of Enlightenment* is a particularly forceful example of their critical theory. The book explores the self-destructive tendencies of modern societies. Its central argument is that instrumental rationality – the form of reasoning which separates facts from value by being solely concerned with practical purposes – has undermined the emancipatory potential of Enlightenment. For instance, Fascism used many of the tools of instrumental reason and modern science in its barbaric destruction and brutal repression. However, democratic states as much as authoritarian ones possess dehumanizing tendencies. These are more subtle but no less damaging – a claim examined in Horkheimer and Adorno's analysis of what they call the 'culture industry', which obliterates individuality and silences critical thinking through 'mass deception'. These arguments have proved to be highly controversial, but they have set many of the terms of subsequent debate and share similar concerns to those raised by postwar North American sociologists over the alienating consequences of mass media consumption.

Consequently, a lasting legacy of this understanding is that the audience is characterized at either an individualistic or a society-wide level, so that individuals are directly affected by the media or use them to gratify personal needs, while society is said to be led in particular directions (Abercrombie and Longhurst, 1998:9). Furthermore, the model of communication used is essentially a linear process of messages passing from senders to receivers in a direct line and assumes that meaning is fixed or disturbed by feedback 'noise' (Fiske, 1982). The North American political scientist Harold Lasswell advanced the classic formulation, which is that communication is ultimately the study of 'who says what to whom in what channel and with what effect' (Briggs and Burke, 2005:4). Finally, the mass communications tradition defined itself as a scientific enterprise and used quantitative methods of data collection to describe observable audience behaviour. Each of these assumptions has been fundamentally challenged by developments in European literary and cultural theory, which provided an alternative to American empirical studies of media audiences.

European Literary and Cultural Theory

The 1970s mark a decisive watershed in the study of audiences, when the mass communication tradition was challenged by the new vocabularies of cultural studies. It is often maintained that the key difference between them is that mass communication research focuses on what texts 'do' to the audience, whereas cultural studies approaches prioritize what a text 'means' (Nightingale, 1996). An important turning point is Stuart Hall's article 'Encoding and Decoding in Television Discourse', originally published in 1973 but subsequently included in numerous edited collections. In it, he distinguished between the encoding of media texts by producers and the ways audiences actively decode meanings – by accepting, negotiating or opposing dominant messages. As Hall (1980b/2003:51) made clear, this approach explicitly challenged the behavioural assumptions of mass communications research, which was solely concerned with the question of media effects on the audience. This tradition was severely limited as:

> The model of power and influence being employed here was paradigmatically empiricist and pluralistic: its primary focus was the individual; it theorized power in terms of the direct influence of A on B's behaviour; it was preoccupied . . . with the process of decision-making. Its ideal experimental test was a before/after one: its ideal model of influence was that of the campaign. (Hall, 1982:59)

Consequently, a whole range of economic processes, social structures and power relations were completely ignored as they were way beyond the theoretical frame of reference.

Underpinning mainstream communications research is a liberal-pluralist conception of power, which is based on a shared consensus of values and is largely understood to be reinforced by the media. In contrast, Hall emphasizes structural conflict. He explains how this comfortable consensus began to be unravelled – initially by the new sociology of deviance (see below) that revealed how differences between subcultural groups and dominant values were not natural but socially constructed, politically enforced and historically variable. This had crucial implications for understanding the media. No longer could the media be seen as *expressing* a natural consensus – 'simply showing things as they were' (Hall, 1982:64). Instead they seek to *impose* a set of dominant values on subordinate groups.

The rediscovery of ideology here involved questioning how the media attempt to secure a 'universal validity and legitimacy for accounts of the world that are partial and particular' (Hall,1982:65). It is important to recognize that he is not advocating a 'conspiracy thesis' where 'programming is depicted as the public voice of a sectional but dominant political ideology' (Hall *et al.*, 1976:60) but rather a 'relative autonomy' between broadcasters and politicians that produces a range of messages, where there is nonetheless a preferred meaning to which the viewer is guided. Likewise, the classical Marxist position that the 'ruling ideas' are those of the 'ruling classes' is rejected in favour of Antonio Gramsci's 'enlarged concept of hegemony' which grasps how political dominance is an uneven process achieved through the combination of coercive power and the active consent of the subordinate majority (Hall, 1982:85). There are some quite complex arguments here and it is important to situate them in intellectual context.

In his discussion of the origins of cultural studies, Hall (1980) identifies 'two paradigms' that have been especially significant. The first he terms 'culturalism' and is a distinctly British tradition that has its roots in the burgeoning New Left movement of the 1950s. It is associated with the approach pioneered by Richard Hoggart (1958) in his *The Uses of Literacy*, a nostalgic account of how working-class culture had been undermined by the advent of a 'new mass culture'. The book contrasts the organic vitality of the working-class culture he grew up with in northern England in the 1930s with the newer postwar commercial culture of loud pop music, 'spicy' magazines, 'juke box boys', noisy 'nickelodeons', American television, cheap 'sex-and-violence' paperback novels and the hack sensationalism of much popular journalism. Although the book was applauded for bringing a new sensitivity to understanding the subtleties of working-class culture, it remains problematically wedded to an older literary tradition of judging cultural worth against particular aesthetic standards.

The aesthetic standards used in the book belong to the 'culture and civilization' tradition of literary criticism established at the University of Cambridge in the 1920s. Among its leading practitioners were I. A. Richards, William Empson and F. R. Leavis who pioneered a way of teaching English Literature that dominated the next five decades. F. R. Leavis and his wife Q. D. Leavis founded the journal *Scrutiny* in 1932, which was devoted to the 'close reading' of touchstone texts while producing some of the earliest critiques of 'mass culture'. A key influence came from a century before in the work of Matthew Arnold (1869/ 1990:6) who had famously defined culture as 'the best that has been thought and said in the world' – a form of human 'civilization' to be defended against the 'anarchy' of the 'raw and uncultivated masses'.

The Leavis circle drew on these ideas to condemn the spread of popular culture for its moral deficiencies and compared it unfavourably with an earlier, folk culture that preceded industrialization. Self-consciously conservative and elitist, they saw their task as defining and defending a canon of great literary works while criticizing popular novels, women's magazines, Hollywood films and popular music as standardized products of an industrialized mass culture. These arguments will now be familiar and were raised by other figures in different countries (such as the Frankfurt School and mass culture critics in North America) and continue to be made today. As Bennett (1981:6) has put it, this was a condescending discourse of the 'cultured' levelled against the culture of those without 'culture' and he explains how popular culture 'was approached from a distance and gingerly, held out at arm's length by outsiders who clearly lacked any fondness for or participation in the forms they were studying'. This is certainly the case with Hoggart (1958) who struggles to make sense of postwar cultural change.

The most enduring influence, though, on culturalism was the socialist literary critic Raymond Williams. Crucially he defined culture as a 'whole way of life' (Williams, 1958/66:16) in contrast to the Leavisite elitist 'selective tradition', while his insistence that 'there are in fact no masses; there are only ways of seeing masses' (ibid.:289) opened the way for a more anthropological understanding of culture than a purely literary-moral one. Williams (1961:64) subsequently maintained that all cultures possess a distinctive 'structure of feeling', which provides a 'particular and characteristic colour' that shapes how the world is experienced in a further effort to overcome antagonistic divisions between 'high' and 'low' culture. Also pivotal to the 'culturalist' paradigm was the social historian Edward Palmer (E. P.) Thompson. In particular, his *Making of the English Working Class* (1963) provided a 'history from below' and clearly understood culture as 'a way of struggle' between classes. For Thompson, class is an historical phenomenon created by people through lived social relations, rather than an inevitable outcome of modes of production.

The combined contributions of Hoggart, Williams and Thompson enabled a more democratic understanding of culture and emphasized the creativity of individuals in making history. By the end of the 1960s the culturalist strategy of privileging human activity as the source of meaning came under increasing attack and many turned to a new body of theory emerging from across the Channel. 'Structuralism' is the second paradigm identified by Hall (1980). It is a product of Continental thinkers and was seen as a way of overcoming the defects in culturalism, which was regarded as theoretically naïve and reductively humanistic through its concentration on individual experience and a broader failure to understand the 'cultural totality' (Hall, 1980:64). The basic premise of structuralism is that for any phenomenon under study there will be a system of structures and sets of relationships that produce meaning. It is the system and the relationship between the different elements that are more important than the individual elements that make up the system. I mentioned earlier that the mass communication tradition worked with a 'linear' model of communication; structuralism provided a very different, 'semiotic' understanding of communication and it was in this focus on language that the impact of structuralist ideas initially registered.

The 'linguistic turn' took many directions but owes its origins to the structural linguistics of Ferdinand de Saussure and Russian Formalist literary critics. Their ideas were developed by the French anthropologist Claude Lévi-Strauss, whose work gave a powerful impetus to structuralism, treated kinship relations, cooking practices and mythic stories as linguistic structures and concluded that the human mind works through binary oppositions to reduce arbitrary data into some kind of order. Likewise, the Marxist philosopher Louis Althusser identified an underlying structure or language of capitalism where individual capitalist societies are particular speech acts, and invoked his own 'Copernican Revolution' by displacing the human subject from the centre of history. This anti-humanism was also at the heart of Jacques Lacan's influential reworking of psychoanalysis by claiming that 'the unconscious is structured like language'. Michel Foucault (1966/94) even claimed to have found the structural codes that govern thinking in particular eras in his *The Order of Things*.

For a time Roland Barthes sought to establish a structuralist 'science of literature' in an effort to distinguish the approach from academic criticism, which relies on aesthetic discrimination and ideological understandings of 'objectivity' and 'good taste'. He set this out in his most accessible book *Mythologies* (Barthes, 1957/93), which contains a collection of short, witty essays on various aspects of popular and high culture as well as an outline of the semiological concepts (like sign, signifier and signified) that inform his approach. His highly influential essay, an 'Introduction to the Structural Analysis of Narrative', published in 1966 (and included in the *Image-Music-Text* collection of essays) provides principles for classifying the endless number of narratives circulating in the world. Yet shortly afterwards Barthes moves from seeing the literary work as a closed entity with precise meanings and general rules that the critic can decode to viewing the text as possessing a multiplicity of meanings that cannot be reduced down to a single core or essence.[2] This insistence on the inherent polysemy of meaning is introduced in his famous essay the 'Death of the Author' where he claims that 'a text is not a line of words releasing a single "theological" meaning (the "message" of the Author-God) but a multi-dimensional space in which a variety of writings, none of them original, blend and clash' (Barthes, 1968/77:146).[3]

Although there were major differences among these thinkers, and we will come back to many of these ideas, structuralism did constitute to an Anglo-American audience a single intellectual movement originating from France in the 1960s. Nearly all the leading figures would soon distance themselves from structuralism, yet much of what was lauded as 'post-structuralism' was already present in these early writings. Nevertheless, the tensions in the culturalism/structuralism divide have not gone away and historians, in particular, were deeply sceptical of structuralism.[4] However, it is the attempts to integrate the culturalist emphasis on lived experience with structuralist approaches to the textual subject that will be a key theme animating this book.

A number of crucial consequences flow from this semiotic understanding of communication. Among the most significant is that it challenges the assumption of audience passivity and opens the way for a more nuanced understanding of audience activity that is 'conceived as interpretive rather than psychological and as political rather than personal' (Ross and Nightingale, 2003:37). We will look in more detail at studies of the 'active audience' in chapter 3 and how attention is drawn to the social contexts of media consumption in this research. However, I now turn to developments in the sociology of deviance that provided a decisive impetus to criminological understandings of the mass media that will be explored in this book.

Criminology and the Mass Media

Investigating the ways in which the press and broadcast news report crime is now an established field in criminology and owes much to the pioneering work of critical scholars in the 1960s and 1970s. The central issue is not whether the media cause troubling 'copy cat' behaviour by young people, but rather how the media promote damaging stereotypes of social groups, especially the young, to uphold the status quo. While the argument that media coverage can create social problems owes much to symbolic interactionism (Becker, 1963) and deviancy amplification (Wilkins, 1964) theories, it was the ground-breaking studies of Jock Young (1971a) on the social meaning of drug-taking and Stan Cohen (1972/80) on the media's construction of the confrontations between mods and rockers, and their edited collections (Cohen, 1971; Cohen and Young, 1973b) which developed the concept of 'moral panic'. At the same time their work provided a radical counter to both Home Office dominated criminology and an empirically based sociology of deviance that 'tended either to be excessively descriptive or else to explain the "predicament" of the young offender almost entirely in terms of poverty and deprivation' (McRobbie, 1994:203). Indeed, both were part of a broader movement in criminology towards more critical positions emerging in the early 1970s that sought to break with this narrow, administrative criminology.

Stan Cohen's (1972) formulation of moral panic has proved to be highly influential as the argument is that demonizing deviants serves to reinforce boundaries of normality and order. The book itself still repays careful reading as it possesses a much greater complexity and is far less mechanistic than the many summaries suggest. There is evidence indicating that he initially intended the term to be 'a modest and descriptive one' (Sparks, 1992:65) as he subsequently cautioned against being 'obsessed with debunking' (Cohen, 1985:156). Nevertheless, in both his and Jock Young's (1971a, 1971b) early studies there was a strong Durkheimian emphasis on how societies are able to cohere through uniting in moral indignation against deviant groups. They both acknowledge the importance of Marshall McLuhan's (1964) celebrated account of the consequences of the shift from print to electronic media, captured in his well-known phrase 'the medium is the message'.

The real message is not the formal content of media but the ways the media extend our senses and alter our social world. Whereas print encouraged 'linear', rational and individualist subjects, through intensifying visual sensations the electronic media produce a 'mosaic' of fragmented experiences that could generate shared collective ideas – a 'global village' that could transcend the divisive nationalisms of the past. McLuhan (1964) argued that the world initially expanded through urbanization and transport developments, but has now 'imploded' as the mass media bring the world closer together again. It is this 'implosive factor' that Cohen and Young (1973b:340) find essential, for the 'media are the major and at times the sole source of information about a whole range of phenomena' and thereby 'points to continual bombardment by images of phenomena that otherwise could be conveniently forgotten'. As Young (1971b:38, emphasis in original) initially put it, because 'of the *implosion* of the mass media, we are greatly aware of the existence of deviants, and because the criterion of inclusion in the media is newsworthiness it is possible for moral panics over a particular type of deviancy to be created by the *sudden* dissemination of information about it'. The influence of McLuhan on their thinking is often overlooked in the vast commentary on the concept and I return to this in chapter 8, where I examine the concept in far more detail than space permits here.

For now it is important to emphasize that both Cohen and Young saw the media's need to maintain circulation in competitive markets as central to the process: the 'ethos of "give the public what it wants" involves a constant play on the normative worries of large segments of the population; it utilizes outgroups as living Rorschach blots on to which collective fears and doubts are projected' (Young, 1973:316). Moreover this is only possible through 'exaggerating grossly the seriousness of events' (Cohen, 1973:228). As Young (1974:241, emphasis in original) then explained, 'newspapers select events which are *atypical*, present them in a *stereotypical* fashion and contrast them against a backcloth of normality which is *overtypical*'. The disproportionate and hostile reaction to a 'condition, episode, person or group' that becomes 'defined as a threat to societal values and interests . . . is presented in a stylized and stereotypical fashion by the mass media' (Cohen, 1972/80:9). Thus they both emphasized how certain kinds of meaning are socially constructed and dramatically amplified through press coverage that serves to generate concern, indignation and panic.

The emphasis on how the media distort reality was subsequently developed through a neo-Marxist understanding of ideology by Stuart Hall and his colleagues at the Birmingham Centre for Contemporary Cultural Studies in their (1978) *Policing the Crisis: Mugging, the State, and Law and Order*. The book can be regarded as the landmark text bridging criminology and cultural studies,[5] and it is here that the somewhat vague Durkheimian notion of social control is replaced by a more rigorous preoccupation with state power, while the politics of signification is prioritized over the sociology of labelling. A further difference is that in Cohen (1972/80:9) moral panics have an 'every now and then', episodic quality occurring at times of 'boundary crisis', whereas Hall *et al.* (1978) use Gramsci to understand the timing of the moral panic that emerged in the early 1970s around mugging as an important element in securing consent at a time of hegemonic crisis.

These quickly proved to be controversial arguments and their analysis has been criticized for claiming that the criminality crisis over mugging was contrived by ruling elites to deflect attention away from the economic crisis facing the British state, while the authors have also been accused of ignoring the impact of crime on the working class. For instance, the moral panic identified by Hall *et al.* was criticized as 'a polemical rather than an analytical concept' (Waddington, 1986:258). While making his case for a 'realistic' approach to crime and control in the 1980s, Young (1987:338) accused the text of Left 'idealism' and located it in the 'Great Denial' of crime as a force of social distress in decaying inner cities. Nevertheless, the overall legacy of this approach is that it is a sustained attempt to analyse the 'social production of news' to reveal the ways that the media 'inculcate and defend the economic, social and political agenda of privileged groups' (Herman and Chomsky, 1988:302). More tellingly it has been argued that

> Hall and his associates based their entire analysis of coverage of a moral panic about mugging on their own reading of mass media content. In limiting themselves to content analyses these researchers failed to answer the central question they posed, namely, whether, the mass media are saturated with official ideology and bourgeois sensibilities that are accepted by people and thereby effect hegemony. An adequate answer to this question requires demonstration, through the concrete activities of mass media operatives, their sources, and their readers, of how hegemony is actually accomplished. What is required is detailed analysis of the social contexts of mass media production and reception, and a view of dominant meanings as the outcome of strategies and struggles rather than as an *a priori* effect of pre-ordained privileged access to particular official sources. (Ericson, 1991:221)

Consequently, more recent studies have explored the relationships between social structures and human agency while holding on to the view that political forces and economic constraints 'limit access to the production, distribution and consumption of information' (Schlesinger and Tumber, 1994:8). Robert Reiner (2007:325–27) defines this work as 'cultural conflict' as it highlights the struggles that take place on newsroom floors between journalists, editors, owners and sources, which we will examine in more detail in chapter 7.

At root, though, are competing interpretations of media power that are either 'pluralist' or 'Marxist' (Schlesinger *et al.*, 1991:399). The pluralist understanding of power was developed by American empirical researchers working in the 'effects' tradition, whereas the Marxist focus on ideology arises from a European tradition of cultural and lit-erary theory. In important respects these are the formative approaches developed in the study of media audiences. A complex dynamic between 'fear' and 'desire' animates these positions. For instance, the concept of moral panic assumes an irrational and fearful response to media representations of crime that in certain respects chimes with Gerbner's cultivation analysis, whereas the notion of active audience has encouraged much research to explore the pleasures of media con-sumption. The next two chapters will explore these themes in more detail.

2

Fearing Crime

In the previous chapter I suggested that a powerful dynamic between 'fear' and 'desire' structures much debate in the media – from worries over the harmful effects of each new medium to the immense pleasures mediated experiences offer. It is clear though that 'fear' dominates public discussion and in this chapter I outline some of the ways in which discourses of fear have become so culturally significant. Fear is a complex human emotion. While fear is ubiquitous and experienced by every living creature, the actual sources of dread are socially distributed. Different societies have developed different ways of living with the dangers that haunt them. Indeed, it is the dark and frightening that is often at the heart of popular entertainment, folklore and mythology. As we will see in later chapters it is a fundamental task of storytelling to draw on these threats and make some reassuring sense of them. Yet contemporary terms like the 'politics of fear', 'fear of crime', 'age of anxiety' and 'risk society' each suggest that we are living in times of such heightened insecurity that danger lurks everywhere and seeps into everything.

A number of important social changes are said to herald this new era and break with the past – the mass media now provide us with round the clock news of crisis, disaster and trauma; rising social mobility brings a greater range of experiences, expectations and troubles; technological innovations have brought with them immense global dangers; and since 9/11 'new' forms of terrorism further contribute to the cultural climate of fear. These themes are pursued in what follows. First, I introduce the criminological debates surrounding 'fear of crime' and as will be quickly established the terrain is somewhat contested. Second, the scholarship on media coverage and changing social contexts will be discussed in tandem as they tend to be treated in isolation. This has led to a problematic assumption that lived realities and collective representations are somehow separate from each other and their quite profound relationships are then consequently neglected. Third, the overall goal is to grasp some of the social forces producing contemporary anxieties and situate them in a more nuanced account of the fears that currently burden us and the world we inhabit.

Fear of Crime in Criminological Context

Although research on the fear of crime was established in the late 1960s – paralleling the growth in more general criminological interest and policy concerns over victims of crime – it had moved to the centre of intense empirical, political and theoretical disputes by the 1980s. Today, the 'fear of crime' is an area of criminological inquiry that constitutes a 'sub-discipline in itself' (Lee, 2001:468) and 'is probably the main legacy of endless, and endlessly repeated, national crime surveys which have consistently identified it as a social problem of striking dimensions' (Ditton *et al.* 1999:83). Few issues trouble the public in Europe and the USA more than crime. Surveys have repeatedly shown that worries over victimization surpass job loss, ill health, road accidents and indebtedness as issues of major concern (Farall and Gadd, 2004:127). Indeed, it has become a well-worn observation that the problems posed by the fear of crime are potentially greater than those caused by crime itself and it was this discovery that prompted the plethora of studies on the topic. Especially since a repeated finding is that women and the elderly are more fearful than others, despite appearing to have the least risks of victimization (Pantazis, 2000:414). Following this logic it is claimed that 'since so few people are crime victims, then the comparatively large levels of survey-discovered fear of crime must invariably be related to media consumption' (Ditton *et al.*, 2004:595). Yet, as we will see, establishing a relationship between unwarranted fear and media use is far from straightforward.

   Part of the difficulty is down to the ways in which the research on fear of crime has developed in criminology, but also how the issues have been framed by the weight of the concerns outlined in the previous chapter. In particular, a critical legacy has emphasized that the mass media distort the 'reality' of social problems (Cohen and Young, 1973b) or 'cultivate' misleading perceptions of a 'mean world' (Gerbner and Gross, 1976). Crucially, it was also felt in official circles that the reporting of crime statistics misled the public.[1] For instance, the policy attractions of criminal victimization surveys have been explained in the following terms:

> It was thought within the Home Office that misperceptions about crime levels, trends and risks were widespread among the public. A survey-based index of crime would demonstrate the possibility – if not the reality – that the index of crime based on offences recorded by the police might be subject to statistical inflation by virtue of changing reporting and recording practices . . . In other words, the survey promised a more informed picture of crime which might help create a more balanced climate of opinion about law and order. (Mayhew and Hough, 1988:157, cited in Walklate, 1998:405)

Thus, a telling factor was the widespread agreement among mainstream criminologists and critical sociologists that the traditional methods of gathering crime statistics (through police reports) seriously underestimated the volume of crime and thereby drew attention to the so-called 'dark figure' of an unknown mass of unreported crimes. 'Dark' because it obscures, but also 'because it is construed as malign, the combination of these two attributes occasioning considerable anxiety' (Valier, 2001:432). Furthermore, the implication is that official agencies, by processing some events as criminal and not others, themselves act as key filters and primary definers of the crime problem.

From the late 1960s in the USA initially, but later elsewhere around the world, interviewing citizens about their personal experiences of crime became commonplace. In addition to trying to obtain a more accurate view of victimization levels these national household crime surveys provide information on the public's beliefs and attitudes towards crime, policing, punishment and prevention. The British Crime Survey was first carried out in 1982 and has been repeated at regular (usually four-year) intervals since. Accompanying national surveys have been an increasing number of local crime surveys, which in the UK have been carried out in various places like Bristol, Sheffield, Merseyside, Islington and Edinburgh. Typically fear of crime is often measured by responses to the question 'How safe do you feel walking alone in this area after dark?', or similar formulations, to which respondents are invited to reply by saying they feel 'very safe', 'fairly safe', 'a bit unsafe' or 'very unsafe'. The use of this question to uncover 'fear of crime' has been widely criticized. The most basic problems are that it fails to explicitly mention crime (Garafalo, 1979) and cannot do justice to the emotional complexity

of fear (Box, Hale and Andrews, 1988), and that through questionnaires respondents are 'forced to use the same language to express
very different feelings' (O'Mahony and Quinn, 1999:232–3). As Evi
Girling and her colleagues (Girling *et al.*, 2000:13) emphasize, these
studies tend to 'discover a lack of "fit" between expert knowledge and
"lay" opinion' that have come to revolve around the question of
whether fear is rational or irrational in an effort to distinguish between
'warranted' estimates of risks and debilitating misperceptions of
threats by particular groups of the public. Home Office research continued to find that both women and the elderly were particularly 'irrational' given the distance between their high levels of expressed fear
and their low levels of actual risk. The conclusion was that women
and the aged were incapable of making rational sense of the risks they
faced.

In polemically staking out his 'left realist' criminology in the 1980s,
Jock Young (1986) sought to distinguish it from both an 'administrative' criminology dominant in the Home Office and a 'left idealist' one
that he claimed denied the seriousness of crime by concentrating on
discourses about crime in the mass media. He subsequently set out
the realist position as being against 'those idealist theories which
portray moral panics as media instigated events without any rational
basis and against those writers who talk glibly of irrational fears of
crime without specifying what a rational fear would look like' (Young,
1987:338). Thus his target is how radical 'denial' unconsciously col-
ludes with administrative criminology's obsession with measuring the
gaps between actual and perceived risks. The latter studies search for
a 'surplus' of fear, as manifest in 'broken windows' (Wilson and
Kelling, 1982), the presence of troubling 'incivilities' (Maxfield,
1984) or other 'perceptions of neighbourhood change' (Skogan and
Maxfield, 1981) that contribute to urban decay, anti-social behaviour
and deteriorating community relations.

A crucial problem though, as Richard Sparks (1992:10) has
argued, is that having raised the question of what a rational fear
would like, Young has hardly begun to explore the ramifications
of the question, let alone suggest credible answers. Instead, the
left realist project was to reclaim the law and order debate from the
right so that people's 'lived realities' of crime are taken seriously
(Crawford *et al.*, 1990). Recalling arguments from the previous
chapter, Deborah Lupton and John Tulloch (1999:510) have suggested that there still remains in this work 'a surprising tendency to
an almost stimulus-response effect (experience of harassment or
crime leads to fear of crime), with little insight into the complexities

and displacements involved, and the extra-rational level at which fear (or lack of fear) is produced and operates'. Through the continual emphasis on 'real' crime they maintain that left realists have problematically ignored the place of cultural and symbolic representations, myths and narratives that are essential to our passage through life and are the very fabric of many daily routines. These are important criticisms and I will return to them below, for other objections quickly surfaced.

Feminists challenged the gendered stereotypes of women as fearful and men as fearless in many of these approaches (see, *inter alia*, Goodey, 1997; Stanko, 1997; Gilchrist *et al.*, 1998; Sutton and Farrall, 2005). Betsy Stanko (1987, 1988) was an early critic and argued that the conceptual thinking underpinning both administrative criminology's national crime surveys and left realism's more geographically focused victimization survey could not adequately grasp women's experiences and fears of sexual danger. By using alternative research methodologies (like ethnographic studies, life histories and individual interviews) significant empirical evidence was unearthed that debunked 'the myth of the safe home' (Stanko, 1988) and then revealed the extent of 'ordinary violence' women regularly face and manage across public and private domains (Stanko, 1990). Such work raises 'fundamental questions of whose standards are used as markers of a reasonable or rational fear' (Walklate, 1998:409) and suggests there are some rather faulty conceptual assumptions behind conventional approaches to researching fear.

While the empirical task of unravelling people's experiences of crime has grown apace, with some attempts to introduce more refined definitional distinctions (Hough, 1995), it remains the case that 'conceptual development has, relatively speaking, stagnated' (Ditton *et al.*, 1999:84). This view echoes Sandra Walklate's (1998:410) point that criminology remains wedded to assuming that fear is measurable and has 'proceeded to ignore the view that fear is something experienced in the immediate threat of physical danger and consequently not measurable at all, let alone by a criminal victimization survey, and continued to pursue the social-scientific imperative of valuing reason over emotion'. What is ignored here is any understanding of fear as a complex human emotion. As Sparks (1992:14) has put it, fear 'is not simply a quantity, of which one possesses larger or smaller amounts: rather, it is a mode of perception, even perhaps a constitutive feature of personal identity'. I return below to some of the attempts that have been made to go beyond narrow, behavioural understandings of these complex social processes. Indeed, recent feminist work (Campbell,

2005) has found that asking how, where and when women feel safe
can give greater insights into the differently structured relationships
women and men have with crime.

Yet it is truly striking how developments in criminology have
occurred largely in ignorance of others in cultural studies, which has
not only contributed to the conceptual poverty of debate but has led
to some odd consequences. Perhaps the most costly is that we still
have 'two extensive but separate literatures on fear of crime, one of
which hardly mentions the possible role of the media and another
that scarcely mentions anything else' (Schlesinger *et al.* 1991:416).
Overcoming this unhelpful separation is one of the main tasks of this
chapter, for 'fear of crime' continues to be 'seen as a function of media
exposure or as a consequence of neighbourhood characteristics'
(Killias and Clerici, 2000:437). I now outline these two literatures,
beginning with the work on the media and then the material on urbanism, which has led to important approaches exploring risk and anxiety
in local contexts.

The Media and Fear of Crime

It is not surprising that the media have received so much attention.
The reasons for this have been well summarized:

> Newspaper, radio and especially television, have a prominent role in
> many popular accounts of fear of crime. One tendency has been to see
> this fear as having no grounding in reality but being merely the product
> of sensational and selective news coverage and lurid dramatizations. It
> is certainly the case that media crime reports inevitably focus on the
> most serious and sensational crimes. Furthermore 'crime waves' can be
> produced by active journalistic imaginations. Given that crime is a con-
> spicuous feature of the media, given that the media is, for many people,
> their major source of vicarious information and given that it accords
> most attention to the types of crime which figure most prominently in
> the public imagination it does not seem unreasonable to assume that the
> media has some influence on perceptions and fear of crime. (Hale,
> 1996:109)

We will look in more detail at the production of crime news in chapter
7, but for now it is important to emphasize that the actual evidence
on media coverage and public fear is decidedly mixed.

Some of the inconsistency is due to methodological discrepancies.
There is substantial variation in the 'ways in which crime news, crime

news exposure and fear of crime have been operationalized in the research literature' (Sacco, 1995:151). Moreover, there are considerable differences between the ways broadsheets, mid-market and tabloid newspapers report crime, while television news reporting, reality crime programming and fictional crime dramas each further complicate the picture. As we saw in the last chapter George Gerbner and his associates' work was particularly influential in establishing that heavy television viewing 'cultivates' a misleading 'mean world view' (Gerbner *et al.*, 1980). These findings were quickly challenged. Reanalysis of the same data set used by Gerbner and his colleagues revealed that once statistical controls for variables like age, income and gender were introduced the causal claims for television viewing become unsustainable (Hirsch, 1980, 1981; Hughes, 1980).

Others found that the media affect judgements of a general, distant world 'out there', but not perceptions of the immediate neighbourhood (Coleman, 1993; Heath and Petraitis, 1987; and Tyler and Cook, 1984). Sparks (1992:148–9) is critical of this overall tradition of research, as it relies on crude forms of content analysis that fail to grasp how television crime dramas address 'some rather fundamental anxieties in ways which are familiar, manageable and intelligible but still involving and exciting' while offering 'no real understanding of why people should wish to view these stories, which are taken to frighten and disturb them, and hence no analysis of the techniques and devices which make it pleasurable to do so'. Many of the chapters that follow will directly take up these themes by foregrounding the dynamic of fear and desire that runs through crime stories. Chapter 6 will follow the anthropologist Lévi-Strauss, by insisting that cultural representations continuously work over and try to resolve the central dilemmas confronted by each society that creates them. The central dilemmas are the key questions of human existence: who we are, where we come from, what happens to us when we die and how we are different from others. Every society has these problems to deal with and each has evolved imaginative ways of living with these worries – by making them recognizable, pleasurable and reassuringly familiar. As we will see in the next chapter, some have argued that the modern mass media play a significant role in securing our trust and even numbing the anxieties provoked by living in a high-risk world.

These arguments help to explain why similar mixed findings characterize research on newspaper reporting and fear of crime. Some researchers have found little or no relationship between newspaper reading and fear (Sacco, 1982; Skogan and Maxfield, 1981; Gomme,

1986; and Chiricos *et al.*, 1997) while others have (Gordon and Heath, 1981; Heath, 1984; Liska and Baccaglini, 1990; Williams and Dickinson, 1993). Like the television analyses outlined above the 'differences between studies that find effects and those that do not find effects often lie in the way media exposure is conceptualized' (Heath and Gilbert, 1996:382). Studies have ranged from detailed content analysis of many newspapers combined with several survey questions examining readership (Gordon and Heath, 1981) to a sole question on how frequently crime stories are read when encountered in newspapers (O'Keefe and Reid-Nash, 1987).

Consequently, the more detailed accounts establish relationships between media and fear, but then find other moderating variables that influence the relationship. For instance, Gordon and Heath's (1981:246) research in three North American cities concluded that readers of those newspapers which devoted the most space to crime exhibit higher levels of fear of crime than those reading papers with less crime coverage. Linda Heath (1984) further demonstrated that newspaper coverage of serious crime in other places was 'reassuring' and reduced anxiety, a phenomenon later described as 'feeling safe by comparison' (Liska and Baccaglini, 1990). Nevertheless both studies found that reports of local crime, especially if they were sensational or random, did increase fear. Similar patterns have been established in the British context where it has been found that readers of tabloid newspapers reporting crime prominently had higher levels of fear than readers of broadsheet newspapers presenting crime less sensationally (Williams and Dickinson, 1993).[2]

As has already been hinted and as Jack Katz (1987:61) makes clear there is in this work a 'disparaging assumption of public naivety underneath the view that people generally read crime news to understand crime'. Instead, he argues that readers are typically sceptical and do not treat press crime coverage as providing the definitive 'empirical truth'. Rather, he suggests that the 'predominance of stories on violent crime in contemporary newspapers can be understood as serving readers' interests in re-creating daily their moral sensibilities through shock and impulses of outrage . . . [it is a] process through which adults in contemporary society work out individual perspectives on moral questions of a quite general yet eminently personal relevance' (Katz, 1987:67). This view anticipates Ditton *et al.*'s (1999:84) more recent finding 'that people are more angry about the threat of victimization than they are afraid of it', suggesting that 'anger' is an ignored emotional response to crime.[3] Katz (1987) though is emphasizing the moral work, collective rituals and emotional experiences that crime news generates. As he puts it, by 'reading crime news, people recognize and use the moral tale within the story to orient themselves towards existential dilemmas they cannot help but confront' (Katz, 1987:70). In other words, he is calling attention to the specific interpretative frameworks readers adopt in relation to the text before them and the world around them.

This point can be developed by looking in more detail at the distinction between 'quality' newspaper titles and the 'tabloid' press. Regarding the former, John Fiske (1992:49) argues that a 'believing subject' is constructed who generally accepts the claims made as true for the 'social reality it produces is the habitat of the masculine, educated middle class, the habitat that is congenial to the various alliances formed by the power-bloc in white patriarchal capitalist societies'. In contrast he claims that the

> last thing that tabloid journalism produces is a believing subject. One of its most characteristic tones of voice is that of sceptical laughter which offers the pleasures of disbelief, the pleasures of not being taken in. The popular pleasure of 'seeing through' them . . . is the historical result of centuries of subordination which the people have not allowed to develop into subjection. (Fiske, 1992:49)

While Fiske (1992) can be criticized for romantically privileging resistance, 'sceptical laughter' does challenge the 'objective rationality' of official discourses found in the upmarket press.

Tabloid journalism works through a carnivalesque language of excess, parody and contradiction. Indeed, it 'makes no effort to present its information to us as an objective set of facts in an unchanging universe' (Fiske, 1992:54). We will return to the problems in Fiske's overall position in the next chapter, as he has been a leading proponent of a particular brand of cultural theory that is keen to show how the 'people' subvert the hegemony of the 'power bloc'. Although he does acknowledge that 'the pleasures of scepticism and of parodic excess' are not always progressive politically (Fiske, 1992:54), he fails to convey how the irreverent modes of address in tabloids actually shore up quite reactionary and entrenched prejudices. But clearly there are different modes of engagement and as we will see in the next chapter studies of media audiences have emphasized that the reader, viewer or listener can occupy multiple subjectivities, which are often driven by unconscious processes as much as conscious choices. This turn to more psychoanalytical understandings of subjectivity is an important one and is anticipated below.

Urbanism, Risk and Anxiety

Since it has proven difficult to establish a straightforward relationship between the media and fear other factors have been explored by researchers to understand the place of crime and vulnerability in people's lives, with one important and influential early study claiming that 'there is no evidence here of any relation between media attentiveness and fear of crime' (Skogan and Maxfield, 1981:179). The authors went on to explain that

> this may contravene a great deal of common wisdom on the role of the media in provoking fear of crime, but a careful reading of the research literature on the subject does not reveal convincing evidence of any stronger linkage between media exposure and fear. In fact, many pronouncements on the subject have been based on the inability of researchers to find other explanations for widely dispersed levels of fear in American cities. (Skogan and Maxfield, 1981:181)

It is in this context that many researchers explored the impact of urban neighbourhood characteristics on the fear of crime, with studies finding that 'victimized populations and fearful populations (which anyway overlap) are structurally bound together by their shared location in social, economic and physical space' (Smith, 1986:117). Much evidence was unearthed emphasizing that those who live in the inner city are more fearful than those who live in the suburbs, towns and villages (Shapland and Vagg, 1985).

Given that city living involves unexpected encounters with anonymous strangers, social diversity and changing urban fortunes, it is claimed that this leads to anxiety, insecurity and uncertainty for some, while others privilege a more utopian reading of the city as a space of democracy, opportunity and progress, through celebrating the urban ideal in contrast to the 'idiocy' of the rural (Hubbard, 2003:58) and suburban monotony. Urban imaginaries revolve around utopian and dystopian discourses that are as old as the Western idea of the city itself (Sennett, 1990). Cities are thus sites of intricately entwined desires and fears that are constructed to protect citizens from danger while offering potential liberation from narrow convention and stifling routine – as well as selling the dream (if less often the reality) of escaping agrarian poverty. Nevertheless, the dystopian image of the city has come to predominate over the last 150 years and has intensified in recent decades as social theorists have identified the rise of a 'risk society' and its associated quest for security as a generalized characteristic of late modernity (Beck, 1986 and Giddens, 1991).

Anthony Giddens (1991) argues that one of the defining features of late modernity is the development of a 'calculative attitude' in individuals and institutions to deal with the issues of risk, trust and security in these troubling times. In this reckoning risk is global in reach, yet is also personalized as it is built into people's subjective concerns about their identity. It provokes an uneasy sense of foreboding. A consequence is that the 'generalized climate of risk' engenders a 'reflexive' consciousness of risk, which thereby 'creates a moral disquiet that individuals can never fully overcome' (Giddens, 1991:185). A major difference between the ways we think of and deal with danger compared with earlier eras lies in the extent to which individuals are now understood as active, reflexive agents. Consequently, risk is primarily conceptualized as a human responsibility, both in its production and management, rather than resulting from fate or destiny, as was thought in pre-modern times. It is important to emphasize that in Ulrich Beck's (1986) original formulation he was not arguing that the past was safer and people less scared, but that modernization creates new hazards and uncertainties previous generations did not have to face.

It is significant that the risks which Beck and others have since focused on are the globalization of perils generated by the scale of technological innovation in the modern era. These include environmental disaster, nuclear war, genetic modification, computer viruses, stock-market meltdown and, in the aftermath of 9/11, international terrorism. Yet accompanying these global risks is a more pervasive 'ambient fear' that 'saturates the social spaces of everyday life' and 'requires us to vigilantly monitor even the banal minutiae of our lives' (Hubbard, 2003:52). Urban fortress living, manifest in the protection of privileged consumption places (private homes, retail parks, heritage centres, leisure complexes) distinguishes between those who belong and those who threaten. According to Zygmunt Bauman (1998:23) 'the new fragmentation of the city space, the shrinkage and disappearance of public space, the falling apart of urban community – and above all the ex-territoriality of the new elite and the forced territoriality of the rest' has generated an intense preoccupation with the protection of territory and the spectacle of security. For example, it has been argued that one of the driving forces behind the introduction of CCTV surveillance systems into British cities and town centres over the last decade or so has been an attempt to arrest their economic decline in the face of fierce competition from safe, secure and sanitized out-of-town retail parks (Bannister and Fyfe, 2001: 810). Each of these defensive responses to insecurity only serves to heighten our awareness of unforeseen danger lurking around every corner.

There is also a lot of money to be made from the trade in safety and security. To take one example, there is the quite extraordinary phenomenon of the 'Sports Utility Vehicle' in the United States. This massive petrol guzzling, quasi-military vehicle had at one point reached 45 per cent of all car sales in the US and is sold as a 'defensive capsule' – a signifier of safety that like the gated communities into which they so often drive is portrayed in advertisements as being immune to the risky urban life outside (Bauman, 2006:143–4). According to Josh Lauer (2005) the SUV first emerged as a status symbol in the early 1980s with the introduction of the military Humvee (which stands for High Mobility Multipurpose Wheeled Vehicle) that was commissioned by the army to replace the jeep and came to popular attention during the first Gulf War. This prompted the development of a civilian version, while the continuing occupation of Iraq has only heightened their popularity.

The massive civilian Hummer was embraced as an ultra-macho novelty vehicle and quickly became one of the most fashionable and popular vehicles in America, with more than a third of its sales to women drivers. Indeed, a recent television advert features a woman driving a Hummer through city streets, with the tagline, 'Slip into something more metal'. Clearly there is something more going on here than an increased risk consciousness, as the SUV is an expensive piece of 'high-end automotive jewellery' in which risk management is transformed into a symbol of conspicuous consumption (Lauer, 2005:163–5). It is significant that in the UK similar over-sized, four-wheeled drive vehicles are frequently derided as 'Chelsea tractors', which indicates their almost ridiculous remove from their original use among working farmers and the rural gentry.

Another rich seam of work has attempted to understand the ways fears and anxieties are socially constructed. Ian Taylor (1996, 1997) has argued that the fear of crime has become a condensed metaphor, which reveals broader concerns over the pace of socio-economic change. As he explains, the rise of defensive middle-class suburban social movements organized around crime prevention 'are activated not just by immediately presenting sets of problems in the specific locality (stories of aggressive young people and actual violence on the hitherto peaceful local High Street) but by deeper fears about joblessness and house prices, and (in the case of parents with suburban children) schooling "for success", child safety, moral socialization . . . and a host of other increasingly agitated concerns' (Taylor, 1997:66).

On this account, worries about crime are intimately bound up with the less easily grasped or articulated troubles generated by changes in economic, moral and social life.

This point is further explored by Evi Girling, Ian Loader and Richard Sparks (2000) in their study of public perceptions of crime in a prosperous English market town where they argue that

> people's responses to crime (in its association with other matters of concern to them) are both informed by, and in turn inform, their *sense of place*; their sense, that is, of both *the place* they inhabit (its histories, divisions, trajectories and so forth), and of *their place* within a wider world of hierarchies, troubles, opportunities and insecurities. (Girling *et al.*, 2000:17, emphasis in original)

The importance of this work is that it attempts to situate people's fears in specific everyday contexts and in doing so it chimes with other recent developments that have highlighted how the individual's social location (Walklate, 1998) and inner personal senses of security (Hollway and Jefferson, 2000) shape perceptions of the wider world around them.

A more polemical account of the 'culture of fear' is contained in Frank Furedi's (1997, 2001, 2007) various depictions of the debilitating consequences of our increased risk consciousness and susceptibility to scaremongering. As he contends in his *Paranoid Parenting* we are creating a generation of intensively reared 'battery children' chained to television or video games where the 'obsessive fear about the safety of children has led to a fundamental redefinition of parenting' (2001:xii). His overall argument is that there has been a major cultural shift away from seeing risk taking as a positive sign of progress towards a more negative 'morality of low expectation'. On this reckoning every human experience is transformed into an ultra-cautious safety situation that encourages us all to become victims. A similar point is made by David Altheide (2002) where he states that a discourse of fear now pervades all social situations and he makes the connection with religious beliefs explicit. In the past organized religion offered salvation from eternal damnation, whereas now the secular state is meant to deliver us from modern fears. No longer afraid of God or the Devil we now fear other humans who embody evil. Historians, however, have questioned whether some periods are more anxious than others and have cautioned against reading evidence partially or selectively to support a broad thesis (Hunt, 1999). Others have accused Furedi and his followers of defending 'a peculiarly

Promethean version of Enlightenment reason, bordering on the caricatured form often critiqued in post-structuralist and postmodern
sociology' (Law and McNeish, 2007:443). Despite these objections
the culture of fear thesis does draw attention to how the meaning and
experiences of fear are continually shaped by social processes.

There is a crucial paradox here. We are currently the 'most tech-
nologically equipped generation in human history' yet we are also 'the
generation most haunted by feelings of insecurity and helplessness'
and as Bauman (2006:101) goes on to explain, citing Robert Castel
(2003:5), in the West we:

> 'live undoubtedly in some of the most secure (*sûres*) societies that ever
> existed', and yet, contrary to the 'objective evidence', we – the most cos-
> seted and pampered people of all – feel more threatened, insecure and
> frightened, more inclined to panic, and more passionate about every-
> thing related to security and safety than the people of most other soci-
> eties on record. (Bauman, 2006:101)

It is clear that the world is undergoing multifaceted cultural, economic and social transformations. Consequently, fear and insecurity
about crime are tangled up 'with the larger consequences of modernity, and find its lived social meaning among people's sense of change
and decay, optimism and foreboding in the neighbourhoods, towns,
cities and wider political communities in which they live and move'
(Hope and Sparks, 2000:5). That such responses vary according to
social position, material advantage and experience of place has been
well documented in the defensive strategies adopted by the prosperous (Taylor, 1996, 1997 and Girling *et al.*, 2000) and the ways less
affluent people living in 'high crime areas' of inner cities manage their
daily lives (Hollway and Jefferson, 2000 and Walklate and Evans,
1999). Although these studies attempt to understand fear of crime as
a locally situated activity they curiously do not directly address media
consumption, audience interpretation and collective representation in
any great detail.

Yet there are strong reasons why it would be unwise to conclude
that the media have no place in shaping popular conceptions of crime
(see also Ditton *et al.*, 2004:598). Part of the problem lies in the lack
of detailed research examining how fear of crime, media use and other
forms of cultural communication interact with the dynamic rhythms
of everyday life. As one recent account puts it, 'in-depth studies of the
ways in which media crime is interpreted within quotidian existences
domestically rooted and geographically located in real (and imagined)

places . . . remain elusive' (Banks, 2005:170). In the next chapter we will see how the local contexts of media use have become central to audience research in cultural studies, suggesting that there is much to be gained in criminology from productive encounters with this work. Before we turn to this material it is important to address other recent developments that have the potential to bear fruit in the future and suggest different ways of conceptualizing such matters as anxiety, fear and risk.

Conceptual Developments

In an effort to develop a richer understanding of fear of crime the work of Mary Douglas (1966, 1985, 1992) is proving influential. Its appeal lies in the way it unravels the emotional complexities of fear and overcomes the limits of the rational/irrational divide. Her anthropology provides a distinctive account of how individuals, communities and institutions collectively think about risk that developed in opposition to those who saw such matters as either mistaken or partial if they differed from expert knowledge. In her early study of purity and danger she argued that what is understood to be dirty, polluting and threatening is culturally specific, and establishes boundaries between Same and Other, while defining social groups and creating moral order. Douglas's (1985, 1992) later writings develop these insights and regard risk as an unforgiving vehicle of blame, in that 'risky' groups are singled out as dangerous and used in cultural relations to sustain social solidarity. Who we blame reveals much about who we are, how we organize our relationships with others and gives shape to the social world by endowing it with moral meaning (Douglas, 1992:6–7). She does not deny that there are 'real risks'; rather her emphasis lies in how certain risks come to perform cultural, moral and political tasks (Douglas, 1992:29). Her work offers a very different way of understanding the causes of public anxiety, but still recognizes that some people worry disproportionately about some dangers rather than others.

The significance of her approach has been recognized by Lupton and Tulloch (1999:511) who have pointed out how distinctions 'between rationality and irrationality in relation to the individual have no meaning in this schema' and for Douglas 'cultural assumptions and meanings always have their use and value to achieve certain, often symbolic ends'. Likewise, Sparks (2001:163) finds in aspects of her work a way of thinking about risk that does not 'imagine putting an end to dispute, but neither does it see us as necessarily entrapped in a "prison-house" of language in a way that makes any kind of rational adjudication or comparative analysis impossible'. Her contribution is one that emphasizes the cultural work that risk performs in the social world. As she puts it, 'fear of danger tends to strengthen the lines of division in a community' and fear 'digs more deeply the cleavages that have been there all the time' (Douglas, 1992:34). The overall argument is that individual perceptions of risk are strongly shaped by prior identifications with different kinds of social organization that sustain cultural boundaries. Thus the implication is that we should 'interpret "moral panics" over the safety of our natural environment not so much as a reasonable response to the "reality" of danger, but rather, as an emotional/cultural reaction to the social experience of marginalization' (Wilkinson, 2001:107). It also helps to explain the paradox that while life expectancy in Western societies has been indisputably increasing, the overwhelming view is that life is fundamentally more risky now than it was a generation ago.

Another important development has been the introduction of psychoanalytical theory into the fear of crime debate. Wendy Hollway and Tony Jefferson (1997, 2000) draw on the key psychoanalytical insight that anxiety is the price we pay for having a sense of self. Their work emphasizes that anxiety is a universal feature of the human condition and that dynamic 'unconscious defences against anxiety are a commonplace and constructive aspect of response to threats' (Hollway and Jefferson, 2000:32). The specific unconscious defence mechanisms they focus on are denial, splitting and projection to explore how threats to the self are managed by these displacing activities. Their overall argument is that anxiety, as a pervasive yet inchoate emotion, lies behind much of the contemporary concerns over fear of crime. Drawing on their research with people living on two council estates in northern England their analysis reveals quite varied and diffuse responses to the threat of crime. The differing responses are informed by individual biography, social location and unconscious defence mechanisms. As they put it, 'a rampant "fear of crime" discourse which might on the face of it be thought to exacerbate fears, could actually serve unconsciously as a relatively reassuring site for displaced anxieties which otherwise would be too threatening to cope with' (Hollway and Jefferson, 1997:263–4). The implication is that fear always has something in its sights, while anxiety is directed towards nothing. When experiencing anxiety the distress is caused by our inability to make sense of the diffuse unease as there is nothing tangible on which to concentrate our dread of the unknown.

According to Freud, fear and anxiety are mutually dependent: 'as anxiety anticipates an experience of helplessness, it leaves us helplessly searching to find an object which is sufficient to translate our anxieties into fear' (Wilkinson, 2001:20). There is some helpful conceptual clarification here as terms like anxiety and fear tend to be used interchangeably and unproblematically in much of the literature. But what is clear is that while the two feelings are closely related our specific fears grow out of inchoate anxieties. Leaving aside the many problems that have been levelled against psychoanalysis generally, which are addressed in the next chapter, it is important to emphasize that Hollway and Jefferson (2000:31) have introduced a notion of human subjectivity that recognizes 'the non-rational, unintentional and emotional aspects of people's actions and experience' that had largely been neglected by criminologists. Nevertheless, sympathetic critics have contended that their approach is more about 'feeling than structure' (Walklate, 1998:411) while others argue that to 'focus only on unconscious displacement tends to ignore both the conscious strategies and various circuits of communication' (Lupton and Tulloch, 1999:515) adopted by their respondents. But replacing the rational, unitary subject with the anxious, fragmented subject need not dispense with a social interpretation of the subject's human situation at particular historical conjunctures. Instead, unconscious processes combine with cognitive choices as well as social structures, like language, so that these aspects of explanation are best seen as complementary rather than alternatives.

In his recent account of *Liquid Fear* Bauman (2006:52) has also argued, in psychoanalytical fashion, that the 'primal fear of death is perhaps the prototype or archetype of fears; the ultimate fear from which all other fears borrow their meanings'. Indeed, he goes on to cite the following passage from Freud:

> We are threatened with suffering from three directions: from our own body, which is doomed to decay and dissolution and which cannot even do without pain and anxiety as warning signals; from the external world, which may rage against us with overwhelming and merciless forces of destruction; and finally from our relations to other men. The suffering which comes from this last source is perhaps more painful than any other. We tend to regard it as a kind of gratuitous addition, although it cannot be any less fatefully inevitable than the suffering which comes from elsewhere. (Freud, cited in Bauman, 2007:52)

In this remarkable passage Freud identifies the three fronts on which the interminable war against dread is fought. Yet it would be wrong to assume that people are constantly afraid – life would be unbearable if that were so – but rather the emotional intensity varies and we find imaginative ways of ignoring or adapting to precarious environments (Tuan, 1979:9). As Walklate (2007:100) has succinctly put it, fear 'is not an ever present feeling or state of mind but burns differently in different contexts'. Nevertheless the passage does show how fear comes from three directions: our own anxious inner worlds, broader external forces and immediate social relations.

In the next chapter we will begin by looking at how psychoanalytical ideas have explained the processes through which audiences identify with what they see on screen or read in books. It provides a way of understanding why violence and horror, when they present no direct danger, are such crowd-pleasers. Indeed, so ingrained are disturbing images (incest, rape, cannibalism, torture, murder and so on) in the masterpieces of Western literature and art that literary critics have suggested that these great works[4] have endured precisely because they enable readers to indulge in the most taboo of fantasies (Fielder, 1982; Schechter, 2005; Trend, 2007). If we are to study crime and the media then we have to confront the role of unconscious, forbidden, subterreanean desires as well as the conscious, often mundane experiences of everyday life – as many of the media texts themselves offer socially acceptable ways of indulging in these pleasures. It is to such matters that we now turn.

3

Making Meaning

It has now become the orthodoxy to insist that media audiences actively work with the texts before them, rather than passively consume the messages sent by powerful cultural industries. In this chapter I explore the implications of what is meant by audience activity and how this enables a more sophisticated understanding of the meanings generated by representations of crime in the mass media. The tensions between culturalist emphases on the importance of lived experiences and structuralist approaches to the textual subject are at their most apparent here. These differences echo broader distinctions between social scientific and more literary traditions of studying the media. Nevertheless, both have come to emphasize how diverse audiences creatively interact with what they see, read and hear. In doing so the shift has been from conceptualizing the audience as an undifferentiated, easily manipulated mass to more culturally specific groups with distinctive identities and subjectivities.

If the central theme of the previous chapter was fear, then the key one here is desire. And if the primal fear of death is the ultimate source of all fears, then it is sexuality that fundamentally organizes all human desires. Initially, this significance registered in psychoanalytical attention to the place of sexual desire in the visual pleasures associated with watching film. The very idea of an active audience implies mediated communication is a two-way, interactive process of meaning exchange that offers not simply idle enjoyment but some liberating potential. Such a view has been criticized for over-estimating the capacity of the audience actively to resist powerful media institutions, but it remains the case that the question of desire raises some important issues around aesthetic taste, cultural relativism and moral judgement that lie at the heart of debates over the worth of popular culture.

Consequently, this chapter will concentrate on these different approaches to media audiences to shed light on important social practices.

Psychoanalysis, Subjectivity and Spectatorship

In cultural, film and literary theory there has been considerable interest in psychoanalytical ideas. Although cinema was born at around the
same time as Sigmund Freud was developing his radical thinking on
the unconscious, it was not until the 1970s that psychoanalytical
theories moved to the centre of debates within media studies. This
renewal of interest was due to the rise of feminist accounts of patriarchal oppression, Jacques Lacan's (1977) influential reworking of
Freudian concepts and Louis Althusser's (1971) understanding of the
media as an 'Ideological State Apparatus'. One important approach
was pioneered by film critics associated with the French journal
Cahiers du cinéma and developed in the British journal *Screen*, which
quickly became known as 'apparatus theory' to explore the analogies
between the film experience, dream states and ideological mechanisms. The work of Jean-Louis Baudry, Christian Metz and Laura
Mulvey provided important contributions that challenged many conventional approaches to studying media audiences in the 1970s and I
will begin by outlining the main contours of their arguments before
moving on to more contemporary figures that have developed psychoanalytical thinking.

Jean-Louis Baudry (1974/92) uses psychoanalysis to grasp the
intensity of experience provoked by cinema – the way it organizes a
heightened 'impression of reality' that is 'more-than-real'. Rather
than analysing the content of images or the stories of particular films
or even genres he uses the term 'apparatus' to explain how cinema
works as an institutional network, which includes the invisible projec-
tor, illuminated screen and audience spectatorship. Baudry emphasizes how the camera lens incorporates the visual use and ideological
values of perspective developed during the Italian Renaissance as it
constructs 'the world in relation to the spectator's vision, and so established the spectator as the centre of the world' (Jancovich, 1995:133).
Thus the values of individualism, possession and elevation of the
visual over other senses are invoked when one stands before a
Renaissance painting or watches a Hollywood movie. The spectator is
'subjected' to the apparatus's positioning and Baudry compares
watching a film to Lacan's theory of the 'mirror phase' of a young
child's development.[1]

Lacan's 'mirror phase' and its relationship to the imaginary and symbolic realms of human subjectivity were crucial elements in how 'apparatus theory' understood the ideological positioning of the subject in cinema spectatorship. Christian Metz (1982) describes cinema as the 'imaginary signifier' in order to grasp the unprecedented range of intense perceptions offered while simultaneously gratifying the narcissistic (seeing an imaginary ideal self reflected on screen), voyeuristic (enjoying looking at others without being seen) and fetishistic (exaggerating the power of things or people to deal with one's fear of them) desires to look among the audience. Metz argues that cinema encourages a form of voyeurism that always includes sadism and insulates the spectator from reciprocal awareness, while the keyhole effect of the screen 'suggests we are looking through an aperture/apparatus upon the actors (a feature it shares with the television screen)' (Allen, 2004:130). There is an important sense in which Metz is emphasizing that in the process of identifying with a film, the spectator is satisfying some basic, primal drives that Freud associated with human sexuality.

Clearly, psychoanalytical theory revolves around quite complex issues of desire, identification and the unconscious. Initially, though, feminists were highly critical of Freud (e.g. Millett, 1969; Firestone, 1970; and Greer, 1971), identifying him as a prime source of patriarchal attitudes, denigrator of women and pathologizer of homosexuality (each view having some truth in it), while Lacan was contemptuous of the women's movement generally. Nevertheless, other feminists did find in both thinkers keys to exploring how gender, sexuality and subjectivity are culturally constructed, rather than pure products of biological destiny. Laura Mulvey's (1975/92) landmark essay 'Visual Pleasure and Narrative Cinema', originally published in *Screen*, is one of the most influential pieces written in contemporary film theory. She argues, like Baudry and Metz, that 'the fascination of film is reinforced by pre-existing patterns of fascination already at work within the individual subject and the social formations that have moulded him [*sic*]' (Mulvey, 1975/92:746).

Mulvey drew on Freudian and Lacanian concepts to argue that the organization of looks in classic Hollywood film is structured to gratify the 'male gaze' in three ways: the look from camera to scene; the look from the spectator to the action; and the looks between characters in the film. She argued that in many of Alfred Hitchcock's thrillers (like *Vertigo*, but also *Marnie* and *Rear Window*) the 'look is central to the plot, oscillating between voyeurism and fetishistic fascination' while the 'heroes are exemplary of the symbolic order and the law – a policeman (*Vertigo*), a dominant male possessing money and power (*Marnie*) – but their erotic drives lead them into compromised situations' (Mulvey, 1975/92:754–5). Her overall point is that the gendered pleasures of the gaze are rendered through voyeurism (the sexual attraction of the threatening woman) and narcissism (identifying with the masculine hero), so that the male characters in the film are positioned in the film as active bearers of the look, while the feminine are coded as passive erotic objects to be desired. Mulvey (1975/92:750–1) further shows how the way in which women are filmed works against the conventional narrative style to 'freeze the flow of action in moments of erotic contemplation' so that the use of close-ups on fragmented body parts (like Marlene Dietrich's legs or Greta Garbo's face) fetishizes the female image. Regardless of the specific content of any particular film the cinematic apparatus works to construct an ideal male spectator that ensures female subordination. In other words, film is addressed to the male unconscious whatever the gender of specific viewers.

Mulvey's article was polemical and hugely influential. There is now broad agreement that mainstream, commercial films and certainly those produced by Hollywood are structured to satisfy male viewing pleasures, with much subsequent work examining the functions of the gaze in specific genres. For instance, Steve Neale (1993) has emphasized that men could be filmed for glamour and bodily display in feminine genres like melodrama and musicals, while in action films men are also subjected to voyeuristic looking as they are ultimately about struggles between hyper-masculine men. Nevertheless, the issue of how totalizing the 'male gaze' is has become a central concern. Tania Modleski (1988) questions Mulvey's readings of Hitchcock's oeuvre as voyeuristic and sadistic, by finding it to be more contradictory as the thrillers allow some expression of female resistance to patriarchal domination. Many of Hitchcock's films (like *Suspicion, Notorious* or *Spellbound*) are actually concerned with a woman attempting to free herself from the control of a man, whereas Gaylyn Studlar (1985/92) finds fault with Metz and Mulvey's insistence that the only visual pleasures on offer are inflexibly masculine and sadistic controlling ones. Instead, she argues that cinematic pleasure is much closer to the submissive pleasures of masochism so that identification is multiple, fluid and crosses gender differences. The implication is that the spectator plays with different subject positions and can occupy contradictory positions (male/female, hero/villain, master/slave) to gratify conflicting desires within the self.

Despite these revisions there have been many criticisms levelled against psychoanalytical approaches to media audiences. Among the most significant is that the psychoanalytical tradition has a universalizing tendency that fails to grasp historical and cultural differences: the 'theory generalizes singular subject identities regardless of obvious differences between people, cultures, and eras' (Pribram, 2004:151). Another objection raised is what Deleuze and Guattari (1972/84:97) call 'the incurable familialism of psychoanalysis'. Their point is that with its totalizing focus on the Oedipal triangle and abstracting the privatized, male-dominated family structures found in modern Europe to stand for eternal processes, psychoanalysis cannot comprehend the role events outside family life play in shaping the unconscious. Others have attempted to contrast the 'autonomous self' of classical Freudian analysis with the 'relational self' of object relations theory to grasp the way we are social beings, while holding onto some notion of the self's inner complexity and turmoil (Chodorow, 1989).

Too often a singular version of psychoanalytical theory is advanced as the key to understanding the dominant meaning of a text. This not only excludes other modes of interpretation but ends up mechanical in much contemporary work, a point well made by Judith Mayne (1993) when she wonders:

How many times does one need to be told that individual film x, or film genre y, articulates the law of the father, assigns the spectator a position of male oedipal desire, marshals castration anxiety in the form of voyeurism and fetishism, before psychoanalysis begins to sound less like the exploration of the unconscious, and more like a master plot? (Mayne, 1993:69, cited in Turner, 1999:141)

Perhaps the most significant consequence of 'these debates was to pose a monolithic picture of patriarchal cinema, rendering the spectator as a passive victim to ideology and the apparatus' (Campbell, 2005:27). As we will see below studies of television audiences have been far more attentive to the social context of viewing than film theorists who have been preoccupied with the close analysis of the textual features and formal patterns of cinema spectatorship. This focus on textual form and pattern is largely due to the fact that film studies developed out of literary studies, where there has been a longstanding interest in psychoanalytical theory and an obvious privileging of the text. In contrast, television studies emerged in the social sciences by pointing out some of the critical failings in *Screen* film theory.

Looking Awry and Sacrificial Violence

Recent years have seen a resurgence of interest in Lacanian psychoanalysis and ideological critique through the work of Slavoj Žižek. He
retains the underlying assumptions of apparatus theorists (that cultural representations support subjectivity), but discards the view that
this can be explained through the predetermined effects of an ideological apparatus stitching subjects into the fabric of the narrative.
Rather, he seeks to show how 'the texts of popular culture serve to
allegorize the drama of lack-in-being that defines the condition of the
subject' (Allen, 2004:136). A good example of this approach is his discussion of two neo-noir films from the 1980s, *Blade Runner* and *Angel
Heart*, in a chapter ostensibly concerned with the question of subjectivity encountered in thinkers like Descartes, Kant and Hegel through
to Lacan (Žižek, 1993). Both films blend familiar noir ingredients
with another genre, science fiction and supernatural horror respectively, yet they each share standard hard-boiled detective quest narratives in which the hero goes on a search that will ultimately end with
his own destruction.

In *Angel Heart*, the private eye Harold Angel sets off on the trail of
a killer who eventually turns out to be himself (having unknowingly
sold his soul to the devil in an occult ritual several years before). At
the film's climax Angel is revealed to have exchanged hearts with a
young soldier, who he now thinks he is, and in the final scene he
screams 'I know who I am' as he descends into hell. In *Blade Runner*,
the hero has to seek a group of human replicant androids at large in a
Los Angeles of the future and terminate them; in the darker director's
cut released in 1992 the hero, Deckard, discovers at the end that he
too is a replicant. In the more conformist compromise 1982 version
the hero is not only less implicated with those he is charged with elim-
inating, but he also escapes with a pretty replicant he hopes to save.
As a result:

> The outcome of the quest is therefore in both cases the radical under-
> mining of self-identity masterminded by a mysterious, all-powerful
> agency, in the first case the Devil himself ('Louis Cipher'), in the second
> case the Tyrell corporation, which succeeded in fabricating replicants
> unaware of their replicant status, i.e., replicants misperceiving them-
> selves as humans. (Žižek, 1993:10)

Both films reveal how memory, which is usually a central prop assuring identity, is mistaken and consequently poses the question of how

real is our reality? For Žižek these texts of popular culture expose the 'traumatic split between the subject available to consciousness, a prey to the fictions of the symbolic order, and the transcendental or unconscious subject . . . and is the manifestation in it of the real' (Kay, 2003:8). In other words, Žižek uses aspects of popular culture to explore the irresolvable split between thinking and being that he sees running through post-Cartesian philosophy. It nicely exemplifies his method of 'looking awry' (Žižek, 1992) at popular culture to render visible aspects of Lacan's notoriously difficult thinking. Similar themes of detection, memory and identity have been pursued in more recent films like *Code 46* (2003), *Memento* (2001) and *Minority Report* (2002) that variously explore the divide between perception and reality.

Another influential theorist who has used aspects of psychoanalysis to grasp how human desire leads inescapably to fierce rivalry and deadly conflict is the French anthropologist and literary theorist René Girard (1979, 1986). His argument is that cultural order and social stability are only possible through repeated acts of collective violence against a lone victim (or group of victims), which through the sacrificial figure of the scapegoat and the dynamics of projection serves to bear the brunt of the aggression and violence previously spread unevenly throughout society. These ideas have been imaginatively taken up by Siobhan Holohan (2005) in an analysis of the scapegoat mechanisms that make certain criminal incidences prone to media spectacle. Through two well-known cases of the 1990s – the murder of Stephen Lawrence in London and the trial of the British au pair Louise Woodward in the United States – Holohan details how media representations construct a sacrificial figure to uphold and strengthen the existing social order.

The first half of the book concentrates on the case of Louise Woodward, who was tried in the American courts for her part in the suspicious death of a baby left in her charge. Holohan begins by detailing the competing representations of the case in the American and British media, which revolved around collapsing family values, exploitative domestic labour and white national identity. While American tabloids tended to portray Woodward as a monstrous child abuser, the British press initially saw her as a victim of economic exploitation. Yet the main reason why the case came to such media prominence, according to Holohan (2005:25), was 'the disjunctive elements of the white woman occupying the structural position of the ethnic worker'. She then situates the case in broader historical, social and political context to examine further the ways in which the story became a morality tale revolving around the disintegrating family in late modernity and mobilizes psychoanalytical arguments on scapegoating to demonstrate how the judicial decision to find Woodward guilty of manslaughter, instead of murder, upheld the symbolic order of American society 'by castrating her as a dangerous surrogate mother' (Holohan, 2005:77).

The second part of the book analyses the legal events and media representations surrounding the murder of Stephen Lawrence. Although ethnic difference was an important aspect of the Woodward case, it is absolutely central to Lawrence. When Lawrence was murdered in 1993 there was scant media interest in the story, yet by the end of the decade there were few left in Britain who were ignorant of the case and the political upheavals that followed in the wake of his parents' campaign for justice. Holohan sets herself the task of examining how Lawrence became a 'virtual white man: that is re-packaged for consumption by the middle-English audience' and she traces how the news media 'sympathetically constructed the Lawrence family as the acceptable face of black Britain' (Holohan, 2005:81). On her reckoning Lawrence becomes middle-English, while his alleged killers are cast as uncivilized thugs from the dangerous classes of the white periphery. There is no doubt that the case marked a significant turning point in representations of class, race and racism (see also Cottle, 2004, 2005; McLaughlin, 2005a and chapter 8). Holohan's overall analysis is a sophisticated textual reading that reveals how media representations of conflict involve sacrificial figures that served to unite society in the face of crisis. There are some quite complex arguments here, but what this more recent work shows is that there still remains considerable potential in using psychoanalytical arguments productively, as subsequent chapters will also demonstrate.

The Active Audience

The tensions between text-centred approaches to interpretation and the culturalist emphasis on lived experience soon became apparent. As I stated in an earlier chapter the 1970s marked a crucial turning point when the mass communication tradition came under increasing attack via the 'rediscovery of ideology' (Hall, 1982). Initially this led to the analysis of the ideological structure of news to show how these texts favour dominant meanings, construct consensus and reproduce the status quo. At the same time the psychoanalytical approaches to film spectatorship outlined above were emerging, which appeared to be worlds away from the socio-psychological empiricism of mass communications research. Both developments privileged the ideological power of the text to position the spectator, but what was missing was any sense of how meaning is generated in everyday life.

It is significant that one of the main challenges to this sovereignty of the text came from studies of television audiences, which emphasized the forms of activity associated with viewing. In doing so this work sought to challenge the widespread assumption that watching the television is predominantly passive in character – whether this be the 'couch potato' slumped in front of the set mindlessly watching whatever 'chewing gum for the eyes' happens to be on or the 'television zombie' who goes on a killing spree imitating what they have just seen. Yet studies emphasizing the 'active audience' also sought to counter the prevailing intellectual trend in cultural studies, which assumed that audience interpretation could be ascertained purely from a close reading of the texts themselves. David Morley (1992:175) is one of the key figures advocating a shift from the '*object of viewing*' to the '*context of viewing*' and the implications of his work have been widely debated.

In Stuart Hall's (1980b/2003) initial formulation of the encoding-decoding model one of its central features was the concept of 'preferred reading' (towards which the text attempts to direct readers) while allowing for the possibility that readers can adopt 'negotiated' or 'oppositional' positions in relation to the text. It is this issue of variation, or 'structured polysemy', that Morley (1980) examines in his landmark study of the *Nationwide* audience. His method was to show an episode of the programme to different focus groups, each with five to ten members and representing a social position – including schoolboys, shop stewards, bank managers, white university arts students and black further education students. Although Morley's study attempted to show how complex audience responses to the media can be, he also emphasized that this variation was not due to individual idiosyncrasies but is an intricate function of socio-economic position and the differing 'cultural competencies' that regulate people's abilities to engage with and make sense of the world. These discursive codes are unevenly distributed according to class, age, gender, ethnicity and other dimensions of cultural identity. In doing so his research sought to show how different audiences understood texts in different ways and that this variation was 'both produced by social inequalities but also acted to legitimate and reproduce them' (Jancovich *et al.*, 2003:5). Morley's findings prompted much critical debate and subsequent empirical research.

The Glasgow University Media Group have consistently applied these methods to content analyses of television news (Glasgow Media Group, 1976, 1980 and 1985) and audience reception studies of industrial disputes (Philo, 1990), AIDS (Kitzinger, 1993), conflict in Northern Ireland (Miller, 1994), mental illness (Philo, 1996), coverage of the Middle East (Philo and Berry, 2004) and child sexual abuse (Skidmore, 1995; Kitzinger, 1999b, 2004). The latter work, for instance, used focus groups to unravel how sexual abuse emerged as a social problem, explored how the participants perceived the risks and imagined possible 'solutions'. This research showed how the media since the mid-1980s began conveying new information about the frequency of sexual abuse and the likelihood of the perpetrator being known to the child. Yet at the same time, the media also emphasized danger from strangers abducting children through a series of highly publicized cases that have only intensified since the research was completed.

Nevertheless, the work demonstrates how media images are integrated into people's everyday lives and social settings, as revealed in the following example:

> a fear of strangers, rather than fathers, step-fathers and uncles, is in many ways easier to sustain (and communicate to children). Research participants with young children spoke of their need to be able to rely on others for child-care. Suspicion of male friends and relatives was viewed as impractical and disempowering, whereas supervising children's freedom of association with strangers was incorporated into their day-to-day routine. People also discussed how fear of child abduction, rather than incest, fitted into their own experiences of parenting (cross-cut by variables such as class and access to supervised child-care or play areas). For example, they described how memories of highly publicised abductions were called to mind whenever their child was late home. (Kitzinger, 1999a: 11)

Clearly, the 'social currency' of media messages depends on the value of particular stories in lived contexts. In this regard, certain crimes come to stand as 'signal crimes' (Innes, 2003) that powerfully shape public understandings of risk and danger.

Morley's overall approach is also a clear influence on Jessica Allen, Sonia Livingstone and Robert Reiner's recent research (see Allen *et al.*, 1998; Livingstone *et al.*, 2001; and Reiner *et al*; 2000, 2001 and 2003). This, highly significantly, is one of the first criminological studies to undertake a wide-scale historical (1945–91) content analysis of media representations of crime across film, newspapers and televisions in Britain. At the same time it attempts to address the issues of audience interpretation through using focus groups.[2] Their findings demonstrate how gender and generation significantly inform audience position. For instance, 'young women are aware of their potential victim status, particularly their vulnerability to male violence, and so they welcomed coverage of such crimes', whereas neither 'younger nor older men in our groups would accept views of themselves as potential victims' (Reiner *et al.*, 2001:189–90). Moreover, the younger 'men were particularly interested in forms of crime media in which the criminal was as much a focus as the law enforcers and in which the moral boundaries between the two were ambiguous or unresolved' (ibid.:190). Young women, in contrast, preferred more 'realistic' depictions or the nature of crime (Reiner *et al.*, 2000:119). These differences are suggestive, but it is important to pause here and briefly discuss the problems in using focus groups to research media audiences.

Critics have argued that the audience is artificially constructed in this kind of research, which raises a number of difficulties. First, the finding of little variation within focus groups suggests that 'a consensualizing process was engendered by the grouping itself' so that the research 'may well have been measuring *that* process, not the normal process of the individual decoding television texts in the family living room' (Turner, 1996:126, emphasis in original). Second, the audience responses are treated in a fairly unsophisticated fashion, rather than analysed as textual constructs themselves. Third, the approach 'does not observe people, but relies on what they choose to tell (they might lie) and on what they are able to tell (what they can articulate about their preferences and choices)' (Bertrand and Hughes, 2005: 55). In other words, the 'talk' generated in focus groups should not be taken as providing a direct window into what people really think and actually do. Fourth, the approach fails to grasp how television, and in particular news programming, articulates a tension between anxiety and security that is ultimately reassuring through its rhythmic ordering of rituals and symbols that we are largely unaware of. As Roger Silverstone (1994) explains:

> Reassurance is not provided only, of course, in the content of reporting. On the contrary. Yet the levels of anxiety that could be raised (and of course may well be either inevitably or deliberately raised) are ameliorated both in terms of the structure of the news as a programme (the tidying of papers, mutual smiles and silent chat following a 'human interest' story complete news bulletins, except under exceptional

circumstances of crisis or catastrophe, all over the world), and in terms
of its reliability and frequency. (Silverstone, 1994:16–17)

Silverstone is emphasizing the everyday quality of television and it is
this sense of routine in social life that has become increasingly important in studies of media audiences.

Media Audiences and Ethnography

Many consequently turned to ethnographic research to grasp audience activity more rigorously than had been attempted thus far. But
as we will see shortly this has also introduced new theoretical problems and methodological difficulties that are not easily resolved. The
1980s saw a plethora of studies on media audiences that more or less
faithfully adhered to ethnographic principles. The best-known examples initially took soap operas as their main focus (Hobson, 1982;
Ang, 1985; and Buckingham, 1987). Morley (1986) took the criticisms of his earlier work seriously and analysed how television is used
in the domestic settings of eighteen families. He found clear gender
differences, with the remote control a powerful symbolic possession
of the man: 'rather as a mace might have featured as an (equally
phallic) physical symbol of authority in an earlier time' (Morley,
1996:322). A finding confirmed in Lull's (1990) study of family
viewing, which also showed how men largely controlled what was
watched. More recent research has claimed that this was too polarized
a view of the negotiations that take place: 'while previous studies have
suggested that men have dominated control over the television, our
evidence indicates that in the 1990s this is relatively rare' (Gauntlett
and Hill, 1999:245). This difference is partly explained by the
different methodologies used and by the proliferation of television sets
in the home over this time period.
    Nevertheless, others further examined the gendering of technologies
in domestic space by showing how the video recorder (Gray, 1992),
home computer (Turkle, 1988) and games consoles (McNamee, 1998)
have predominantly 'masculinized' cultural meanings. This is not
simply about 'boys' toys' or a 'matter of "technological incompetence"
on the part of the women concerned, who are 'unable' to work the
video, but who 'routinely operate more complex forms of domestic
technology, such as automatic washing machines (which their hus-
bands are correspondingly "unable" to operate)' (Morley, 1996:323).
The issues of domestic labour, leisure time and new technology in

the household are bound up with cultural competencies that encourage suitable dispositions towards consumption. Likewise, Brunsdon (1997) demonstrated how the ownership of satellite dishes by the early 1990s came to say much about the social status of the household – a highly conspicuous sign of the 'low' taste of the occupants, while the increasing number of dishes on a street is regarded as a symptom of neighbourhood decline.

What united this work overall was an emphasis on action, choice and creativity in an effort to dislodge the power of the text. This position is taken to its farthest limits in John Fiske's (1987) account of the semiotic experience 'television culture' delivers. Thus he stresses the subversive, popular tactics used by media audiences to evade the dominant meanings inscribed in mass-produced culture. As he went on to explain:

> People can and do make their own culture, albeit within conditions that are not of their own choosing. How much power is available within this terrain, and how fixedly its boundaries are determined are matters of considerable debate, in which I align myself with those who propose that ideological and hegemonic theories of popular culture have overestimated the power of the determinations and underestimated that of the viewer. (Fiske, 1989:57)

For Fiske popular culture is a battleground where a struggle is fought between the forces of ideological incorporation and subordinate resistance is played out. His position is undoubtedly an extreme one and emphasizes the subversive power of the audience to play with textual meanings.

By the 1990s critics were alarmed at the romantic optimism of what became known as the 'new revisionism' (Curran, 1990) and 'cultural populism' (McGuigan, 1992) of active audience theorists (Seaman, 1992). Meagan Morris (1990:21) was one of the first to condemn this 'banality' by suggesting that 'somewhere in some English publisher's vault there is a master disk from which thousands of versions of the same article about pleasure, resistance and the politics of consumption are being run off under different names with minor variations'. Her overall point is that the uncritical celebration of media audiences to resist blunts any radical edge in this work and takes the notion of cultural democracy too far. It risks falling into a 'complacent relativism, by which the interpretive contribution of the audience is perceived to be of such a scale and range as to render the very idea of media power naïve' (Corner, 1991:281). Similarly, Curran (1990:

151) contends that while this 'new revisionism' presents itself as original and challenging, all it amounts to is 'old pluralist dishes being reheated and presented as new cuisine'.

In other words, the recent studies have reinvented the wheel of 'uses and gratifications' research discussed in chapter 2, while espousing an understanding of audience creativity that chimes all too easily with prevailing free market political ideologies declaring the sovereignty of consumer choice. This is the main target of Jim McGuigan's (1992) critique of the facile populism of such work, which he sees as sharing with the rise of postmodern uncertainty an uncritical endorsement of liberal philosophy combined with a general crisis of aesthetic and moral judgement. His argument is that these studies ignore the broader economic, political and social context in which popular culture is produced and thereby overestimates the degree of freedom open to the individual to create meaning in their everyday lives. Although McGuigan voices a number of important concerns, his alternative approach is one that is essentially a return to political-economic analyses of culture and modernist certainties that are themselves reductive and elitist.

Studies of audiences are unavoidably involved in making judgements about the cultural worth of the texts consumed. An extremely helpful way of understanding the issues at stake here is through Andrew Sayer's (2005:122–33) discussion of the 'posh and the good' in his analysis of how people experience class inequalities. Posh is a marker of high class position, but only obliquely relates to the good, while descriptions of the common often equate with the rough, the bad, lowly and cheap. As he explains:

> the contingent relation between the posh and the good does not mean that the posh cannot indeed be good; social theory is posh, for example, but it can also be good (though it is worth asking if it is not sometimes merely posh!). Equally, the common might indeed be bad. To challenge the symbolic domination involved in the conflation of the posh and good and the common and the bad is not to deny such possibilities. (Sayer, 2005:124)

Rather, it makes explicit the relationship between aesthetic judgement and broader social values that may reinforce inequalities. It also cautions against rejecting highbrow cultural forms simply because they are valued by the dominant, but calls into question whether these things are actually worthwhile (or are largely status symbols). The same goes for dismissing popular cultural forms simply on the grounds that they are liked by the many. There are some important normative issues at stake here, not least in how we define the merits of particular texts, but the point I want to emphasize is that cultural criticism will always involve questions of morality and politics as much as aesthetics.

The Uses of Ethnography

Although many proponents of the 'active audience' would reject the term ethnography to describe their own research practice it is clear that ethnographic methods have become the preferred way of studying media audiences (good examples include Gillespie, 1995; Hermes, 1995; Jancovich *et al.*, 2003; Livingstone, 2002; Lotz, 2000; Seiter, 1999). Mark Banks (2005) is one of the first to study how media use and fear of crime vary in local contexts. Specifically, he examines how media representations of crime are incorporated into the lives of two middle-class households in Manchester. His study is clearly influenced by the developments just outlined and certainly benefits from them. Thus he begins by situating media technologies in the 'moral economy' of the household and locates the possible textual readings in the contested 'politics of the sitting room' (Morley, 1992). His argument is that 'the meanings generated by media remain understandable only in the context of the study of everyday life, where the daily experiences of home and social life, reproduced in private and public routine and ritual, shape patterns of meaning, identity and experience' (Banks, 2005:172). Importantly, he demonstrates how feelings of community belonging and personal security are bound up with attachments to particular localities that shape the interpretation of mediated crime stories.

Another example is Joke Hermes's (2000, 2005, with Stello, 2000) research on a small, disparate group of Dutch crime fiction readers. She proposes that they share an 'interpretive community' that enables the readers to form a sense of who they are. It is a form of cultural competence and citizenship that acts as a bond between groups of readers who may never actually meet while mobilizing a distinctive kind of liberal, middle-class identity. However, it is her more general argument that is crucial here. She insists that there is a tendency to 'overrate the meaningfulness of any single text once it is part of an everyday setting' (Hermes, 2000:352). Her target is the now familiar one of the privileging of textual analysis; instead she emphasizes audience experiences to reveal how texts are used in the complex rhythms of everyday life. Building on her earlier work, Hermes (1995) argues that not all media texts are *meaningful* to audiences. Instead, what diffuse audiences are doing is drawing from the endless media stream that flows around them to construct social worlds that suit them and how they imagine themselves to be. In the case of her crime fiction readers the 'rationale behind the social subjectivities mobilized by detective novel reading is to achieve a particular type of "middle-classness"' (Hermes, 2005:71). Questions of identity and everyday life also figure prominently in the much more constrained worlds of total institutions.

The last example I will discuss is Yvonne Jewkes's (2002) research on how prisoners use diverse media forms to survive the pressures of prison life. She explains how the media

> have the potential to increase social learning and develop various aspects of socialization, and may advance cultural competence, extending the social dominance of some individuals over others. They can also provide a means of avoidance of other people, allowing some individuals (perhaps notably, vulnerable prisoners) to 'tune out' of the prison culture. They deny present realities, evoke memories and allow inmates to transcend the confines of space and time. (Jewkes, 2002:187–8)

As such her work also reveals how media technologies are crucial ways of securing social order and conformity in environments where relations between the keepers and the kept are fraught at the best of times. The real strength of her study is the way it gets at the dynamic between acquiescent mediated pleasures and creeping social control, while being an innovative example of ethnographic media research.

The virtues of ethnographic audience research have been intensely disputed. It has long been accepted that anthropologists, who developed ethnography for studying distant and unfamiliar cultures, would insist that the technique has been used in partial and selective ways. For instance, Janice Radway (1988:367) argued that the initial ethnographic studies of media audiences had been 'narrowly circumscribed' as the whole cultural field has been cordoned and sectioned off through a 'preoccupation with a single medium or genre'. Furthermore, traditional ethnography is long-term and involves an immersion in the culture, whereas most audience studies observe for short periods while interviews are not themselves treated as texts. There is a tendency to fall 'back on a realist treatment of language, analysing transcription of speech as a pure and direct expression of the mind of the subject' (Seiter, 1999:29). The current problems with ethnographies of media audiences have been summarized in the following way:

First, there is the technical and perhaps insurmountable problem imposed by current anthropology's demand that observations be unobtrusive and context-bound, leading to thick descriptions, with purist critical researchers warning against falling into the trap of generalization. Is it heresy to suggest that this model is technically unrealistic? Can research be conducted unobtrusively while peeping over the shoulder of a teenager who insists he or she is not performing for the researcher? And how does the distortion of the picture by the researchers' presence in the subjects' home compare with the distortion of anonymous answers to questionnaires into which certain parameters of context are introduced? (Liebes, 2005:371)

By raising these questions Tamar Liebes is not suggesting that media ethnographers should abandon situating audiences in the complexity of everyday life, but is pointing to the limitations of the ethnographic method at a time when it has become the orthodoxy among researchers.

John Hartley (1987) was another early critic of ethnographic studies of audiences by arguing that any analysis of the 'the *Nationwide* audience' or 'the *EastEnders* audience' has to artificially create such an audience to study it at all. Although Hartley's argument is ultimately textual, seeing audiences as the product of discursive regimes he draws attention to how there are different ways of watching television. This has been developed by Nicholas Abercrombie (1996:182) where he identifies two parallel modes of involvement: the literary mode and the video mode. The literary mode requires an almost fierce concentration of effort and stresses order, in that the correct sequence of activities must be adhered to gain from the text. The best example of this would be reading a novel. While this mode does not deny that pleasure may be acquired from a text, consumption is, nevertheless, primarily a very serious matter and implies a dedicated commitment to the cultural object.

The video mode on the other hand implies that appropriation does not necessarily follow the 'correct' narrative order. Moreover, in this mode the audience may not be giving their full and undivided attention to the particular cultural object. For instance, they may be doing several different things at the same time, or using a number of other texts simultaneously. Importantly, these two forms of appropriation are not equally valued. The video mode is generally treated as inferior to the literary mode, as it is that favoured in the use of popular culture, especially television, where for much of the time the set is on nobody is paying that much attention and he suggests that it is precisely because television is so closely integrated into the fabric of domestic

life that it is so widely ignored, glimpsed or grazed. Nevertheless any
text can be theoretically appropriated in either mode, but they are very
differently judged, for as

> far as television is concerned, video mode is very similar to the distracted
> or inattentive mode of viewing . . . This explains the contempt with
> which men frequently greet women's viewing of soap opera. It is not
> only the content of the soaps that is derided, but also the distracted way
> in which they are watched. Men's watching, on the other hand, is much
> more in literary mode, which tends to attract greater social approval.
> (Abercrombie, 1996:183)

Abercrombie argues that audiences have developed new skills of
engagement with new media, and he points to a number of studies
(Ang, 1991; Mace, 1992; Root, 1986) that have examined this issue
in relation to television viewing – in particular, how skills of television
use have developed over the last fifty years, in which there has been a
movement from intense concentration to distracted appropriation
and a concomitant development in knowledge among audiences of
how television is produced and how it achieves its effects.

This argument echoes John Ellis's (1982) account of the differences
between television and cinema, in which he draws a clear distinction
between the gaze, which follows psychoanalytical theories of spectatorship and is associated with cinema, and the glance, which is more
characteristic of how television is viewed. As we have seen, television
is a domestic medium and due to its place in ordering household routines (Silverstone, 1994) is rarely looked at in the same way as films
are in a cinema. Indeed, television is ultimately visually illustrated
talk:

> Paradoxically, while cinema, advertising and magazines provide power-
> ful *visual* images, which are more crucial in conveying meaning and in
> giving the audience pleasure, television is actually rather more depen-
> dent on *talk* for its effect . . . Television is intended to be received in a
> domestic context which is characterized by conversational interchanges
> and it mirrors and interacts with the conversational lives of its audiences.
> (Abercrombie and Longhurst, 1998: 109–10, emphasis in original)

The implication is that television is an oral, rather than a literate
medium, so that the tools of literary and film criticism will be unable
to grasp these distinctive qualities, which Fiske and Hartley (1978)
have likened to the equivalent of a 'bard' in modern culture. The
'bardic function' takes a number of roles. Just as the 'traditional bard

rendered the central concerns of his day into verse . . . television renders our own everyday perceptions' into its own specialized language system (Fiske and Hartley, 1978:86). What is more, television is endlessly talked about in ways that are both referential and critical (Liebes and Katz, 1993).

These arguments have led to much debate over the differences between television and other media as well as isolating questions of textual interpretation from how audiences use texts. The important task is to work across these divisions, while being mindful that there are no easy syntheses of conflicting positions. A useful way of conceptualizing audience investments in the media is to recognize that 'they are *both* social – to do with meanings – *and* psychic – to do with desires, anxieties and pleasures' (Thornham and Purvis, 2005:96, emphasis in original). The overall point of this chapter has been to show how both the social and psychic realms are crucial if the rich textures of mediated experience are to be fully grasped. The next three chapters will concentrate on the texts themselves and provide an historical overview of the different ways in which crime has been represented in the media.

PART II

Representations

4
The Print Revolution

In this second part of the book I introduce a more historical lens to view forms of cultural representation and social processes. Consequently, this chapter deals with the rise of the print media – in the form of books, newspapers and pamphlets from around 1500 until 1800 and details the many ways in which crime came to be represented. Historians would describe the period as 'early modern' and distinguish it from the medieval era that preceded it in many ways. Among the most important are the declining power of the Church and corresponding growth in the rationalizing authority of law, science and state. The advent of printing and spread of individualization associated with these developments revolutionized social life. Yet it is important to recognize the complexity of the cultural mix here, where oral, literate and visual forms of communication intermingle and co-exist. In this period English society is neither purely oral (that had disappeared some time ago) nor yet fully literate (teaching the mass to read would only happen late into the nineteenth century) while the visual (religious iconography in particular) is already powerful. I also want to emphasize the diverse range and sheer invention of crime coverage over this period, where criminals are cast as popular heroes and their executions great festive spectacles sustaining an extensive gallows literature.

My overall point is that our contemporary representations of crime and punishment possess a long ancestry. Although I will be presenting a chronology and mapping of different genres they do borrow from each other and offer an often bewildering blend of fact and fantasy that defies neat categorization or even clear distinction. I begin with a broad account of popular culture in the oral tradition and emphasize the importance of carnivalesque rituals in pre-modern worlds. Then I chart the origins of early modern crime reporting and the rich assortment of narratives that came rolling off the printing presses during this period. At the same time the novel gradually emerges, enabling new ways of representing human experience by assimilating other modes of writing and transforming these earlier genres by concentrating on wayward characters. The celebration of individualism found in the novel is closely associated with the rise of the public sphere and Enlightenment philosophy that would fundamentally change political power and pave the way for our modern sensibilities.

The Oral Tradition and the Carnivalesque

It is hard now to comprehend the importance of oral communication from antiquity to the Middle Ages. One of the key differences between oral and literate cultures is that:

> We are no longer linked to our past by an oral tradition which implies direct contact with others (storytellers, priests, wise men or elders), but by books amassed in libraries, books from which we endeavour – with extreme difficulty – to form a picture of their authors. (Lévi-Strauss, 1950/68:366)

In the oral tradition, songs, stories and poems were designed to be performed and came in dynamic rather than rigid form, where singers and storytellers collectively borrowed, circulated and reworked each other's tales, themes and tunes (Briggs and Burke, 2005:6). The texts often used rhyming schemes and standard metaphors to help performers initially memorize and then flamboyantly improvise stories before their audiences. Indeed, what is now called medieval literature was produced to be heard, not read (Chaytor, 1945). Much recent scholarship has emphasized the complexities of oral cultures, which had all too often been dismissed as 'simple' or 'illiterate'.

The rise of literate culture begins slowly and unevenly in the twelfth and thirteenth centuries, but significantly evolves from around 1450 with the invention of movable metal type and the birth of a printing press in Western Europe. The print revolution, along with gunpowder and the compass, was genuinely epoch-making. It established literacy as an essential quality of the refined, preserved knowledge and undermined religious authority by making conflicting views on topics more widely available (Eisenstein, 1979). It is important to emphasize that up until the middle of the nineteenth century most poor Europeans remained illiterate or semi-literate, and most Europeans were poor. Morcover, the prospect of literate masses provoked considerable alarm well into the nineteenth century: it 'was feared that should "the million" be able to read, the natural order of society would be irremediably upset, existing economic and political systems would collapse, and civilization itself would be threatened' (Leps, 1992:71). In England, universal elementary education was only introduced in the 1870s to enable the 'lower orders' to read the Bible or penny newspapers, instil morality and promote patriotism – the thought that education could provide enlightenment or social mobility would have been regarded as totally objectionable. The emergence of a national press and universal state education crucially enabled the formation of a shared sense of unifying interests, thus laying the foundation of 'nation' consciousness in 'imagined communities' (Anderson, 1991).

It is also important to recognize the highly significant role played by images in pre-modern worlds. In particular, religious iconography provided both information and indoctrination. Pope Gregory the Great (c.540–604) is said to have 'described images as doing for those who could not read, the great majority, what writing did for those who could' (Briggs and Burke, 2005:7). The images in and on medieval cathedrals and churches, from wood carvings and stone gargoyles through to the stained glass windows, formed an elaborate system of visual communication to instruct the many who could not understand the Latin used by priests during Mass. Religious worship, festivals and ceremonies also played an important ritual role that has remained significant. It has been noted how the

> early theatre was bound up with religious observance, giving a sacred element to performance almost automatically. Attendance at festivals of drama in ancient Greece, for example, was primarily to honour Dionysus. There were similar intimate connections between worship and drama in medieval Europe. Alongside the Mass and during the Christian festivals at Easter and Christmas, there would be small dramatic presentations to accompany the more formal worship. At the same time, performances outside the street depended on Bible stories. The trade guilds in particular would use such stories for the plays that they put on each year. (Abercrombie and Longhurst, 1998:45)

Another important ritual occasion for pre-industrial societies was the carnival. Here the established customs, rigid hierarchies and social rules were temporarily overturned at fairs, feasts, processions, wakes and other forms of popular festivity that often accompanied the formal religious feasts.

The significance of the carnivalesque was initially recognized by the Russian literary theorist Mikhail Bakhtin and has become a crucial 'cultural analytic' to grasp the forbidden pleasures of transgression (Stallybrass and White, 1986). For Bakhtin (1984) the carnivalesque is a metaphor for the temporary, licensed suspension and reversal of order – when the world is turned upside down and inside out, when the low becomes high and the high turns low, as kings become fools, criminals make laws, donkeys give masses, men dress as women – all for a brief period of time. It is on these occasions that transgressive desires can be temporarily enjoyed, strict hierarchies reversed and vulgar excess indulged. Bakhtin's crucial point is that in the Middle Ages the carnival played a major role in the life of ordinary people, who inhabited a dual world existence: one serious, governed by the authority of the church, the feudal system of work and official state ceremonies, the other unofficial, characterized by reversal, excess, parody and laughter.

Bakhtin also defined the literary genre of 'grotesque realism', orig-inally medieval, as one opposed to all forms of high art and literature. It includes parody and other forms of discourse that 'bring down to earth' the authoritarian, the narrow-minded and the mighty through mockery as the 'people's laughter which characterized all the forms of grotesque realism from immemorial times was linked with the bodily lower stratum' (Bakhtin, 1984:20). Thus the human body is depicted in earthy, profane and degraded terms, where the lower regions (belly, bowels, genitals) rule the upper parts (head, reason, the heavens). As he explains, via Cervantes's (1615) novel *Don Quixote*, the character Sancho Panza conveys through 'his potbelly, appetite, his abundant defecation, are on the absolute lower level of grotesque realism of the gay bodily grave . . . which has been dug for Don Quixote's abstract and deadened idealism' (Bakhtin, 1984:22). Much of the comedy in the book derives from this clash of romantic idealism, grotesque realism and absurd self-delusion.

Indeed, the book can be read as an early satire on the 'media effects' tradition, by warning readers that novels can turn you mad. It begins with a middle-aged country-gentleman scholar, driven insane by reading too many chivalric romances, setting off on a quest round the country in search of adventures as the self-styled knight Don Quixote. Famous episodes include persuading a village farmer, Sancho Panza, to join him as his squire (and ride a donkey), attacks on 'giants' (wind-mills) and armies of 'enemies' (sheep), and later in the book they keep coming across characters who have actually read about them. We will see later how this textual play between fact and fantasy is a defining characteristic of early novels. For now it is important to note that while the practice of carnival diminished in Europe, largely as a result of Church persecution and subsequent Puritanism, its symbolic significance is now sustained in 'places on the margin' (Shields, 1991), bohemian lifestyles (Featherstone, 1992) and numerous cultural representations.[1] The main focus of the chapter now turns to the impact of the print revolution on crime writing.

Crime Reporting

The origins of crime journalism lie firmly in the oral tradition. In fact descriptions of outcast criminal underworlds flourished during the break-up of feudalism while providing major sources of popular entertainment and social criticism. It has been argued that broadside ballads, which told a story through song, worked as 'a kind of musical journalism, the forerunner of the popular prose newspapers and a continuation of the folk tradition of minstrelsy' (Shepherd, 1972:21). The most familiar to us now will be the Robin Hood ballad cycle, but many others – like the mid-fourteenth century *Tale of Gamelyn* (see McCall, 2004:100–1) – revolve around a noble band of robbers. Famously, they steal from the undeserving rich to give to the dispossessed poor, while highlighting the malign presence of corrupt officialdom and an overfed, tyrannical clergy.

Although these were idealized champions of the peasantry there was a clear political vision at work in the songs and myths built on these bandits merrily redistributing wealth, righting wrongs and fighting injustice. As Eric Hobsbawm (1969/2001:47) suggests, while in 'real life most Robin Hoods were far from noble' the legend itself represents an important symbol of justice and primitive form of social protest. Thus 'social bandit' mythology is ultimately concerned with upholding the traditional order of things by having the protagonists rise up and fight those who abuse authority or rule unjustly (Faller, 1987:121). Crucially, they do not demand revolutionary change but the restoration of fair rule – in the case of Robin Hood he stands against the usurping Prince John and waits for the rightful King to return. They do not seek to do away with feudal oppression or establish a free and equal society, but they nonetheless 'do prove that justice is possible, that poor men need not be humble, helpless and meek' (Hobsbawm, 1969/2001:61).

These bandit ballads belong to a critical tradition of crime reporting that has never been very pronounced in written form. The main reason is that printed crime reports, from their immediate inception, were subjected to state intervention and vigorous censorship. Gradually printed pamphlets or broadsides, which presented news narratives in the form of prose or rhyming ballad, began to replace handwritten newsletters by the start of the sixteenth century. Among these diverse publications were the cony-catching pamphlets – 'cony' meant 'victim' in the jargon of the pickpockets, dice-cheats, confidence tricksters and assorted villains that populated Tudor London. Mary McIntosh (1971:101) contends that not only did these 'craft thieves' have their own slang (cant), neighbourhoods (sanctuaries) and meeting places but there were in fact two 'distinct criminal underworlds at this period: that of the wayfaring rogues and vagabonds who lived by stealing and begging – often under false pretences; and that of the London-based thieves and tricksters'. It is even said that just like other kinds of craft occupation 'thieves had their company, which handled their contributory pension fund', with a 'training school for pickpockets and cutpurses near Billingsgate' while St Paul's was just one of the many places where the craft thieves plied their trade (Picard, 2003:277–8).[2]

An example of a cony-catching pamphlet is Thomas Harman's (1566) *Caveat for Common Cursitors*, which describes twenty-three kinds of vagabond and the dangers posed to the country by this 'rascal rabblement'. Harman was a judge from Kent and interviewed travellers to produce one of the first sociologies of crime (Barrett and Harrison, 1999). His pamphlet also included a glossary of canting language (the distinctive slang vocabulary used in the underworlds), a form that would influence the popular canting dictionaries of subsequent centuries. These dictionaries and glossaries gave a sense of the highly skilled specialisms of professional criminals while representing them as a disturbing alien presence.

A torrent of measures designed to control the publishing trade by licensing or suppression were introduced, which included in 1557 the granting to the Guild of Stationers almost total control over printing and the power to search for illegal presses and destroy their publications. Censorship was a major preoccupation of early modern European states and churches, both the newly Protestant and Catholic alike, where the prime targets were heresy, sedition and immorality. The Catholic Church, for example, established an *Index librorum prohibitorum* in 1559 that was continuously revised and updated over the next four hundred years.[3] In principle, pamphlets were meant to be subjected to the same strict censorship rules as books and plays, but there is evidence that many 'lewd and scandalous' tracts made it uncensored onto the streets (Picard, 2003:240). Printers found numerous ways of evading religious and political censorship; material banned in one city or region would frequently be printed in another thus encouraging a lucrative and dynamic trade in forbidden literature.

The reporting of rebellions and treason rarely challenged the state's version of events. Such loyalty should not be surprising. Much of it was published by the Royal printers and written by state officials, often going to considerable lengths to disguise its indoctrinating form, source and content – one strategy was to present the propaganda as a letter from a gentleman to a doubting friend (Chibnall, 1980:181). The fact that such pamphlets still exist suggests that they were responses to 'underground' accounts that have not survived (Shaaber, 1929:46). It also points to the persistence of a much stronger oral culture, publicly discussing ideas, rumours and gossip in the inns, playhouses and street markets that were part of the fabric of everyday life. Thus it is important to 'look not at print alone but at the media system as a whole'; as 'only a minority of the population could read, let alone write, it follows that oral communication must have continued to predominate in the so-called age of the printing-press' (Briggs and Burke, 2005:64). The overall point is that oral, print and visual media have co-existed and interacted from the sixteenth century onwards, but that the oral tradition belongs 'to an "other history" of histories, pantomime and song' that is often neglected or disregarded (Linebaugh, 2003:8).

Aside from sedition[4] the other staples of Tudor and Stuart crime reporting were murder and witchcraft. Although the tone of the many broadsides and pamphlets detailing the exploits of criminals and witches was overtly moral and warned of the temptations of sin, this approach was accompanied by a sensationalism that relishes in the telling of the 'terrible' events, 'bloody' atrocities, 'strange and inhuman murders' and so forth encountered in the pages. Peter Lake (1993:259) quotes from a typical pamphlet from 1606 describing how a female robber turned into a 'tragical midwife' by ripping open the belly of a pregnant woman with a knife and cutting out a child's tongue. Accounts of witchcraft thrived in the late sixteenth and early seventeenth centuries and, like the murder tracts, called on the reader to beware of the danger that surrounded them.

Yet much historiography has shown that accusations of witchcraft often resulted from disputes between village neighbours, with

persecution only one of the many methods used for coping with suspects (Briggs, 1996; Clark, 1997). Likewise, recent scholarship on
the ways Tudor and Stuart England managed cultural difficulties
(ranging from monstrous births, bestial intercourse, cross-dressing,
serial infanticide, clergy mocking, sexual debauchery and irregular
burials) has revealed a society that 'preferred to accommodate rather
than eliminate difference' (Cressy, 2000:282). The broadsheets and
pamphlets that sensationally reported these events had both commercial and evangelical aims, seeking to exploit a metropolitan
appetite for news of perplexing phenomena while lacing their
accounts with spiritual warnings and religious guidance to avoid censorship and keep to a didactic form.

Although the meaning of murder and witchcraft from these printed
sources was fairly clear in the seventeenth century other, more
ambiguous, narratives of crime and criminality came to the fore as the
century progressed and the boundaries of tolerance were stretched.
The century was characterized by political, economic, social and religious upheaval that included civil war, the loss of ancient customary
rights, a compromised restoration, two separate Protestant solutions
to succession crises and the introduction of the 'bloody code' of criminal statutes as the new political order sought to establish its power
through the terror of the gallows. Hal Gladfelder's (2001:10) invalu-
able analysis of the main genres of criminal narrative helps us to grasp
the incredible assortment of publications that came pouring off the
presses during this turbulent era. The main forms of publication up
to the beginning of the eighteenth century were what he defines as
'criminal anatomies' as well as picaresque and providential fictions,
news reports, executions and gallows literature, trial reports and a
flourishing trade in criminal biography. Each of these I now outline.

Criminal Narratives

Criminal anatomies included the cony-catching pamphlets, canting
dictionaries and moralizing tracts on deviance, described above,
which constructed the criminal as an alien other – the Irish in particular were persistently held to be criminal. In stark contrast, the comic
picaresque and tragic providential fictions of the period offer greater
uncertainty and more psychological complexity in their tales of
episodic coincidence and bloody revenge. The picaresque form of
narrative emerged in sixteenth-century Spain as an account of a
rogue's adventures (the Spanish for rogue is *picaro*), who living on his

wits survives through a series of journeys, satirizing and exposing the pretences of the diverse social worlds in which he finds himself. The genre quickly spread across Europe, with Thomas Nashe's (1594) *The Unfortunate Traveller* one of the earliest English representatives, while the publication of *The English Rogue Described* by Richard Head in 1665 marks the full realization of this narrative form.

The picaresque has been understood as a response to the crisis of status inconsistency that occurred following the demise of feudalism (McKeon, 1987:238) and the accompanying rise of a wandering, pauperized population with no station in life (Linebaugh, 2003:120). Providential fictions are unambiguous and are self-consciously tales of divine retribution and moral polemic, as exemplified in the thirty stories collected in the 1621 compilation, *The Triumph of God's Revenge, against the Crying, and Execrable Sinne of Murther*. These tales were not about contemporary English crime, but took the form of dramatic tragedy set in the past and on the Continent. Characteristically, they demonstrated how 'the messy business of revenge, adultery and murder is structured through the discourses of retributive religion so that Providence intervenes to ensure that God's justice prevails' (Biressi, 2001:47). While these anatomies and fictions drew on an earlier culture and diverse literary styles, crime reports and gallows literature grew out of the new printing technologies and improved means of distribution into and out of Restoration London. These developments enabled news of disturbing crimes and exemplary hangings to be bought as broadsides or pamphlets shortly after their occurrence to exploit topical interest as quickly as possible.

There is much evidence to suggest that crime reports dominated coverage of nearly all the available newspapers at this time (Black, 1987:80–1). A typical example is *A Full and True Account of the Apprehending, taking and Examination of one Mr. Harris, and carried before Justice Tully, Sworn against by Mr. Swagg, to be that Notorious Highwayman that used to Rob on the Black Mare on Hounslow-Heath: then Committed to the Gatehouse, August the 11th, 1704*, which was published in London only days after the crime it describes (cited in Bell, 1992:5). As historians have emphasized, these accounts brought an immediacy that profoundly altered perceptions of the world (Eisenstein, 1979). By closing the distance between readers and the represented they drew 'the threat of criminality into social spaces' that might otherwise have been thought safe from harm (Gladfelder, 2001:11). Immediacy was also the key to the gallows journalism that claimed to record the 'last dying speeches' of those condemned to hang. These execution reports were formulaic, beginning with a confession of guilt, a cataloguing of crimes and a final repentance. They were also immensely popular. The long-running, periodically printed pamphlet entitled *The Ordinary of Newgate, His Account of the Behaviour, Confession and Dying Words of the Malefactors who were Executed at Tyburn* is one of the most famous examples.

Tyburn, Newgate and the Old Bailey were significant places in the cultural landscape and class structure of eighteenth-century London. At the Old Bailey trials small property-holders met 'to hear and determine' offences and from the large number of petty criminals paraded before them they selected a handful to hang every six weeks in what Dr Johnson described as the 'legal massacre' at Tyburn (Linebaugh, 2003:74). Newgate Prison, situated next to the Old Bailey, was where the condemned were confined before their execution at Tyburn. The Ordinary of Newgate's *Account* began in 1684 and its popularity lasted until well into the middle of the eighteenth century. It provided personal details of the lives of the condemned, describing their sometimes penitent, other times defiant, conduct while awaiting execution. The commercial success of this gallows literature is confirmed by the fierce competition between publications, with rival titles striving to get their work out first while claiming that the Ordinary was inauthentic and driven by mercenary principles (Rawlings, 1992:5–6). The literature's influence can also be seen in the way many 'Sheriffs and Secretaries of State kept an attentive ear to these gallows' utterances, and were prompt to intervene when the words spoken might question the Hanoverian Succession, the doctrine of private property, the sovereignty of money or approved norms of sexual conduct' (Linebaugh, 2003:90).

Like the gallows speeches of the condemned, criminal trial reports grew directly out of legal ritual and reflected the increasing importance of the law over religion as the main ideological force from the end of the seventeenth century (Sharpe, 1984, 1987). The publication of detailed reports of Old Bailey trial sessions opened up considerable commercial possibilities and by the 1680s they had become an officially protected monopoly (Langbein, 1983). Much like the criminal anatomies, the trial reports detailed the transgressive underworlds and shadowy practices of deviant metropolitan subcultures in ways that were both fascinating and repulsive to the middling sort who avidly consumed them. Gladfelder (2001:21–3) gives the example of an antisodomite campaign orchestrated by the Societies for the Reformation of Manners, which led to a series of widely reported Old Bailey trials in the 1720s, to illustrate the way in which homoeroticism was inscribed with alien otherness. One witness, a constable working for the reforming societies, described what he observed at Mother Clap's molly house (one of the popular taverns where gay men met) in the following fashion:

> I found between 40 and 50 Men making Love to one another, as they call'd it. Sometimes they would sit on one another's Laps, kissing in a lewd Manner, and using their Hands indecently. Then they would get up, Dance and make Curtsies, and mimick the voices of Women . . . Then they'd hug, and play, and toy, and go out by Couples into another Room on same Floor, to be marry'd, as they call'd it. (cited in Norton, 1992:55)

The passage gives a sense of how the lingering detail, typical of these trial reports, overwhelms whatever juridical interest there might have been in the case. However, the very accumulation of detail and presentation of conflicting witness accounts in trial reports suggested that the link between crime and the gallows was less certain and more imprecise than many of the other narrative genres allowed.

It is this ambiguity that lies at the heart of criminal biography, a genre that did much to individualize deviance and grant celebrity to notorious law-breakers. It has been estimated that between two and three thousand biographies have survived from the eighteenth century, which gives an indication of their popularity. The plot structures often bore striking similarities and echoed the redemptive patterns of the dying speeches (Rawlings, 1998:6–7), but through the narrating of a highwayman's adventures, gentleman thief's memoirs or master criminal's exploits they were raised 'above the sordid and brutalizing petty deviance of the regular Tyburn procession' (Chibnall, 1980:185). Examples abound and here I will only concentrate on a few of the well known. Jack Sheppard, an unremarkable thief, was once the most infamous person in eighteenth-century England.

Born in 1702 and hanged at Tyburn in 1724 for housebreaking, his notoriety arose from the ingenuity with which he was able to escape different prisons, including Newgate. Sheppard's fame was largely a product of newspapers 'building up a popular image' of him and Philip Rawlings (1992:40–1) insists that it is in the context that his biography, *The History of the Remarkable Life of John Sheppard*, must be read – as an imaginative response to the way newspapers constructed his escapes and media celebrity. There remains considerable debate over who produced the text. Some argue *The History* was written by Daniel Defoe following a series of meetings with Sheppard during his final confinement (Gladfelder, 2001:90). It was not at all unusual for the biographies to be published anonymously; such was the disreputability of the literary trade in the eighteenth century. Authors were often compared to thieves and their work to prostitution. A group of these writers became known as 'Grub Street', after the place in London where many émigré journalists lived (Rogers, 1972). Terms like this and 'hacks' still persist from the eighteenth century and are used collectively to disparage writers who are hired, like hackney carriages, to make a living. The profession was also a risky one, with prosecutions for seditious and blasphemous libel aimed at repressing opposing voices an ongoing state activity. Defoe himself was imprisoned many times, mostly for debt but occasionally over his political writings, including a five-month stretch in Newgate following the 1702 publication of his *The Shortest Way with the Dissenters*, a pamphlet satirizing High Church extremism.

Perhaps the most enduring heroic figure from this literature is the highwayman. Among the most celebrated is Captain James Hind, who was hanged, quartered and disembowelled in 1652, with some thirteen separate works about him surviving in the British Library (Faller, 1987:12). Claude Du Vall was equally infamous, executed in 1670, and prompting a glut of life-and-crimes biographies, which include the *Memoires of Monsieur Du Vall*, described as 'a hit-or-miss collection of ironic reflections and asides, mostly directed against the French and against women who are sexually drawn to handsome robbers' (Gladfelder, 2001:85). By the 1720s the characteristic features of criminal biography had taken shape, so that when Dick Turpin was hanged in York for horse-stealing in 1739 the media machinery for transforming him into a mythical figure was already well established.

Casting the highwayman as epic hero was attractive to the early eighteenth-century press for a number of reasons. There were clear continuities with the earlier outlaw ballad tradition, but the fact that most highwaymen were footpads possessing few of the genteel graces of the well-armed horseman in the popular literature meant that the highwayman's allure was heightened in comparison with the reality of street crime. The footpad used brutal methods to rob passers-by in the heart of the city in contrast to the heath (the wasteland beyond the suburbs) where the mounted highwayman worked at 'a tolerable distance . . . from the usual realms of human activity' (Faller, 1987:179–180). By concentrating on a few notorious individuals the press of this period hovered ambiguously between celebration and condemnation. Ultimately they 'were steering a middle course' that accepted 'the rules of the crime game – the framework of law, justice, the justice (of inevitable) punishment – but they were awarding the prize of celebrity status to those who played attractively and gave the authorities a good run for their money' (Chibnall, 1980:186). Yet this double-sided status of the criminal clearly posed problems; by upsetting social categories the mass of words, songs and images circulating around the gallows did not simply present the condemned as an example to be avoided and feared, but as one to be admired and desired. Similar tensions would also reveal themselves with the advent of the novel.

Authorship and the Novel

In his influential account of the *Rise of the Novel*, Ian Watt (1957/72:15) maintained that writers like Shakespeare, Chaucer and Milton recycled traditional plots as the feudal world view held that there could be nothing new: 'since Nature is essentially complete and unchanging, its records, whether scriptural, legendary or historical, constitute a definitive repertoire of human experience'. Then the novel arrived. Now regarded as one of the pinnacle forms of Western civilization, Watt argued that the novel was born out of the growth of middle-class individualism in the eighteenth century. He claimed that it fundamentally challenged feudal beliefs by thoroughly subordinating 'plot to the pattern of the autobiographical (and this) is as defiant an assertion of the primacy of individual experience in the novel as "cogito ergo sum" was in philosophy' (ibid.). Nevertheless, what we now regard as literature only begins to take shape in the early nineteenth century during the Romantic era, when poets like Coleridge, Wordsworth and Shelley advanced an understanding of human creativity that was fundamentally opposed to the grim realities of existence appearing in the newly industrializing England. Before then the distinctions we now make between fact and fiction were understood differently and it took much effort to defend the view that while 'fiction was not the truth of history it was nevertheless truth in some other, more profound sense' (Nelson, 1973:8).

Although there are problems with understanding the novel as an exclusively middle-class form, the close relationship between individualism and transgression is central to its development. As recent scholarship has demonstrated, the eighteenth-century novel is saturated with criminal narratives, and this is no longer on the mythic scale of Elizabethan tragedy, but is rather everywhere and an

inescapable part of urban life. Lennard Davis (1983:125) has gone so
far as to suggest that 'without the appearance of the whore, the rogue,
the cutpurse, the cheat, the thief or the outsider it would be impossible to imagine the genre of the novel'. This representation of criminality served competing functions and was immediately perceived to
be dangerous. As Gladfelder (2001:7) explains, commentators were
'unsettled from the outset by the genre's concentration on the experience of a range of socially disruptive figures familiar from the network
of criminal narrative: socially climbing servants (as in *Pamela*), illegit-
imate and outcast children (as in *Tom Jones*), runaway and fortune-
hunting adventurers (as in *Robinson Crusoe*)'. Authors like Samuel
Richardson, Henry Fielding and Daniel Defoe were so troubled by
their own fictional preoccupations with unruly characters that they
criticized each other and their readers for being fascinated with the
lowly and perverse. Fielding (1741) had even corrosively parodied
Richardson's virtuous heroine Pamela in *Shamela* by portraying her as
a devious upstart, and in doing so began his own career as a novelist.

It is also important to recognize that these early authors were
drawing on, and in some cases transcending, already existing literary
forms by introducing fresh arenas of complexity to their novel characterizations. Daniel Defoe is the archetype, deploying his skills as
journalist, pamphleteer, spy, historian and biographer in the fiction he
would produce towards the end of his life and is now famous for. With
the publication in 1719 of *Robinson Crusoe*, Defoe's feigned autobiography of a shipwrecked mariner, he created a text open to many
different readings, which include spiritual rebirth, adventure story,
economic allegory and distillation of colonial attitudes to name a few.
It was also the first of the fictional autobiographies that he went on
to write in the 1720s and include *Moll Flanders*, *Colonel Jack* and
Roxana. If *Robinson* exemplifies an indebtedness to the formal,
Puritan procedures of spiritual autobiography – telling a tale from
sinful youth through to repentant conversion and divine deliverance –
then the later writing draws on the criminal biographies, gallows
speeches and picaresque conventions to provide a detailed picture of
the chaotic uncertainty of human existence and the struggles over
power, status and property in a world where the old certainties were
beginning to unravel.

Moll Flanders takes the form of a gallows confessional and includes
a spiritual rebirth in Newgate at the depths of her misfortune. So the
story is ostensibly about a woman who ultimately makes the right
choice by repenting and is rewarded with a happier life on earth. Yet,
the story is riven with duplicity. She often pretends to be someone else

and manages to deceive other characters, readers and mostly herself. The split between the old penitent Moll narrating the tale and the young protagonist blind to her fate brings a comic irony to the plot. This ironic structure is further enlivened by the many layers of hypocrisy and deception revealed in the various episodes encountered in the text, including Moll unwittingly marrying her brother, becoming an adept thief and finally realizing that she 'had been no less than a Whore and an Adulteress all this while' (Defoe, 1722/1989:177). It has been convincingly argued that the book, like others from this period, exhibits a 'categorical instability' since the novel as a literary institution was yet to take a coherent form and these works signal a 'change in attitudes about how truth and virtue are most authentically signified' (McKeon, 1987:20).

Although a distinction between 'factual' and 'imaginative' writing had long been recognized, Lennard Davis (1980:120) points to how authors of novels in the seventeenth and early eighteenth centuries almost routinely 'begin their works with a preface asserting that they are presenting not a fiction but a factual account of a real series of events' and then announce that they are merely 'the literary editor of someone else's papers, journals, or oral history'. This deliberate denial of authorship is present in Defoe – in the opening of the preface to *Moll Flanders* he goes to some lengths to claim that the work is not fiction, but a factual account. The book opens with the complaint, 'The World is so taken up of late with Novels and Romances that it will be hard for a private History to be taken for Genuine' and goes on to explain that while

the original of this Story is put into new Words, and the Stile of the famous Lady we here speak of is a little alter'd, particularly she is made to tell her own tale in modester Words than she told it at first; the Copy which came first to Hand, having been written in Language more like one still in *Newgate*, than one grown Penitent and Humble, as she afterwards pretends to be. (Defoe, 1722/1989:37)

Defoe is clearly casting Moll as an unreliable narrator and presenting the story as an edited transcription of words originally too vulgar and distasteful for the more cultured reader.

Jonathan Swift (1726/1994:1) was quick to send up the technique in his *Gulliver's Travels*, which opens with an enraged 'Letter From Captain Gulliver to his Cousin Sympson' scandalized at the liberties the latter has taken in the presentation of his text: 'in the account of the Academy of Projectors, and several discourses to my master

Houyhnhnm, you have either omitted some material circumstances,
or minced or changed them in such a manner, that I do hardly know
my own work'. There then follows a response from Richard Sympson
entitled 'The Publisher To The Reader', informing us that:

> This volume would have been at least twice as large, if I had not made
> bold to strike out innumerable passages relating to the winds and tides,
> as well as to the variations and bearings in the several voyages; together
> with the minute descriptions of the management of the ship in storms,
> in the style of sailors: likewise the account of the longitudes and lati-
> tudes; wherein I have reason to apprehend that Mr. Gulliver may be a
> little dissatisfied: but I was resolved to fit the work as much as possible
> to the general capacity of reader. (Swift, 1994, orig. pub. 1726:6–7)

Swift made no secret of his contempt for the newly emerging narrative form of the novel, the modern, egocentric subjectivity it encouraged and its unbridled celebration of British civilization. Hence,
Gulliver begins his travels as a self-confident giant of a man and ends
his odyssey finding the human species so abhorrent that he prefers the
company of horses.

Nevertheless, there is considerable debate over whether these forms
of authorial disavowal were a way of overcoming puritan sanctions
against heretical works of the imagination or a literary device designed
to ensure a realist quality to the work. It is evident that divisions
between fact and fiction were blurred and that eighteenth-century
novels played with this fluidity to the extent that a question remains
over whether it was actually possible to write fiction without simultaneously maintaining that it was factual.

Another key paradox is that for what we would now regard as a news
story to appear in print during the eighteenth century it would frequently have to be presented in the form of fiction. For instance, when
Dr Johnson wrote accounts of the English parliamentary sessions for
the *Gentleman's Magazine* he used satirical allegory to say that he was
chronicling the debates of the 'Senate of Lilliput' and used the
anagram of Walelop to stand for Walpole (cited in Davis, 1980:133–
4). In many respects, this use of fiction was a strategy designed to
avoid the seditious libel laws set up to regulate the press. It took some
time for this 'categorical instability' to solidify and marks 'a major cultural transition in attitudes towards how to tell the truth in narrative'
(McKeon, 1987:20). Even after the revision of the Stamp Act in
1724, which sought to separate news (that was now taxable) from
fiction (which was not), there remained considerable confusion over
how exactly to differentiate news from novels for at least the next

quarter of a century. Yet by the end of the eighteenth century the characteristic features of the novel are in place, for authors and readers alike.

It is therefore important to recognize that the novel emerges from a voracious fusion of specific practices (including letter writing, diary keeping and trial reporting), multiple types of writing (broadsheets, political pamphlets, as well as conduct guides, travel narratives and criminal biographies) and institutional sites (like libraries, coffeehouses and other meeting places) that made possible this new, imaginative way of representing human experience. One of the remarkable features of the novel's emergence is how it came to confine 'meaningful, significant, and serious narrative to the actual and familiar world of more or less daily experience and to banish or trivialize the older and manifestly unrealistic genres of epic and romance' (Richetti, 1996:4). To understand this cultural transformation we need to grasp the social forces prompting such changes in aesthetic, moral and political judgements. Critical explanations, as we will now see, have tended to concentrate on the formation of a 'public sphere' where the expanding bourgeois and urban professional classes could meet and establish their views during this most seemingly polite of centuries.

The Public Sphere and Enlightenment

The term 'public sphere' was initially coined by the German sociologist Jürgen Habermas (1962/89) in a pioneering study of communication processes and social change. His argument is that the eighteenth century marked a decisive stage in the development of rational debate. The emergence of capitalism at this time brought with it the commodification of culture and opened up the liberal, democratic possibility of well-informed individuals resolving their differences through enlightened reason rather than brute force. Crucial to the argument is that a new space opened up between the disintegrating feudal authorities (church, nobility, patronage), expanding capitalist markets, urban trade corporations and newly evolving nation-states requiring continuous administration, standing armies and the legal exertion of authority. The 'public sphere' was much more than a purely discursive realm but was grounded in a network of social spaces and institutions that regulated manners and promoted urbane conduct. These included new, refined sites where conversation could flourish in meeting places like coffee-houses, tea gardens, assembly rooms, salons, spas and resorts, debating societies and learned associations –

all of which had relatively low entry costs and were in principle open to everyone.

It was the energy released by the emerging capitalist markets that stimulated the growth of these public sphere institutions and enabled Enlightenment philosophy to take cultural expression. Moreover, it has been argued that the rise of newspapers, journals, periodicals and especially literature 'served the emancipation movement of the middle class as an instrument to gain self-esteem and to articulate its demands against the absolutist state and the hierarchical society' (Hohendahl, 1982:52). In the English context early eighteenth-century periodicals like *Tatler* and *Spectator* were 'animated by moral correction and satiric ridicule of a licentious, socially regressive aristocracy'; but their key consensual influence lay in consolidating new class relationships, by codifying 'the practices whereby the English bourgeoisie may negotiate an historic alliance with its social superiors' (Eagleton, 1984:10). An important element in Habermas's argument is that for the first time particular groups and individuals could shape public opinion and influence political practice free from manipulation. Yet by the nineteenth century he claims that the public sphere becomes contaminated and weakened through becoming 'refeudalized' – in that advertising, public relations and other techniques of information management have returned the public sphere to trivial spectacle and subordinated it to selective commercial interests.

Extending this argument to the early twenty-first century we can see how political spin doctors, global media corporations and tabloid celebrity marketing have replaced monarchs, church and nobility as the patrons and sponsors of much mass communication. Of course, critics have disputed the appropriateness of the feudal analogy to contemporary media, whereas others claim that he has idealized the bourgeois public sphere. In practice many were excluded from these forums of rational debate and they were dominated by rich, white men in periwigs seeking to protect their interests by only selectively adopting Enlightenment principles. Habermas's (1985) response to these criticisms is an acknowledgement that social interests shape communication, but he insists the Enlightenment remains an unfinished project as the possibilities of communicative rationality have yet to be realized.

The Enlightenment's 'Age of Reason' crucially broke with the cyclical view of history and the understanding that nothing fundamentally new could be thought. Although Enlightenment intellectuals inherited many of the assumptions of the classical tradition, they challenged the orthodoxy of the past by looking to the future and founding a new era based on the powers of reason, science and liberty. The radical idea was that knowledge progressed and that reason would bring liberation from the barbarism of the feudal Dark Ages. They included French philosophers like Descartes, Montesquieu and Rousseau who were systematically critical of the despotic regimes in which they found themselves. The light of reason would oppose faith, superstition, tradition and prejudice to bring about true Enlightenment. Meanwhile, a quarrel raged between 'the Ancients and the Moderns' with various writers arguing that the new science of physics pioneered by Galileo, Boyle and Newton was far superior to anything produced in antiquity. These developments encouraged European intellectuals to see humanity afresh. Central to the cultural and political project of Enlightenment was the assertion that individuals, through the reasoning powers of their sense experiences, could determine their own destinies. Penal reformers, among others, drew on these ideas to critique capital punishment and the savagery of the 'Bloody Code', which helped to establish the new system of imprisonment as the just response to crime (Carrabine *et al.*, 2004).

The famous *Encyclopédie*, published in thirty-five volumes between 1751 and 1765, included Diderot, Voltaire and Rousseau among the many contributors who did much to spread and popularize these philosophical ideas. Initially only the very rich could buy the whole series, but cheaper editions followed and were widely discussed in the burgeoning coffee-houses and other places of egalitarian assembly. Indeed, the significance of coffee-houses was that they provided a radically new kind of social institution, 'free from the "grotesque bodies" of the alehouse', and they promoted themselves as '*decent* places to go' where for 'one penny *any* man could sit and drink' (Stallybrass and White, 1986:95–6, emphasis in original). These 'penny universities' claimed moral superiority over the alehouse by being places of productive leisure rather than unruly consumption, thus allowing the Protestant ethic of sobriety and profit to be realized in one telling space.

By the middle of the eighteenth century Rousseau's proclamation that 'Man is born free, and everywhere he is in chains' controversially reversed the conventional Christian view that humans are intrinsically corrupt and in need of religious salvation while also suggesting the universal right to liberty. Yet it took the French and American Revolutions to give legal force to the political theory that declared 'all men are created equal' (except, of course, slaves, women, indigenous populations, children, etc.), while the Terror that subsequently engulfed France at the end of the eighteenth century revealed that populist governments can disregard human freedom as easily as absolutist monarchies. As revolutionaries replaced aristocrats on the guillotine in the years after the French Declaration of the Rights of Man and Citizen, the executions provided 'a practical refutation of its claim that "rights" were natural, let alone inalienable and sacred' (Robertson, 2000:5). It was Jeremy Bentham who mounted an influential liberal attack on natural rights and unjust legal systems, which became a pivotal force driving social reform in the nineteenth century. Even then there was considerable suspicion surrounding a 'standing police force', not least because of fears of Continental systems of police spies and that ran contrary to English liberty.[5] Contemporary policing developed from a patchwork of parochial systems with towns and parishes relying on the community-based 'watch', local constables and private 'thief-takers' before the controversial introduction of a metropolitan police force in 1829 to regulate urban life.

It is clear that the combined processes of population growth, expanding cities, nascent industrialization and bourgeois revolution radically transformed social structures. Crucial to the American and French Revolutions was the right to freedom of speech and the press, which had been anticipated in the 'Wilkes and Liberty' movement of the 1760s in England. John Wilkes was a radical politician who successfully mobilized popular support through the media – including his newspaper the *North Briton*, political demonstrations and handbills – for the right of the people to have a free press and full knowledge of state activity. Consequently, it is important to recognize that the loosening of government control over the press resulted from struggles between political groups and lobbying by economic interests, as well as from the strategic positioning by particular publications, rather than from the noble accomplishment of policy decisions on freedom of speech (Leps, 1992:73). As the next chapter will demonstrate, successive governments had attempted to curb press freedom through the law courts, but the authorities came to realize that taxation was a far more effective way of silencing the radical titles (Curran, 2003:7). At the same time much of the popular literature documented in this chapter gradually went and a whole new aesthetic develops that comes to glorify crime and its detection by representing criminality as one of the fine arts.

5
Entertaining the Nation

All media provide entertainment. A criticism often levelled at the media, especially television programmes and tabloid journalism, is that the content is unchallenging and serves to distract audiences away from more serious issues. One of the key themes running through this chapter will be the blurring of distinctions between informing and entertaining the public. I begin with the press in the nineteenth century before turning to developments in crime fiction, which picks up the threads from the last chapter and finishes with an account of 'reality TV' – that much derided emblem of ratings-driven sensationalism that has threatened to overwhelm our television screens in the last decade. Throughout the chapter I will be situating these more recognizably modern (some would say postmodern) representations of crime in their historical, commercial and cultural contexts.

The chapter covers representations of crime in the news and as entertainment but, as we have seen, rigid distinctions between true and fictional accounts of crime are not only hard to sustain in practice, but frequently the differences are imperceptible. This is not to suggest that people are incapable of distinguishing between the real and the imaginary, but to insist that media audiences commute on a daily basis between books, magazines, newspapers, computers, television, cinema, radio and so forth in ways that veer from vague distraction to fierce concentration. Moreover, understandings of crime in everyday life are continually informed by representations of crime in popular culture. What is now offered is a sense of the more contemporary range of criminal narratives that can be regularly encountered through television-viewing, cinema-going and reading newspapers, while indicating some changes and continuities with the concerns outlined in the previous chapter.

The 'New Journalism' and 'Jack the Ripper'

The tensions between informing, educating and entertaining the public have figured extensively in debates over the functions of a mass-produced press. Indeed, only with the arrival of a weekly 'pauper press' in the early decades of the nineteenth century does some notion of a national-consensual 'public interest' emerge. By attracting a largely working-class readership, these radical titles stood in contrast to the 'respectable press' and fought hard campaigns against stamp duty – a tax largely designed to eliminate them. The mainstream news-papers were scarcely respectable. There is clear evidence of heavy and direct bribery of journalists, with official advertising 'steered to papers favourable to Government opinion' (Williams, 1978:46). Meanwhile the editors and distributors of the radical pauper press faced impris-onment for dealing in unstamped newspapers as well as ongoing per-secutions for seditious and blasphemous libel. Arguably, far from heralding a new era of press freedom and liberty this period witnessed a far more effective system of press censorship in the form of market forces. Advertisers were reluctant to become associated with contro-versial, illegal unstamped publications and thus placed their adver-tisements with the 'respectable' press, whose propertied readership could afford the products advertised (Allan, 2004:13). This lack of investment meant that the radical press struggled to find the capital necessary keep up with the quickly improving print and distribution technologies.

According to James Curran (2003:9) the main 'rivals to the radical press within the working class (of whom well over half were literate or semi-literate by the 1830s) were almanacs, printed ballads, gallow-sheets and chapbooks'. It is also important to emphasize that the popular literature on crime continued to be diverse, as explained in the following passage:

> The nineteenth century had inherited from the eighteenth a tradition of crime-writing broad enough to suit all pocketbooks and degrees of lit-eracy: for the masses, criminal biographies, dying speeches, ballads, and news posters in single sheets (broadsides) on the streets; for those who had the time, skills, and money, Sessions Papers or reports of recent crime in newspapers; for the literate lower classes, fuller reports and chaplains' accounts in pamphlets or chap-books (cheap, miniature books); for the 'respectable' reader, the leisured student of crime, his-torical compilations in books. All of these genres circulated news of sensational crimes – indeed, made sensationalism possible – in the nineteenth century as literacy increased. (Knelman, 1998:25)

Accompanying this popular literature was a ~~~~
culture centred on the diffusion of printed images i~~~~
azines (Anderson, 1991) and the publication of sta~~~~
representation that enabled yet another picture of cri~~~~
formed. Crime surveys were debated in parliament, re~~~~
press and provided a stark contrast to the melodramatic ~~~~
Gothic fiction – then an immensely popular genre emerging~~~~
broader Romantic movement against modern forms of ra~~~~ ...sm
that fetishized fact and the Enlightenment project itself.[1] It has even
been suggested that criminal statistics 'were as influential in the
nineteenth century as television pictures of isolated incidents are in
the twentieth century in creating an image of that unseen but threatening world that surrounds every individual' (Sindall, 1990:26).

The standard accounts of the British press emphasize the importance of advertising revenue and legal emancipation as the forces
delivering press freedom by the middle of the nineteenth century. It
is from this period that the notion that the press constitute an independent 'fourth estate' gains currency, as a means of monitoring the
activities of the state executive and shaping public debate. The term
deliberately invokes the medieval concept of estate – of aristocracy,
clergy and commoners – to establish the democratic role played by the
press in scrutinizing the government on behalf of the people.
Following the abolition of the 'taxes on knowledge' in the 1850s newspapers expanded rapidly in the second half of the century. It was from
then that the 'new journalism', defined through its 'attention to crime,
sexual violence and human oddities' came to prominence in contrast
to the dry political commentary of earlier times (Williams, 1961:195).
The 'new journalism' sought to democratize reporting and make it
more attuned to daily life, thus 'human interest' stories were introduced to expose the secrets of the rich and prompt sympathy for the
poor. The 'new journalism' and what is also referred to as the
'Northcliffe revolution' – in which powerful 'press barons' (again,
note the feudal connotation) come to set the public agenda – laid the
foundations of modern news reporting.

Yet much of what was termed 'new' and revolutionary was really an
extension of the styles and techniques pioneered in the Sunday newspapers like *The News of the World*, *Reynolds' Newspaper* and
Lloyd's Weekly Newspaper in the 1840s. As Judith Walkowitz
(1992:84) explains, the 'Sundays had already reshaped the staid
format of news reporting of respectable dailies by incorporating narrative codes of popular literature, organized around themes of sex and
crime'. By adapting these techniques to a more elite readership the

new journalists hoped to construct a 'Government by Journalism' that would help expand critical public opinion in the 1880s. Editors and proprietors sought a wider audience by deliberately moving away from the ponderous self-importance of the older, 'obsolete journalism' towards a more sensational mode of address:

> This was particularly the case with the reporting of crime which drew on the colourful layout, profuse illustrations and the sensational 'human interest' type of story of publications like the 'Illustrated Police News'. In placing crime second only to war in his hierarchy of selling values, Northcliffe was only following the lead of the popular Sunday papers of an earlier generation. Northcliffe was certainly not the first to discover that, in the words of Kingsley Martin, 'in times of peace a first class sex murder is the best tonic for a tired sub-editor on a dull evening'; but the editor of the 'Evening News' was still excited to discover that he was able to calculate with reasonable accuracy the increase in circulation that a really messy murder would secure. (Chibnall, 1980:206)

The unsolved 'Whitechapel Murders' of autumn 1888 have become part of collective memory partly due to the mystery surrounding the identity of 'Jack the Ripper', but also, the distinctive cultural elements drawn on to make sense of the sadistic brutality involved have ensured the continuing exploitation of Ripper mythology by the media. It has been argued that the saturation 'coverage given to the Ripper murders clearly illustrates how the press could use crime reports to produce a consensual position supportive of established power relations, while increasing circulation and taking on the role of champion of truth, and of the just cause' (Leps, 1992:116).

It is significant that the murders from the outset were confined to Whitechapel, a decaying district in the East End of London synonymous with squalor, sex and crime. To contemporary, 'respectable' observers it had become known as 'the abyss' – an alien, dangerous and ungovernable place full of immorality, menace and disease (Stedman Jones, 1971). Newspaper coverage of the murders frequently contrasted this illicit landscape with descriptions of the grinding poverty in which many of the inhabitants lived. It was portrayed as 'a magnet not only for a "vast floating population – the waifs and strays of our thoroughfares" – but also for young West End bloods and for scores of respectable "slummers" who visited and even settled in the area' (Walkowitz, 1992:196). The fact that the murders could go on happening, followed the same pattern and involved anatomically precise acts of sexual mutilation lent a supernatural quality to the violence. Very early on Gothic fiction provided a lens and framework to understand the grotesque butchery of female bodies. In particular, Robert Louis Stevenson's (1886) *The Strange Case of Dr Jekyll and Mr Hyde* presented the most popular form of explanation: steeped as it is in multiple personality theory and Lombrosian criminal anthropology, it helped to 'furnish the idea that the Ripper might be "respectable" and therefore untraceable' (Biressi, 2001:66). Published just two years before the Ripper murders Stevenson's 'shilling shocker' not only presented a schizophrenic personality in the final throes of sadistic, apelike degeneracy and mental collapse, but also brought the primitive, debauched and monstrous into civilized, metropolitan life.[2]

Speculation about a mad, upper-class doctor dementedly punishing working-class prostitutes also played on widespread fears of the medical profession, which had already been subject to a series of scandals that 'cast a dark shadow over medical research into the "mysteries" of the female sex' (Walkowitz, 1992:210). For instance, until the repeal of the Contagious Diseases Act in 1886 the authorities could medically examine any woman suspected of being a prostitute and therefore a disease risk. If tensions in class and gender relations were revealed in these explanations, then race was to the fore in other competing accounts. It was supposed that the ritualistic elements of the murders pointed to religious fanaticism and the large Jewish immigrant population of Whitechapel was immediately put under suspicion. These very different responses to the murders exposed the extent of social antagonism in late Victorian London and eventually justified measures – like slum clearance, ending child prostitution and other social hygiene reforms – that sought to contain the disorder unleashed by the Ripper. The sexualization of the popular press will be explored in more detail in chapter 7 for I now turn to popular fiction in the nineteenth century.

The Origins of Detective Fiction

Of all the genres of popular fiction the detective story is probably the most studied, partly because its beginnings can be fixed with relative certainty. It is generally agreed that Edgar Allan Poe's 1841 story 'The Murders in the Rue Morgue' provides the crucial innovation of organizing the narrative around the intellectual genius of a detective hero, Auguste Dupin, who reconstructs the scene of a crime to apprehend the guilty culprit through the clues left behind. Of course, Conan Doyle subsequently translated the formula into the highly successful series of Sherlock Holmes stories, the first of which appeared in 1887.

In this literature crime and its detection becomes primarily an intellectual struggle between two great minds. Thomas De Quincey's 1827 essay 'On Murder Considered as One of the Fine Arts' provided an early attempt to reconfigure the aesthetic of crime writing by emphasizing the sublime qualities of violent murder. Intentionally controversial, his assertion was that the 'mass excitements of crime – ballads and broadsheets were everywhere at the time – are in fact functionally the same as elite admiration of stupendous Alpine views and staggering feats by Byronic heroes' (Knight, 2004:18). This is a crucial and lasting aesthetic change.

Gothic fiction and the Romantic movement are unmistakeable influences on the detective genre. Emerging in response to the eighteenth-century Enlightenment, the Gothic looked back to the pre-modern and revolved around motifs like suspense, terror and the supernatural. The Romantics included poets like Coleridge, Wordsworth, Shelley and Byron, who highlighted the dangers of excessive rationality and ugly industrialism and emphasized the need to retain the older, 'natural' institutions of the past. The movement, as a whole, is characterized by the privileging of aesthetic over utilitarian standards. Although this literature does not yet present the dilettante detective it does create an unsettling atmosphere of menace and foreboding. It has even been claimed that the 'fear of bourgeois civilization is summed up in two names: Frankenstein and Dracula' as they express 'the anxiety that the future will be monstrous' (Moretti, 1983:83–84). Consequently, the innovation Poe performed was to transform these motifs into his detective fiction. In the Dupin stories Poe established many of the trappings of the modern detective story. As commentators have pointed out, the character has a contradictory identity, in that his method of detection is both artistic and scientific. In this 'he foreshadows the later generic detectives of the twentieth century, who combine a bohemian artistic intuition and a disciplined rigour, the rational and the irrational' (McCracken, 1998:52). The eccentric brilliance of the urbane amateur sleuth is later underlined in Sherlock Holmes, who is most definitely not a policeman, but a decadent intellectual (who frequently escapes into music and cocaine).

It is the combination of reason and unreason that sustains detective stories. For instance, Dupin eventually reveals that the mysterious murders in the Rue Morgue were committed by an escaped orang-utan. This explanation is totally rational in the context of the narrative, but at the same time quite bizarre. As Scott McCracken (1998:52) suggests, the detective story oscillates between the idea that modern life can be mastered and read but at the same time threatening, since that order is delicate and vulnerable to the destructive forces of nature or pre-modern threats. One historical shift that is important for the emergence of detective fiction is the transformation of punishment based on arbitrary power to the rule of law. In other words, this genre of fiction emerged at a time when Western countries had only recently moved from a judicial process based on torture and confession to one centred on trial by evidence (Bloch, 1965/96: 246). Detective fiction articulates Enlightenment discourses of individualism, science and rationality. According to the literary critic Walter Benjamin the stories frequently comment on the urban experience by saying much about the development of policing and surveillance.

For Benjamin, the origins of detective fiction are to be found in the rapid expansion of cities in the nineteenth century and the impersonality this urban sprawl brought to social relations. He suggests that the original content of the detective story was the 'obliteration of the individual's traces in the big city crowd' (Benjamin, 1983:43). The literary context in which Benjamin (1983) discusses Poe's detective stories is through the figure of the flâneur. Historically, the term flâneurs referred to a group of writers and journalists who in the serial feature sections of Paris newspapers, and in books known as *physiologies*, wrote depictions of city life from a position of privileged spectatorship (Brand, 1991:6). Benjamin's argument is that the flâneur was a precursor to the detective as they both suggest that the city can be read.[3] Poe's achievement was two-fold. First, he linked crime with the urban crowd. Second, he provided, in Dupin, a figure that could read and master the dangerous city. In the nineteenth century the myth and reality of intrepid urban exploration became a defining feature of bourgeois male subjectivity. Walkowitz (1992:18) also explains how men like 'Frederick Engels, Charles Dickens, and Henry Mayhew were the most distinguished among a throng of missionaries and explorers, men who tried to read the "illegible" city, transforming what appeared to be a chaotic, haphazard environment into a social text that was "integrated, knowable, and ordered".'

Benjamin further argues that the development of a penetrating gaze that could master the city is not just restricted to the world of fiction. In fact it closely corresponded to the new mechanisms of surveillance that rendered the urban legible to the gaze of power. This was achieved precisely through the bureaucratic reduction of individuality down to a set of knowable traces. Benjamin clearly anticipates Foucault's (1977) analysis of Jeremy Bentham's Panopticon, which was designed to be a model prison in which the surveillance of prisoners was to be complete and total. So the argument can be made that the 'private eye' of detective fiction complements this public eye of power, through rendering society totally visible to the gaze of power. In fact, it has been suggested that the Sherlock Holmes stories embody the totalitarian aspiration of a transparent society. As every 'story reiterates Bentham's Panopticon ideal: the model prison that signals the metamorphosis of liberalism into total scrutability' (Moretti, 1983:143). A further theme introduced in classic detective fiction and sustained throughout the twentieth century is the ideological positioning of women:

> Doyle's repetition intensifies and makes plainer the misogynistic dynamic of the Poe tales – with their dismembered mothers, abortive shopgirls and adulterous queens, and the central pairing of male-bonded detective and narrator – establishing 221B Baker Street as a universally accessible men's club. (Hutchings, 2001:114)

Moreover, the early stories tend to represent crime as a puzzle to be solved and chronicle disorder in the respectable bourgeois family.[4] Or more precisely they chart the corrosive power of greed upon Victorian social relations (Young, 1996:99).

I have dealt at length with some central themes in classic detective fiction, not least because there are important continuities that inform subsequent developments in the genre, but some significant differences appear as the twentieth century progressed, which I now outline.

The 'Golden Age' and 'Hard-Boiled' Detection

The 'Golden Age' is the term used to refer to the novels of authors like Agatha Christie, Dorothy Sayers and G. K. Chesterton which were produced in the twentieth-century inter-war period. In these stories the detective remains an eccentric, amateur sleuth but there are some significant changes. For what is seen here is not only a shift from dangerous city streets to the seemingly tranquil English countryside, but also crime, or more accurately the murder mystery, is an event that takes place in the upper reaches of the class structure. This social milieu means that the 'ordinary' policeman (and it is usually a 'he') has no chance of solving the mystery, since he possesses neither the standing necessary to gain access to nor the graces to move easily in this social setting. The *ordinary* policeman stands by while the *extraordinary* detective solves the mystery. Consequently, the detective is an ambiguous figure, who is inside, but with a certain distance from, the social setting of crime (Clarke, 2001:79). Predominantly, this role is occupied by an amateur, or at least someone who is not a member of the police force. Crucially though the sleuth remains a flâneur who can penetrate the social codes of the elites. For instance, Agatha Christie's Miss Marple is as much a flâneur as her urban counterparts. She is able to play the part of the innocent old lady, an anonymous type, yet also possesses the observational powers to see what others do not see and thereby solve the mystery.

While there is a shift in tone, from the gloom and menace of Poe to a more familiar comedy of manners in the Golden Age mysteries, and an accompanying change in location to the ubiquitous English country house, there are important continuities with the earlier work. The stories remain preoccupied with disorder and the destructive force of greed upon family relationships. This theme is developed in the inter-war period, for while the upper classes present themselves as self-confidently imperial, powerful and respected in public, where everyone knows their place and acts accordingly, yet in private they 'keep killing one another – and when one of them is murdered, there is a long queue of likely candidates for the role of chief suspect' (Clarke, 2001:76). The mystery is an effect of intimate, family relationships going wrong rather than a result of a dangerous world 'out there' and the victim is typically cast unsympathetically and deserving of their fate. The victim is usually the harsh, hot-tempered and stupid father opposed to a marriage, or an unremitting cad whose impending marriage to the decent girl interferes with her preference for an upright young man. Worst of all the victim has posed as a gentleman but has concealed some dark secret that he has used to exploit the rituals of status (Grella, 1988:96–7).

It has been argued that the great appeal of this literature in the inter-war years was nostalgia following the destruction wrought by the Great War, ensuing economic crises and revolutionary upheavals:

> The country-house and drawing-room settings of the novels . . . are not a reflection of contemporary life, but a recollection of Paradise Lost. Through them, the Good Life of antebellum days was relived – in imagination if not in reality. (Mandel, 1984:30)

In stark contrast to the English murder mystery an entirely different kind of detective fiction was being developed in the United States, most famously in the work of Raymond Chandler and his archetypal 'private eye' Philip Marlowe. This genre is usually regarded as 'hard-boiled' detective fiction in that the narrative seeks to offer a sense of social realism in its murky urban settings, its focus on low life and the use of gritty, everyday language. This literature also provided the basis for the development of film noir in Hollywood in the 1940s and 1950s, which offered frequently bleak outlooks on the urban condition as opposed to the musicals, melodramas and screwball comedies that were being produced in the 1930s. In fact, the term film noir was coined by postwar French film critics, once American pictures began to be shown again after the Second World War, when these critics noticed the dramatic contrasts in the ambiguous existential content and distinctive visual style of the films that Hollywood produced during and after the war.

In many ways these stories and films returned crime to the mean streets of cities and we can see many motifs that Poe introduced are set conventions in hard-boiled fiction and film noir. For instance, the figure of the detached, intuitive and smart investigator and the city as a dark, dangerous setting return to centre stage. Similarly, wealth, power and status are key elements in these stories and films, but they function in very different ways from the English murder mystery. The imaginary social order of America here is one where the city provides the context in which money links a variety of social groups, which would include the old rich, businessmen, gangsters, con men and corrupt police departments in tangled relationships (Clarke, 2001:82). The highly stylized look and generic codes of noir include the 'weak hero sucked into a life of crime by the treacherous femme fatale, the tough private eye hoping to outwit the criminals who owned his city, the maze of rain-slick streets leading nowhere, the hallucinatory contrasts between glaring white faces and deep black skies, the lush orchestral scores ratcheting up moments of emotional intensity still further' (Leitch, 2002:33–4). This distinctive visual style was influenced by German expressionist cinema (many of whose chief exponents had fled to Hollywood in the 1930s), while the moody urban thrillers were told through voice-over, ominous flashback and surreal dream sequences.

The narrative tension in these stories is animated by the conflict between an amoral, corrupt world and the isolated moral code of the detective. Like all mythic heroes he mediates between opposing forces and reconciles them, one way or another. The detective must be socially mobile enough to work in a whole variety of urban settings without becoming contaminated. In fact it has been argued that the Private Investigator is the moral conscience of America. The classic 'everyman' figure, who stands for all the 'little people' who are not part of the centres of power and influence, but whose lives are threatened by their corruption (Clarkc, 2001:84–5). This is the conservative limit of the genre. Even though it reveals widespread corruption it is a literary and cinematic form that defends the social system (Messent, 1997:7–8). So while individual crimes might be solved, nothing ever changes in the larger social and political climate – the basic source of corruption remains untouched. Nevertheless, new gender relationships are introduced, particularly in the form of the 'femme fatale' who lures male protagonists to their doom. The sense of women as profoundly dangerous is central to noir. Indeed, the mystery surrounding the temptress often overshadows the mystery surrounding the crime and the narrative displays an inability 'to cope with the woman-question' (Kuhn, 1982:35). The inevitable doom that surrounds the fall guy tapped into Second World War anxieties, and the subsequent return of troubled veterans, Cold War menace, McCarthyism and rapid social change in the postwar era were all themes explored in later films.

The Police Procedural

Since the 1950s the police have been the focus of narrative attention in detective fiction, not least because the 'imaginary social order in which gifted amateurs could carry out investigations under the noses . . . of humble policemen could hardly be sustained (except as a pastiche) in the postwar context' (Clarke, 2001:86). James Ellroy, the author of *L.A. Confidential,* has remarked that he 'consciously abandoned the private eye tradition', since the 'last time a private eye investigated a homicide was never' (cited in Messent, 1997:11). This emphasizes the fact that private eyes are quite simply irrelevant to contemporary criminal justice investigations, and that the figure is purely a romantic fantasy. In response, the detective story has moved its social milieu to the occupational world of the police procedural where stories are based in police settings, and detection becomes professionalized. Of course, in some versions the narrative form does not change very much, the same themes are simply moved to the world of the police. It still remains a matter of the detective's extraordinary ability to reveal the truth beneath the surface of appearances, albeit now accompanied by the apparatus of organized detection while still displaying personal eccentricities in characters like Morse, Frost, Dalziel and Pascoe.

It has been argued though that the 'TV cop programme is one of the most interesting genres broadcast on television' as it 'is a genre that is continually being "reinvented" as new variations are tried in an attempt to replace tiring cornerstones of the schedules' (Lacey, 2000:229). Moreover, there is an important sense in which 'detective fictions might be considered to be phenomena which bear the imprint of their times' (Sparks, 1993:99). For instance, the popular detective series *Inspector Morse* (1987–93, with subsequent single films) has been situated in the context of a broader discussion of 'heritage television' that offers 'a certain image of England, partly through its dominant structure of feeling, an elegiac nostalgia, and partly through its production values and export destiny, which offer the (tasteful) pleasures of money on the screen' (Brunsdon, 1998:230). Other versions rework what Reiner (1992:200) has termed 'community police narratives', which are as old as television itself. In the British context, the exemplar is *Dixon of Dock Green* (1955–76), which came to be displaced by the ruthless vigilantism of *The Sweeney* (1975–8), but staged a highly successful comeback in such series as *The Bill* (1984–), *Juliet Bravo* (1980–5), *Heartbeat* (1992–) and the influential American series *Hill Street Blues* (1981–9). Since the mid-1990s the TV police procedural has undergone further change, partly in response to the phenomenal success of medical drama series like *Casualty* (1986–), *Holby City* (1999–) and *ER* (1994–).

There has been a corresponding move towards the 'medicalization of crime' in the genre with the focus shifting away from the police as the solvers of mysteries on to forensic pathologists and criminal psychologists (Brunsdon, 1998:242). Examples of this genre hybridity include *Cracker* (1993–), *Dangerfield* (1995–99), *Silent Witness* (1996–), *Waking the Dead* (2000–) and *Wire in the Blood* (2002–), which are part of a broader diversification of the police procedural formula in an effort to increase and keep audiences in an increasingly competitive television market. This influence can be seen in how the American producer of *CSI: Crime Scene Investigation* (2000–) 'had demanded a show so stylistically different that a channel-surfing audience would be forced to stop and view the unusual looking images' (cited in Lury, 2005:38). Competition for TV audiences in an era of hundreds of cable channels has meant that prime-time programming has had to develop distinctive visual styles and elaborate story arcs to seduce viewers.

Cinematic representations of crime fighting tend to explore the tensions between the 'good cop' and the occupational world in which he functions. This is very close to the Private Eye form, in which the 'loner' battles against the bureaucracy and incompetence of the police department. The classic example of this is the Dirty Harry series of films. The first, which was released in 1971, heralded an innovation of tainted-cop investigation dramas. Harry Callaghan is the police officer dedicated to terminating a serial killer on the loose in San Francisco. To get his man he will rarely play by the book and he defies both his conservative bosses and the political establishment in tracking down the killer. The indignant, crusading policeman embodies both a late 1960s counterculture ideology, through his defiance of authority, and a right-wing distrust of the government.

In fact, one famous film critic complained that 'this action genre has always had a certain fascist potential, and now it has finally surfaced' in Dirty Harry (Kael, 1972, cited in Sparks, 1996:354). There is no doubt that the film applauds Harry's vigilantism, and Harry Callaghan, played by Clint Eastwood, is an unbreakable straight-arrow who remains completely uncontaminated in his search for the psycho. In later variations on the same narrative pattern, cop and killer become doppelgängers and a far more morally ambiguous story is told, such as in the more recent films *Face/Off* (1997) and *Heat* (1995), whereas in the Harry films they remain distinct adversaries in a straightforward battle between good and evil. And like its hero, the films believe that evil can be contained, whereas in later films like *L.A. Confidential* (1997), malevolence is systemic and no cop operates with Harry's moral purity (Hirsch, 1999:157). Similar double-crossing themes are explored in *The Departed* (2006) where Matt Damon and Leonardo DiCaprio are cast as metaphysical doppelgängers infiltrating the hostile worlds of the police and the mob respectively.

Born to be Bad

Much of the crime fiction discussed so far has been concerned with a narrative structure that starts with an opposition between law-abiding citizens and criminals. Yet there is another genre of films that focus on professional criminals, on characters who pursue a criminal way of life before the film or story begins which would include the classic original gangster films of the 1930s up to the underworld epics of the *Godfather* cycle or *Goodfellas* (1990), and the more recent television series *The Sopranos* (1999–2007). This genre puts a new dynamic on family relationships in mob tales. The latter successfully exploits the dynamics of 'must-see' television consumption by presenting 'large ensemble casts in well-crafted multi-layered narratives that explore a side of American society missing from the early formulaic action series like *Starsky and Hutch* or *Kojak*' (Rixon, 2003:58). In fact, *The Sopranos* is closer to Jacobean tragedy than crime drama, dealing with blood, comedy and action on an epic scale – and is routinely described as the best thing on television.

Another staple of Hollywood cinema has been the failed heist, which was cleverly reworked in *Reservoir Dogs* (1992) and the myriad of imitations that followed in the success of Quentin Tarantino's postmodern reworking of what had become a stale genre. Of course, he also provided a fresh spin to crime films in *Pulp Fiction* (1994), which transformed hit men into likeable, tragicomic heroes. In contrast, British crime cinema has traditionally concentrated on tough men in seedy low-life characterizations of professional crime worlds (such as *Brighton Rock*, 1947; *Get Carter*, 1971; *The Long Good Friday*, 1981; *The Krays*, 1990). While many of these films had reached iconic status in the 1990s 'lads' press, important changes occurred in British crime film during that decade. The social milieu of crime switched from the underworld to the underclass, or to be more precise a number of key films examine the 'predicament of the jobless underclass male' (Monk, 1999:174). From the feel-good comedy of *The Full Monty* (1997) to the grim heroin drama of *Trainspotting* (1996) films explored the consequences of the economic decline and social destruction wrought by Thatcherism in places blighted by deindustrialization, where crime is a 'normal' fact of daily life. The humour returns in *Hot Fuzz* (2007) which imaginatively transports the high-octane Hollywood action thriller to a sleepy Somerset town and plays as much on the audience's knowledge of American genre movies as the dull ordinariness of British life.

The most famous cinematic examination of the criminal psyche is Alfred Hitchcock's *Psycho* (1960), which 'looked like nothing audiences had ever seen on television, or in movie theatres either' (Leitch, 2002:40). The plot centres on Norman Bates, a motel proprietor, his mummified mother and frenzied destruction of any woman he is sexually attracted to. *Psycho* spawned a cycle of films that explain crime in terms of psychological abnormality, as in *Cape Fear* (1961, 1991), *Repulsion* (1965) and *Badlands* (1973). Over the last couple of decades the serial killer has become a central figure, which highlights the return of the threat of irrationality to the genre. While classical crime fiction derives its narrative tension from the opposing forces of reason and unreason, in much of the detective fiction in the twentieth century, crimes are motivated and their causes can be traced somewhere back to relationships of love, greed or revenge among the principal players in the drama. Yet with the advent of the serial killer, there is the creation of 'innocent victims'. In this imaginary social order, crime is a totally random event and it appears as if out of nowhere, making violence unpredictable and symbolically much more dangerous than in previous fictional representations of crime (Clarke, 1996:83). The films and stories lay a great stress on the ways in which the serial killer can pass for normal and will not stand out as a deranged individual. Quite the reverse is the case; he blends invisibly into social life. For instance, the serial killer in *Se7en* (1995), played by Kevin Spacey, is referred to only as 'John Doe' (the term used for unnamed corpses).

In the conventional detective story, the murderer is in many respects 'normal' in that they belong to a particular social type with predictable motives, such as love, revenge, money and so on. By contrast, the detective is 'extraordinary', with special qualities that permit a solution where the less brilliant will fail. In the case of the serial killer, this pattern is inverted. *Silence of the Lambs* (1991), for example, features Dr. Hannibal Lecter as a brilliant psychiatrist who is serving a life-sentence for his cannibalistic serial killing activities, but is called on to help the FBI ensnare another homicidal psychopath. It is the murderer who is extraordinary with the ability to appear normal, while the detective is part of a collective enterprise and is increasingly dependent on the abilities of others, such as forensics, psychologists and so on, to arrive at a solution (Clarke, 1996:84). Yet this theme of inversion is, in many respects, a defining characteristic of Gothic melodrama, in that the 'transgression of all boundaries [is] a conscious narrative agenda' (Simpson, 2000:19), while it is the oscillation between reassurance and danger that sustains the narrative tension in serial killer texts.

In other words, the appearance of the serial killer in fiction owes an enormous debt to Gothic horror, which relies heavily on the establishment of normality prior to the terror being unleashed and the ensuing violation of the comforting patterns of daily life. More recently, the true-life thriller *Zodiac* (2007) combines elements of the police procedural, urban paranoia and newsroom movie as it concentrates on the men who pursue the serial killer. Based on the spree of motiveless killings in late 1960s California the murderer (the self-styled Zodiac) was never brought to justice and the film follows the obsessions of the journalists and detectives frustrated in their decade-long hunt as they hit dead ends, false trails and disinformation. Instead of focusing on the charismatic serial killer the film constructs a pervading sense of menace surrounding the journalists and detectives as their lives and families are put at risk as they become increasingly obsessed with the case.

Themes of disruption, excess and inversion are central to the carnivalesque cinema of directors like David Lynch, David Cronenburg and the Coen Brothers. Films like *Blood Simple* (1984), *Blue Velvet* (1986) and *Wild at Heart* (1990) abound with grotesque figures moving in social worlds where casual violence is endemic and provoke 'perverse laughter at its excess' (Fuery, 2000:130). The dark comic humour that infuses these narratives becomes a defining feature of films like *Shallow Grave* (1994), *Pulp Fiction* (1994), and *Lock, Stock, and Two Smoking Barrels* (1999). David Cronenburg's films also work with figures of the grotesque – often to extremely unsettling effect by focusing on the impact of technology on the human body. More recently his *A History of Violence* (2005) marks something of a departure, as it explores the savagery underlying suburban American life by focusing on a lone hero's attempts to defend his family from hostile outsiders. Yet the film borrows and subverts familiar themes from hard-boiled thrillers and classic Westerns, ultimately to expose the amoral values behind both genres. Likewise David Lynch's (2000) *Mulholland Drive* ostensibly seems to be a film about cinematic language, whose last half-hour provides a series of mystifying events that obliterates distinctions between fantasy and reality, and invites any number of postmodern interpretations.[5]

While these are recent developments in US crime cinema, British television viewers were treated to the *Prime Suspect* (1991–2006) series that explored the struggles faced by Detective Inspector Jane Tennison, played by Helen Mirren, to work in the male occupational culture of the police. Further transgressive themes were explored in *Between the Lines* (1992–4), which examined police corruption and featured Siobhan Redmond playing Detective Sergeant Maureen Connell – British television's first lesbian detective. These advances were conspicuous feminist interventions into a conventionally masculine genre, yet much recent American programming has been defined as 'post-feminist' due to the political ambivalence presented in popular series like *Buffy the Vampire Slayer* (1997–2003), *Ally McBeal* (1997–2002) and *Sex and the City* (1998–2004). In these texts feminism occupies 'a spectral, shadowy, almost hated existence' (McRobbie, 2005:192). As the following passage explains:

> All of these series are generic hybrids, merging elements of soap opera, series drama, comedy, fantasy and, in the case of *Buffy*, horror. All are aimed primarily at a female audience, feature young, independent,

usually single women in an urban environment, and engage with issues generated by 'second wave' feminism, but in an ironic, playful and style-conscious manner which might be seen as antithetical to an earlier generation of feminists. (Thornham and Purvis, 2005:126)

The chapter now turns to a consideration of how genre hybridity has further reshaped the broadcasting landscape.

Reality TV

There is an important sense in which the proliferation of 'reality' TV programming (a term which covers 'docu-soaps', lifestyle 'make-overs' and 'factual entertainment' formats) represents a crisis in the documentary form – the pinnacle of public service broadcasting. The reasons for the demise of documentary and the 'daytime-ization' of prime-time television are complex, but would include the interplay of the market, the expansion of satellite broadcasting and the standardization of programming style to maximize audiences (Palmer, 1998:363). The impact of the market has meant that producers are required to make more and cheaper programming where a substantial proportion of viewers are turning away from terrestrial broadcasting to watch sport and film on satellite and cable (Brunsdon *et al.*, 2001:31). It is important to locate this style of programming in the context of these broader transformations, not simply because the formats share similar modes of address, production values and genre hybridity but also because they raise important questions about the relationships between the media, democracy and the public sphere.

One of the earliest and best-known reality TV programmes is *Crimewatch UK*, which was first broadcast in 1984, and regularly attracts audiences of between eight and thirteen million viewers – figures that are close to soap opera popularity and far greater than the main national news programmes (Dobash *et al.*, 1998:38). The success of *Crimewatch* lies in its blurring of the boundaries between fact, fiction and entertainment. For instance, fact and public appeal are merged with dramatization and fiction so that while it is 'intended to mobilize audiences to help the police solve crimes, it also entertains, using crime stories with murder, armed robbery with violence, and sexual crime as staple items' (Dobash *et al.*, 1998:38). However, a key difference between *Crimewatch* and the more recent programmes lies not simply in the use of CCTV footage as opposed to dramatized reconstruction, but that 'both the "everyday-ness" of the crimes portrayed . . . and the frequency of their occurrence in "everyday life" is highlighted in both the rhetoric and the aesthetic which are characteristic of programmes such as *Crime Beat, Police Camera Action* and *Car Wars*' (Brunsdon *et al.*, 2001:47). In other words, not only is the dull monotony of everyday crime emphasized but 'the address to the viewer as a threatened consumer is key to these programmes' (Brunsdon *et al.*, 2001:49), in that the viewer-consumer is continually warned that they must take responsibility for crime prevention.

There is considerable debate over whether these new forms of programming are a more democratic way of representing crime or are part of a broader governmental project activating the citizenship against the figure of the criminal. For instance, it has been argued that 'what we are witnessing through hybridization and new reality and access genres is the democratization of an old public service discourse, dominated by experts and a very official kind of talk, and the creation of a new mixed public sphere, where common knowledge and everyday experience play a much larger role' (Bondebjerg, 1996:29). A much more critical reading of reality TV is offered by Palmer (1998, 2000) who clearly laments the contemporary loss of the documentary project, with its ambition to create an informed citizenry by expanding public understanding through exposing injustice. As he puts it, 'such programming works against the documentary ethos, confirming stereotypes rather than exploring the cracks and fissures in the system and thereby introducing the ambiguity vital to healthy debate' (Palmer, 1998:374).

In important respects these arguments return us to the debates that began this chapter. Many of the criticisms directed at 'infotainment' worry over the 'dumbing down' of public debate and diminution of modernist forms of political communication. Likewise, the discussion of the origins of detective fiction argued that the figure of the detective was closely related to the new forms of discipline and surveillance associated with modernity. The panopticon offered idealized forms of power relationships in which the *few see the many* to pierce the murky surface of appearances and thus discover the causes of crime. This metaphor of detection remains a highly significant theme in contemporary fiction. Yet it is important to recognize that accompanying these processes are complementary forms of what Thomas Mathiesen (1997:219) has described as synopticism, that enables the *many to see the few*. The panoptic and synoptic also produce a further development – a desire to be watched:

> One thing that reality television has shown is that we are a nation not only of voyeurs but also of exhibitionists. The contestants on the likes of *Big Brother* are there in the vain hope of being spotted for a future of never-ending fame and fortune; the characters in docu-soaps likewise. (Leishman and Mason, 2003:124)

The fusion of panopticism and synopticism is also now an unmistakeable feature of news reporting. The omniscience of CCTV surveillance has provided incredibly moving 'visual obituaries' that in the UK include 'James Bulger being led to his death from a shopping mall, Jill Dando shopping in Hammersmith, and Damilola Taylor skipping across a paved square in Peckham' (McCahill, 2003:194).

Mathiesen's (1997) argument is a crucial one. It shows how the rise of the mass media has close corollaries with the spectacle of crime in popular culture and the rigorous deployment of surveillance technologies in public and private space. In this regard reality TV would seem to be the latest manifestation of this trend, not simply because the programming relies on grainy CCTV footage and insists that the public must take responsibility for crime control, but rather that the gaze of the viewer is crucial to understanding the place of crime. Mathiesen (1997) goes so far as to describe his thesis as the 'viewer society', to emphasize the significance of synopticism. To develop this point, Bauman's (1994) argument that the global reach of media technology has brought a new barbarism into our homes is especially important in developing a more nuanced understanding of mediated violence.

Global news stories involving war, terrorism, hatred, killing and starvation have meant that now ordinary interactions take place against this backcloth of cruelty. Bauman claims that the sheer volume of these images has a desensitizing effect on viewers and produces a mass indifference to the spectacle of cruelty. Consequently, there is a stark contrast 'between viewers whose main experience of violence is mediated and those who are living within the orbit of the constant threat of its eruption' (Stevenson, 1999:132). Indeed, it has been estimated that only a seventh of the world's population live in relatively secure democratic zones of peace, while the rest live in zones where warlords, random acts of violence, civil and international wars are commonplace (Keane, 1996). Since 9/11 the pursuit of security in the face of international terrorism has posed a considerable 'threat to the very liberties it purports to protect' (Zedner, 2005:507).

For Stan Cohen (1996) the atrocities that have become a daily part of life in so many parts of the world are a consequence of the collapse of distinctions between political dispute and criminal violence. In his subsequent work he has maintained that people engage in complex 'states of denial' rather than weary 'compassion fatigue' when confronted with the mediatized suffering of distant others (Cohen, 2001; Cohen and Seu, 2002). Yet critics wonder why there is this cultural demand that we ought to have a moral responsibility to care for the suffering of distant others (Tester, 2001; Wilkinson, 2005). Appeals to 'collective sympathy' are distinctly modern phenomena (Turner, 1993) and date from the eighteenth century when shared feelings for human suffering became a defining feature of 'moral individualism' and prompted much social reform (Wilkinson, 2005:142).

In an important article Claire Valier and Ronnie Lippens (2004) have attempted to formulate what kind of response can be called 'just' to the routine parade of images of suffering we are regularly confronted with and those that do passionately 'move us'. They go on to explore the possibility of an unconditional ethical response to the face of the other that is presented in 'moving images' of mothers of murdered children. These arguments can usefully connect with Rob Stones's (2002) call for a 'civic imagination' that enlarges our concern for the suffering of distant others, Susan Sontag's (2003) deliberations on the obligations of conscience and Angela McRobbie's (2006) account of vulnerability, violence and cosmopolitanism. It is on the 'ethics of representation' (Holohan, 2005:148) that much future work needs to be done and I return to some of these issues in the final chapter.

6
Telling Stories

In the last couple of chapters I have outlined some of the important developments in the representation of crime in the mass media. Here I introduce more systematic ways of understanding these different regimes of textual representation. As we have already seen there remains considerable debate over how actively media audiences derive meaning from texts in their daily routines and other approaches that privilege textual analysis as a largely self-contained activity. Of course, the problem revolves around keeping the analysis of the distinctive textual properties distinct from the quite complex spectatorial processes (ranging from intense identification to bored indifference) that audiences engage in. One of the main reasons why textual analysis has been able to develop quite independently from studies of readers, viewers and listeners is the longstanding interest in why storytelling is such a universal feature of human existence. We not only tell stories, but stories also tell us. They are good to think with. Roland Barthes (1977/90:136), for instance, suggests that falling in love involves telling ourselves stories about falling in love and in this sense 'mass culture is a machine for showing desire'.

It is also important to recognize that this interest in storytelling is not purely restricted to the world of fiction. As Ken Plummer has influentially put it:

'Stories' have recently moved centre stage in social thought. In anthropology, they are seen as pathways to understanding culture. In psychology, they are the bases of identity. In history, they provide the tropes for making sense of the past. In psychoanalysis, they provide 'narrative truths' for analysis. In philosophy they are the bases for new forms of 'world-making' and the key to creating communities. Even economics has

> recognized its 'storied character' . . . Sociologists may be the last to enter
> this field explicitly, although much of their work over the past century has
> in one way or another implicitly been concerned both with the gathering
> of other people's stories (through interviews and the like) as well as telling
> their own stories (of modernity, of class, of the degradation of work). But
> a clear 'narrative moment' has now been sensed. (Plummer, 1995:18–19)

Criminology is also experiencing something of a narrative turn with
recent studies of film (Rafter, 2000), literature (Ruggiero, 2003) and
celebrity (Schmid, 2005) each demonstrating the cultural work performed through these different ways of telling stories. Indeed, both
Nicole Rafter (2007) and Philip Rawlings (1998) have independently
argued that crime films and the 'true crime' genre (their respective
subjects) constitute a *popular criminology* that operates parallel to, but
some distance from, academic criminology – where the rejection of
the former 'by academics often seems tinged with a lofty disdain for
the prurience of such work' (Rawlings, 1998:2). However, that disregard is hard to sustain given that it is popular criminology that provides the most significant source of public understandings of crime,
justice and punishment.

In this chapter I introduce the more systematic ways of analysing
the formal properties of stories that have been developed in literary
theory and structural anthropology, before applying these arguments
to the police procedural genre on television. I have chosen the police
procedural to illustrate these points, but other genres (courtroom
dramas and prison films are the most obvious) could just as easily have
been chosen. It is also worth emphasizing that police officers are
themselves acutely aware of the gulf between mediated public expectations of their role and the mundane responsibilities that fill much
day-to-day police work, but at the same time they understand that
media images are a crucial part of policing. Consequently, this shapes
how they 'perform' in the street so that their activities and reputations
are in turn policed by the media (Perlmutter, 2000).

I begin though with an account of why stories of wrongdoing are
central to storytelling and introduce Aristotle's still influential discussion of representation before turning to the modern analysis of narrative in linguistics and anthropology, which I will argue enables a more
sophisticated understanding of popular criminology to emerge. It has
been suggested that the enduring popularity of crime films is due to
the way they:

> provide escape from daily life, opportunities to solve mysteries, chances
> to identify with powerful and competent heroes, and discussions of

morality that are comfortingly unambiguous. Their predictable plots and stock characters, far from disappointing audiences, deliver the plea-sure of variations on the familiar . . . They offer access to places most of us never get to in person, such as drug factories, police interrogation rooms, glamorous nightclubs and prison cells. Good crime films portray these places in terms so vivid, gripping and emotionally compelling that we identify with their characters even when we know that the stories are in large part fantasies. Opening a window on exotica, crime films enable viewers to become voyeurs, secret observers of the personal and even intimate lives of characters very different from themselves. Crime films also offer us the pleasurable opportunity to pursue justice, often at the side of a charismatic and capable hero. (Rafter, 2000:9)

In what follows I will introduce the systematic attempts that have been made to grasp how forms of representation do this cultural work.

Narrative

Since stories are central to social activity they have received consider-able attention. One of the earliest studies of narrative was Aristotle's *De Poetica* (*Poetics*), which sought to identify how various kinds of poems and plays have certain themes in common. Written in the fourth century BC, the book emphasizes the importance of genre classification and reflective emulation in a discussion of epic poetry, tragedy, comedy and music. It is widely regarded as the founding text of literary criticism in the West (Eco, 1990/2006).

Aristotle not only classified works on the basis of shared traits but also insisted that art mirrored nature. Thus he established a 'mimetic' theory of representation – that is, he claimed that literature, painting, music, sculpture and so forth work by imitating the truth of the world. Aristotle's broader point is that human beings are prone to construct likenesses, and then to respond to these imitations with pleasure. In doing so, we satisfy our innate desires for knowledge by exercising the uniquely human power of understanding through recognition.

This theory of reflection has been highly influential. In the eighteenth century, for instance, Dr Johnson famously defended Shakespeare as 'the poet that holds up to his readers a faithful mirror of manners and of life' (cited in Bell, 1992:21). It is to be found in subsequent debates over the merits of 'realism' in nineteenth-century novels, conventions which were subsequently challenged in modernist and postmodernist fiction. Rafter's (2000) fundamental point is that crime films 'mirror' social relations and I will return to her important work below. Besides introducing the idea of mimesis to explain how stories work Aristotle also claimed that 'character' and 'action' are essential elements of a plot. Indeed, he is the first to have stated that a plot has to have a beginning, a middle and an end, and not necessarily in that order – in the *Odyssey*, for example, the wanderings of Odysseus are told through flashbacks and shifts in the centre of the narrative as the hero returns home. In Greek tragedy, the hero usually makes errors because the gods intervene in mortal lives, whereas in Shakespearean tragedy they arise through fundamental flaws in the central protagonist's character (Hamlet's indecision, Macbeth's ambition, Othello's jealousy and Lear's pride are the examples usually given).

Stories of transgression are absolutely central to every culture's imaginary origins, typically situated in some dreadful primordial event – as in Eve's temptation in the Garden of Eden or Prometheus's theft of fire from the gods. The process of discovery can thus be seen as a universal feature of narratives, while the mystery that lies at the heart of tragedy generates unsettling experiences of disorder, uncertainty, suffering and death. For Aristotle, the archetype is Sophocles's *Oedipus Tyrannos*. In the play, the climactic moment of recognition is when Oedipus's discovery of his true origins also reveals his shocking crimes (unknowingly marrying his mother and unwittingly murdering his father). The tragic power is derived from Oedipus's gradual realization that the monstrous lies within himself and that he alone is responsible for all the terrible misfortunes that surround him (a city where plague rages, his children cursed, a wife who hangs herself and his obstinate inability to see the whole before him). Indeed, what defines Oedipus is how little he truly knows himself – an enduring theme that psychoanalytical theory is fundamentally indebted to.

The modern analysis of narrative begins with the 'linguistic turn' in social thought in the early twentieth century. Vladimir Propp's (1928/68) *Morphology of the Folk Tale* remains one of the most influential studies of narrative and has proven to have considerable generality. From an analysis of a large number of Russian folk tales he identified common features they shared, which he reduced to seven 'spheres of action' and thirty-one fixed elements that could be combined in different ways. Any individual folk tale brings together these 'spheres of action' so that heroes follow quests, have helpers, fight villains, fall in love, marry princesses and so on. What Propp provides is an account of character functions as a narrative unfolds, which follow certain rules that have not changed much over centuries. Propp's method, which offers a detailed classification of sequences in folk tales, is often contrasted with that developed by the French structural anthropologist Claude Lévi-Strauss. In books like *Structural Anthropology* (1950), *The Savage Mind* (1962) and *The Raw and the Cooked* (1964), Lévi-Strauss sought to move anthropology away from studying the specific content of myths and rituals towards a more structural understanding of the general systems of signification based on patterns of binary opposition.

In short, Propp's approach considers what happens in a text, whereas Lévi-Strauss is concerned with how a text achieves meaning. For Lévi-Strauss all myths are derived from a set of binary oppositions, or conflicting elements, that can be combined in a finite number of ways. These binary oppositions (like good and evil, us and them, man and woman) often lie beneath the surface of any myth, but the story will always revolve around them and the hero will seek to reconcile these competing forces. In a sense myths are fragments of a meaningful whole, which has an underlying structure that is not always directly apparent to empirical observation. In *Tristes Tropiques* he makes the methodological claim that geology, psychoanalysis and Marxism are his 'three mistresses', for each showed 'that understanding consists in the reduction of one type of reality to another; that true reality is never the most obvious, and that the nature of truth is already indicated by the care it takes to remain elusive' (Lévi-Strauss, 1955/73:57–8). It is the impulse of the savage *mind* (as much as the modern one) to impose form on content and this marks the origin of all thought. Accordingly cultural forms result from the human mind attempting to order the arbitrary environment into a manageable series of classifications and prohibitions. Myths are manifestations of universal mental processes that organize and structure reality. For instance, he identifies Oedipal-type myths forbidding incestuous relations underlying stories amid people, places and times as far apart as native North American tribes and Ancient Greek city states. His more general point is that collective representations, whether these are myths, music, cooking, kinship or engineering, communicate specific cultural codes that shape social life into meaningful arrangements.

Many have applied these analyses to popular culture. The structuralist literary critic Tzvetan Todorov (1966/2000) has discussed these arguments in relation to detective fiction, which he divides into three kinds of mystery: the whodunit, the thriller and the suspense novel. He argues that they all contain two stories – the crime and the investigation. In the whodunit, the first story is the murder which has happened before the novel begins and it is the second story, the investigation, that the novel actually tells and which excites our interest. In thrillers the two stories are fused, so that the first story is suppressed and the second vitalized. The crime no longer takes place before the action; instead 'the narrative coincides with the action' and looks forward rather than back (Todorov, 1966/2000:141). Suspense novels combine elements of the whodunit and thriller. They keep the mystery of the whodunit but shift attention to the investigation, and the detective may well be in danger and a suspect in the investigation – as in the 'hard-boiled' fiction of Dashiell Hammett and Raymond Chandler. Todorov connects his analysis of detective narratives to the Russian Formalist distinction between the *fabula* and the *sjuzet*. The *fabula* is the events as they happened, while the *sjuzet* is the way they are told. This is a fundamental point. It suggests that narratives have a dual structure: what actually happened (story) and the way of telling it (discourse). Furthermore, it is the way these two levels interact that has preoccupied much literary theory as many modernist and postmodernist texts subvert and unsettle our familiarity with these narrative functions.

One of the best-known examples of this kind of structuralist analysis is Umberto Eco's (1979) study of the thirteen James Bond novels written by Ian Fleming. In this piece Eco sets himself the task of identifying the underlying structure of rules that have made the series so popular. As he puts it, the presence of these 'rules explains and determines the success of the "007 saga" – a success which, singularly, has been due both to the mass consensus and to the appreciation of more sophisticated readers' (Eco, 1979:146). According to Eco there are a number of reasons for their success: the opposition of character and values; a sequential structure of play situations; a Manichean ideology; and distinctive literary techniques. He begins by demonstrating how the stories are constructed around four opposing characters (Bond, M, Villain and Woman) and competing values (like Duty-Sacrifice, Chance-Planning, Perversion-Innocence and so forth). Each of the characters conveys one or more these values, so that 'Bond represents Beauty and Virility as opposed to the Villain, who often appears monstrous and sexually impotent' (Eco, 1979:149). Related to this finite series of binary oppositions is the organization of these elements into a series of premeditated moves that pushes the story invariably forward, like a game of chess. While their sequencing may change the basic structure remains the same: 'Bond moves and mates in eight moves' (Eco, 1979:156).

Following on from the binary oppositions and sequential moves lies the Manichean ideology structuring the narratives, which 'sees the world as made up of good and bad forces in conflict' (Eco, 1979:187).

By seeking 'elementary oppositions' Fleming is following the reactionary 'path of fable' and Eco compares the Bond novels to the 'archetypal elements' found in fairy tales:

> M is the King and Bond is the Knight entrusted with a mission; Bond is the Knight and the Villain is the Dragon; that Lady and Villain stand for Beauty and Beast; Bond restores Lady to the fullness of spirit and to her senses – he is the Prince who rescues Sleeping Beauty; between the Free World and the Soviet Union, England and the non-Anglo-Saxon countries is realized the primitive epic relationship between the Privileged Race and the Lower Race, between White and Black, Good and Bad. (Eco, 1979:161)

Eco (1979) is careful to detail the skilful way Fleming deploys literary techniques – weaving epic simplicity with minute description that borders on kitsch.

Eco's analysis was originally developed in the 1960s and shares many of the same assumptions as the French literary critic Roland Barthes, who attempted to relate the signs of popular culture to social forces and class relations. Barthes's (1966/77) essay, an 'Introduction to the Structural Analysis of Narrative', is a key distillation of Propp, Lévi-Strauss, Todorov and Eco's thinking. At this time Barthes was establishing a structuralist 'science of literature' in an effort to distinguish the approach from academic literary criticism, which relies on aesthetic discrimination and ideological understandings of 'objectivity' and 'good taste'. Instead, structuralist interpretation involves an immanent study of the work aimed at revealing the internal relationships of theme, imagery and structure. For example, he explains that when 'Bond orders a whiskey while waiting for his plane, the whiskey as indice has a polysemic value, is a kind of symbolic node grouping several signifieds (modernity, wealth, leisure); as a functional unit, however, the ordering of the whiskey has to run step by step through numerous relays (consumption, waiting, departure, etc.) in order to find its final meaning' (Barthes, 1966/77:118).

The shock waves generated by structuralism continue to be felt. By lifting the lid off the way literary texts work structuralism presents a relentless demystification of culture. It is no accident that analyses of Superman comics, cowboy movies, James Bond novels, and wrestling matches sit effortlessly alongside erudite discussions of ancient myth, Aristotelian poetics, tragic drama, modernist fiction and the avant-garde. In doing so the structuralist method is profoundly challenging 'literature's claim to be a unique form of discourse: since deep structures could be dug out of Mickey Spillane as well as Sir Philip Sidney, and no doubt the same ones, it was no longer easy to assign literature an ontologically privileged status' (Eagleton, 1996:93). Key advantages of the structuralist approach include the way it reveals layers of significance that would otherwise remain hidden, emphasizes how meaning is socially constructed and powerfully challenges common-sense assumptions. Establishment critics were quick to point out how much of what is presented is simply a spurious scientificity, and dubbed this obscurant 'new criticism' the 'new fraud' (Picard, 1965). Others complained that the method reduces cultural phenomena down to underlying structures and thereby glosses over surface complexity that adds to the richness of the text (Hawkes, 1977).

The most serious limitation of the method though is the resolute ahistoricism of structuralism: it treats the text as an isolated object fixed in space rather than as a changing series of relations moving through time. This point has been well made by Tony Bennett and Janet Woollacott (1987) when they criticize Eco for failing to grasp the 'inter-textuality' of James Bond, how he functions as a 'mobile signifier' whose meaning has shifted over time in relation to the highly successful series of films, merchandizing spin-offs and whole range of cultural practices inspired by the Bond phenomenon. Their entire book is devoted to proving that the meaning of Bond can never be fixed and they chronicle how the meanings have shifted in postwar culture. Initially, Bond was a purely literary figure and functioned as a pre-eminently English hero, embodying the imaginary, nostalgic possibility that England might again return to the centre of world affairs – at a time when its status was in rapid decline. Yet by the 1960s, when the films went into production, Bond was ideologically repositioned and extracted from the 1950s Cold War climate of the novels. The early films vividly captured the mood of 'swinging Britain' and furnished 'a mythic encapsulation of the then prominent ideological themes of classlessness and modernity' (Bennett and Woollacott, 1987:34).

Although Bond was less central to the popular cinema of the 1970s, the films became an institutionalized ritual on television – especially when ITV began the regular broadcast of a Bond film on Christmas Day from 1975 and established him as 'a way of life' for British viewers. More recently, the channel has taken to broadcasting the entire series over summer months as a means of retaining audiences in the face of increased competition. Consequently, they argue that it makes little sense to conceive of texts as relatively fixed structural codes; instead they regard Bond as a floating cultural icon that is continually reconfigured over time. It is also important to emphasize that the concept of intertextuality implies that all texts are related to each other and that each text will lie somewhere between convention and invention (Cawelti, 1971). In doing so, every text must necessarily 'participate' in genre as 'there is no genreless text' (Derrida, 1980/2000), but also flirt with more than one genre at any time.

Genre

Although the study of genre can be traced from antiquity up to the eighteenth century (when genres were understood as ideal types of artistic expression to be replicated and polished), by the nineteenth century cultural producers came to regard classical genres (the epic-lyric-dramatic triad) as constraining forms of representation. Opposition to them was one of the defining features of the European Romantic movement and later entered into the aesthetic flourishing of modernism in the early twentieth century. Consequently, genres have long been equated with mass marketing, commercial branding and popular culture as opposed to genuine artistic vision. Todorov (1973) has explained that one of the reasons why literary critics have tended to shun genre analysis is that to identify a particular work as belonging to part of a genre is to instantly denigrate it. Yet film scholars have deployed the concept of genre to distinguish between different film narratives, with each genre having its own rules, conventions and visual styles that 'transcend individual films and which supervise both their construction by the film-maker, and their reading by an audience' (Ryall, 1975:28). This influential definition recognizes the social character of genre by highlighting the interplay of institutional production, audience interpretation and textual difference. Cinematic genres include Westerns, thrillers and musicals, while television displays a much wider range of genres – which includes situation comedies, soap operas, costume dramas, sporting events, police serials, news programmes, game shows, crime thrillers as well as feature films. Certainly, for those who study television, the concept of genre is a way of handling the medium's considerable breadth as a cultural form by dividing it into more distinct elements – examining news programming or game shows rather than the whole of what is broadcast on television.

One influential kind of genre analysis is to compare the typical narrative structure of one genre with another. For example, John Fiske (1987) discusses the differences between soap operas and *The A Team*, a popular action series from the 1980s, to raise a number of important issues. The first, as many commentators have also pointed out, is that soap operas rely on an 'open' rather than 'closed' narrative, where a number of disparate story lines are interspersed throughout the programme. Some of these stories may reach a resolution, but the soap itself does not. In contrast, the drama series, situation comedy or police procedural will contain a narrative problem that is often resolved at the end of each episode. Soap operas concentrate on the personal and emotional lives of their characters as well as featuring strong women and spineless, devious or dissolute men. These, and other aspects of the genre, contrast strongly with the heroic masculinity displayed in male tales like action series, where men forcefully drive the narrative. There is also a close approximation between real time and story time, which is unlike any other fictional genre (Kilborn, 1992). Problems dealt with by particular stories can take the same length of time to be resolved in real life as they do in the soap opera. Analysing differences like these is an extremely helpful way of grasping the distinctive codes, conventions and expectations genres deploy.

The police series is one of the most popular genres on television and it is also a genre that makes explicit claims to represent police work realistically. Police series like *The Bill* or *CSI: Crime Scene Investigation* conform to the generic requirements of realism (believability, credible scenes and plausible characters) to make their fictional world convincing. Yet despite the appearance of realism it has been argued that popular television drama series function as myth in the structuralist sense outlined above. Police series represent, but at the same time conceal and displace, social antagonisms. They do this by turning actual social contradictions 'into "timeless" oppositions between good and evil through a narrative structure of disruption/quest/restoration (or its contemporary form of crime/pursuit/arrest)' (Thornham and Purvis, 2005:81).

Geoff Hurd (1979) demonstrates how this displacement occurs by considering the major oppositions structuring the narratives. In an influential analysis of *The Sweeney* (1975–8) and *Z Cars* (1962–78), but applicable to many other police series, he identifies the following seven binary oppositions operating in the programmes:

police	crime
law	rule
professional	organization
authority	bureaucracy
intuition	technology
masses	intellectuals
comradeship	rank

According to Hurd, each of these oppositions are resolved within the drama so that those terms on the left column are the ones that are privileged over those on the right. To take a couple of examples, a typical tension explored is that between authority and bureaucracy, where the hero's authority is gained from their skill at catching criminals on the streets rather than their position in large, complex bureaucratic institutions. Furthermore, relationships are structured by antagonisms between comradeship and rank – where the camaraderie and mutual respect of the detectives and ordinary policemen is played off against the formal relationships with senior policemen, who typically are more concerned with their position in the organizational hierarchy and public image than with the dirty business of fighting crime.

The structuring of the fictional world of the police along this set of oppositions is 'psychologically authentic', but 'the drama is emptied of its potentially disruptive conflict by divorcing the activity of policing from any class analysis of power relationships within society' (Hurd, 1979:133–4). On this view, the police series does portray social conflicts realistically, but the deeper contradictions (such as the repressive role of the police) are concealed and displaced into these mythical oppositions. Crucially, the police series only concentrates on the role of the police in containing crime and catching criminals, yet by doing so it excludes two thirds of the judicial process: courts and prisons. Their absence though is resolved in the piece by defining them as separate institutions – a point which is emphasized by the place of other genres (courtroom dramas, prison dramas) on screen. But it is not only criminal justice institutions that are excluded from the stories. Usually, only policemen have rounded, developed characters. Everybody else – gangsters, villains, the public and women – appear as flat stereotypes in contrast to the depth of the main police characters to reiterate the superiority and infallibility of the force.[1]

In his ethnographic study of Minneapolis police patrol officers David Perlmutter (2000) examined how media representations informed their abilities to police. He explains how the myths of media police sharply contrast with the reality experienced on the street[2] and generate unrealistic expectations among the public, especially when they do not act like their media portraits. This cycle of perceptional influence is one of the most important findings from the two years he spent observing police work:

> That factor, that cops *know* whereas others do not because they cannot
> or will not learn or have not been there, contributes to group solidarity

among the men and women in blue. It also places them in a unique societal position to comment on violence in media and its 'realism'. This
dichotomy is the fundamental challenge to the self-perception of cops
and their own estimate of their value to society. People think they know
what it is like to be a cop because they have seen so many cops on TV
and in films. Whether such portrayals are 'realistic' is almost besides the
point: Real cops live out complex work lives and have onerous duties that
simply are not expressible in any other way than to be there among them,
day after day, dog shift after dog shift. TV is not there, yet TV is with
them, and they know it. (Perlmutter, 2000:52, emphasis in original)

The significance of this passage is that questions over the accuracy or
otherwise of media representations of policing miss the point – for the
myth and reality are intimately entwined. As Sparks (1993:149) has
indicated, 'Cop shows do not presume that we believe the world to be
divided neatly into heroes and villains: but they do presuppose that at
some level we would like it to be so.' As we have seen, these elementary oppositions not only structure narratives, but in important ways
help to give order and shape to social life.

Nick Lacey (2000:163–7) has carefully applied Hurd's series of
binary oppositions to the more recent American police series *NYPD
Blue* (1993–) as a way of assessing how generic a particular programme is and what, if any, innovations have been introduced.
Although *NYPD Blue* introduced rapid editing, handheld cameras
and telephoto lens to give 'an "edgy" feeling to the *mise-en-scène*' it
remains overwhelmingly faithful to the generic principles identified by
Hurd (Lacey, 2000:166). Of course, genres do change. To capture
some of this dynamism it is important to grasp how police procedurals were transformed from their slow-moving, quasi-documentary
origins in the 1950s into fast-paced, stylish entertainment for the
1970s up to more recent developments that have seen the genre diversify and dominate television schedules.

The Origins of Police Procedurals

Initially, British television productions sought to realistically represent
changes in policing – a tradition established most famously in the
parochial paternalism of *Dixon of Dock Green* (1955–76). As Alan
Clarke (1983:45) observed, Dixon formed such a powerful icon that
the *Financial Times* bemoaned the demise of 'the George Dixon type
of policing' in its analysis of urban riots in the early 1980s. Indeed, he
goes on to explain that such 'is the power of media imagery that this

description could still be used to summon up not just the memory of a popular entertainment but a style of policing the "real" crime problem' (ibid.). The fictional George Dixon is the archetypal 'bobby on the beat' and remains a yardstick against which the police continue to be compared. Although he came to look increasingly outdated as the years progressed it is important to recognize that when it was first introduced the programme was praised for its realism, as it centred on an ordinary, working-class policeman on the beat, rather than the more idealized detectives of other crime dramas.[3]

Likewise, *Z Cars* (1962–78) was initially conceived as a documentary about people's lives rather than a police drama and was praised for its attempt to accurately track changes in policing during the 1960s, such as the introduction of panda cars and consequent decline of foot patrols. Set in the fictional world of Newtown (based on Kirkby, Liverpool) – a slum-clearance housing estate experiencing anomic community disintegration – the episodes privileged character over plot and weaved a number of distinct stories across each fast-paced episode so that the cast of regular policemen were foregrounded in turn in separate episodes. Hurd (1979:118–19) even notes how the chief constable of Lancashire withdrew his support for the original series 'on the grounds that the presentation of policemen as "human beings", not immune from the pressures of and problems of everyday life, might undermine public confidence'. This decision was reversed once the success of *Z Cars* became apparent, which at the time was regarded as innovative and gripping television viewing. Significantly, the early episodes were not only transmitted live from a new BBC studio but used an unusually large number of filmed sequences and back projections inserted into the drama to increase the documentary feel of the programmes (Leishman and Mason, 2003:55).

By the 1970s the police series genre turns from a preoccupation with the complexities of community policing towards more aggressive tales of crime, pursuit and capture. The shift from 'police procedural' to 'action series' is explained by both changing conventions of representation and a growing sense of crisis in social relations from the late 1960s onwards. The change initially registered on American television screens, where three distinctive elements were introduced that transformed the genre:

> These were violence, action sequences and the increasingly prominent role accorded to music in the development of the narrative. Action sequences covered everything from the variants on the car chase to the

> choreography of the stunts in series like *Kojak* and *Starsky and Hutch*.
> Indeed, the title sequence of *Starsky and Hutch* is an excellent example
> of what 'action' means in the context. The two heroes are introduced
> squealing around in cars and corners in a rapid car chase . . . This sense
> of urgency is underpinned by a musical score which drives the action at
> a relentless pace. (Clarke, 1986:220)

As concerns the introduction of vivid violence into the police series he
contends that the real breakthrough occurred in the graphic cinema of
directors like Serge Leone (*Once Upon a Time in the West*, 1969), Sam
Peckinpah (*The Wild Bunch*, 1969) and Arthur Penn (*Bonnie and Clyde*,
1967).[4] By lingering on the visceral qualities of violence spaghetti
Westerns discredited the bloodless conventions of classic horse operas.
The films made by Don Siegel starring Clint Eastwood are particularly
important here. Over a short period of time Eastwood is transformed
from the mysterious, amoral 'man with no name' gunslinger of Leone's
mid-1960s 'Dollar' movies to the ruthless cowboy cop flown to New
York in *Coogan's Bluff* (1968) and reaches apotheosis in his portrayal of
the maverick detective 'Dirty Harry' Callaghan (*Dirty Harry*, 1971 and
Magnum Force, 1973). These films were at the forefront of the spate of
police movies over this period, which helped shape the view that violence was a way of life for the police in North American cities.

Television not only borrowed these cinematic developments but
also tamed them. As Sparks (1992:28) points out, 'Kojak is as hard-
pressed by the tide of crime as Eastwood's Harry Callaghan, but he is
also humorous and graceful.' Against the funky, stylish 'new wave' of
1970s American TV cops (like *Kojak*, *Rockford*, *Starsky and Hutch*)
the homegrown likes of *Dixon* and *Z Cars* suddenly looked hopelessly
old-fashioned.

While it was the BBC that tended to screen the highly successful
American imports as well as the – by now plodding – domestic procedural fables, it was ITV that produced the iconoclastic *The Sweeney*
(1975–8), based on the Metropolitan police's 'Flying Squad' (a specialized unit concentrating on serious crime in London). The series
centred around the character Jack Regan (played by John Thaw), a
tough, individualistic detective who shared with his American counterparts a self-righteous belief in the validity of his methods, even if
they involved a smattering of violence and a bending of the rules. *The
Sweeney* was very much a product of the times:

> What the new series offered was a closed unit of characters who would
> appear regularly enough to develop into individual characters against a
> background of serious crime. It should be remembered that the concept

of 'serious crime' had assumed particular connotations by the 1970s: it
referred to crimes involving large sums of money and large amounts of
violence and usually both. *The Sweeney* legitimated the transition to violence as part of the routine of police work by locating the fiction within
the framework of that section of the police force most likely to deal with
violence . . . The Flying Squad was an ideal vehicle for this fictional representation both in terms of the internal logistics of the genre and the
concerns of the law and order debate outside of the series. (Clarke,
1986:221)

Clarke here is careful to acknowledge both the socio-political context
and specific generic innovations that heralded this change in direction
for the police series.

This is not to suggest that there is a simple, direct correspondence
between crime on the streets and on screen. It is important to avoid
'viewing fictions as simply reflecting the conditions of their formulation, hence mistaking them for historical documents of a more
straightforward kind, or one attributes an undue role to them in
bringing about the events they seem to describe' (Sparks, 1992:28–
9). The process is, as Clarke (1986:222–3) insists, one of mediated
refraction than pure reflection. *The Sweeney* was not a faithful representation of policing in 1970s London – the authenticity of the series
was derived from a combination of the audience's limited knowledge
of policing, previous police shows, broader public order debates and
rising crime rates. Nevertheless, it is clear that as a genre, the television police series is 'a privileged site for the staging of the trauma of
the break-up of the postwar settlement' (Brunsdon, 1998:223). By
the 1970s, the 'law and order' decade, there is a darker mood per-
meating police dramas and this does speak to the perceived crisis in
authority of the Heath and Nixon years, which contrasts strongly
with the rather cosy, consensual picture of policing established in the
previous decades.

Continuity and Change

In important respects *Dixon, Z Cars* and *The Sweeney* have set the
generic conventions for the many subsequent representations of
British policing. *The Bill* (1984–) is the longest-running example,
which has maintained a large audience through many changes in tone
and format over the last couple of decades. From quasi-documentary
beginnings to current soap opera plotting the series has consistently
sought to incorporate developments occurring elsewhere, both in real

life and in other programmes, into its fictional world. Like *Z Cars* it is an ensemble piece and includes multiple, overlapping stories involving different departments in the Sun Hill police station. In addition, the lineage of the earlier dramas is also apparent in *The Bill* through

> two long-standing characters from the series in the 1980s and early 1990s who were direct descendants from earlier police procedurals. Sergeant Bob Cryer was an updated George Dixon. Although considerably younger, Cryer had the same friendly nature, paternal concern for fellow officers and the public, and a similarly strong sense of what was morally right . . . Cryer's colleague, Detective Inspector Frank Burnside, was an anachronism straight out of *The Sweeney* . . . In order to fit into the precise framework created for *The Bill*, Burnside had to be a 'watered down' version of *The Sweeney*'s Jack Regan, as too much violence and illegality would have been out of step with the ideology underpinning the series. (Leishman and Mason, 2003:64)

At the same time the series attempted to break similar ground as the innovative American police series *Hill Street Blues* (1981–9), which gave strong roles to women, involved a multi-ethnic cast and used a naturalistic, documentary style to give a realistic feel to the series. The series marked a significant break with the buddy machismo of series like *The Sweeney* and *Starsky and Hutch*, while new British police procedurals like *The Gentle Touch* (1980–4) and *Juliet Bravo* (1980–5) placed female characters in leading roles in an effort to diversify the genre and emphasize the caring aspects of police work.

It is debatable how far these series did challenge conventional gender stereotypes, yet it is clear that *The Bill* has attempted to broaden forms of cultural representation. In this context, the widespread persistence of racial discrimination and sexual harassment was brought to a head by a series of high-profile cases brought by serving officers in the 1980s, which did much to expose the white 'hegemonic masculinity' structuring the occupational culture of the police (Walklate, 2000). The landmark case brought by former Assistant Chief Constable Alison Halford in the early 1990s was crucial. At the time she was Britain's highest-ranking woman officer and she filed a case against the Merseyside police authority after her applications for promotion were turned down nine times, while less qualified men succeeded. The case received extensive publicity, revealing a cop canteen culture riven with drunkenness and misogyny – issues that the *Prime Suspect* series of dramas explicitly examined.

The first, broadcast in 1991, launched DCI Jane Tennison (Helen Mirren) into the traditionally male role of leading a serial murder investigation, where the 'genre-innovative narrative is that of Jane Tennison's progress from "that bitch" to a well respected "guv'nor", supported by her men when her removal is threatened by those upstairs, and finally extracting a confession' (Brunsdon, 1998:233). Subsequent cases further explored equal opportunities issues: *Prime Suspect II* (1992) dealt with racism in the police force and *Prime Suspect III* (1993) confronted male child sex abuse. Yet her career progress comes at a personal cost: 'the triumphs achieved by Jane Tennison are bought at a high price: a successful detective but not a successful woman' (Eaton, 1995:175). It is thus no surprise that the final drama, broadcast in 2006, centres on Tennison's battles with alcoholism and failing private life as she attempts to solve her last case before retirement.

The last two decades have also seen the return of classic detective series that recall the earlier 'whodunit' English tradition discussed in the last chapter combined with the newer procedural elements outlined above. Chief among the many are the two-hour films of *Inspector Morse* (1987–93, with subsequent single films), which featured John Thaw in the role of Morse (he was previously cast as Regan in *The Sweeney*) and knowingly plays on this generic past – while '*The Sweeney* was aggressively contemporary in a way which contrasts strongly with *Morse*, the two share the invocation of what is presented as old-fashioned integrity' (Brunsdon, 1998:229). This romantic, individualistic focus is revived across a whole plethora of dramas featuring regional detectives like Barnaby, Dalziel, Frost, Wycliffe and Vincent that tend to be largely predictable, if no less entertaining, formulaic exercises.

One important exception is *Between the Lines* (1992–4), which examined corruption in the police force and rather than simply suggesting a few 'bad apples' the stench of a 'rotten barrel' pervaded the series:

> Instead of providing reassurance that the police were capable of tackling individual and institutional corruption, the series laid out the complexities of policing contemporary society, taking in not only corruption, but also addressing other key areas of 1990s policing – public-order policing, drugs, racism, sexual harassment and discrimination, rule-bending and the increasing involvement of the police in firearms incidents. (Mawby, 2003:223)

The first series, in particular, was also an excellent example of the 'hybrid serialized series' (Brunsdon, 1998:237) in that it offered both involving, episode-bound stories and a continuous, developing narrative arc that sustained audience interest across the episodes, while the theme of police corruption chimed with increased public concerns over police accountability and conduct.

Similar themes are explored in *Ghosts* (2005–), which also examined the tensions between personal and professional ethics by focusing on an undercover unit dedicated to rooting out corruption in the force, but did much to reveal the moral dilemmas and increasingly paranoid nature of contemporary policing. In this way, *Between the Lines* paved the way for the arrival of new hybrid procedural dramas. These focus on policing by agencies other than the police, and include *The Knock* (1994–2001) series revolving around the adventures of an undercover Customs investigative team and, more recently, *Spooks* (2003–), which is based on the activities of an MI5 counter-terrorism section. Likewise, *The X Files* (1993–2002) was a particularly influential example of this genre mixing. By blending elements of the detective narrative with science fiction, paranormal horror and romantic comedy it heralded 'must see' television viewing that programme makers have been attempting to produce in the wake of a fragmenting audience dispersed across multi-channels and time-shift hard disc recorders. This last point reminds us that market considerations powerfully shape popular cultural forms and it is to issues of institutional context, production processes and media organizations that the book will turn in the next chapter.

Another crucial police drama series of the late 1990s that offered both a keen awareness of genre history and a relentlessly bleak picture of contemporary Britain is *The Cops* (1998–2001). Set in the fictional northern urban town of 'Stanton' the series opened with police officers snorting cocaine and committing various other crimes, like assaulting members of the public. The series itself was shot in the 'reality TV' style, using shaky camera work, a virtually unknown cast and uneven sound to blur the boundaries between fiction and documentary, while the officers are most often shown doing a difficult job in quite desperate circumstances. The officers' deviance is situated in everyday situations, and, like *Z Cars* and later *The Bill*, the series has portrayed the police as human beings with all their personal failings and occasional acts of heroism. Over the last few years *The Bill* too has responded to all these developments by including some dangerous and corrupt police officers who have tried their hand at every conceivable kind of rule-breaking while the more ordinary characters have developed major moral flaws: revelations about PC Jim Carver's alcoholism, PC 'Smiffy' Smith's extreme right-wing sympathies and Sergeant Boyden's homophobia were just some of the story lines that underlined this new change in direction, and the series has recently seen an influx of new, younger characters (often played by actors from other soaps like *EastEnders* and *Hollyoaks*) in an effort to keep audiences. Indeed, the BBC's Holby franchise has just moved into police precinct territory with its *Holby Blue* (2007–) set in the same oddly anonymous West Country city as its medical dramas, suggesting television producers still see the procedural as a ratings winner.

One of the more imaginative developments in recent police dramas is *Life on Mars* (2006–7), which centres on a modern, forensically minded DI Sam Tyler transported 'back to the nick in time'. Here he is confronted with the unreconstructed alpha-male policing methods of 1970s cop shows in the iconic, camel-coated shape of Chief Inspector Gene Hunt, who 'never fitted anyone up who didn't deserve it' and his fellow hard-drinking, rule-bending Manchester CID officers. The series has great fun playing with the contrasts between then and now, and should no doubt generate further spin-offs,[5] but is no simple exercise in nostalgia as it maintains an ambivalence towards the past. Of course, it is a highly stylized piece and is from the makers of *Spooks* (2003–) and *Hustle* (2004–). These confident ensemble dramas share similar production values, privileging cinematic glamour over drab realism and involving good-looking characters in fast-moving, improbable plots and visually striking settings.

The final generic innovation, which was touched on in the last chapter, is the response of police procedurals to the phenomenal success of medical dramas – which by the mid-1990s had reached epidemic proportions, as television newspaper critics often joke. Examples include *Cracker* (1993–), *Dangerfield* (1995–), *Silent Witness* (1996–), *Waking the Dead* (2000–) and *Wire in the Blood* (2002–). Like other hybrid procedurals they can ask some important questions about who can police, who is responsible and who is policed. But all too often there is a 'tendency towards a spectacularization of the body and site of crime' (Brunsdon, 1998:242) in these moves towards the medicalization of crime. Much the same has happened across the Atlantic. Following the complex moral difficulties presented in police procedurals like *NYPD Blue* (1993–) and *Homicide* (1993–), the forensic empiricism of *Law and Order* (1990–) and *CSI: Crime Scene Investigation* (2000–) have sought to return some of the guaranteed certainties of science to TV policework. Indeed, the *CSI* franchise has received much recent attention precisely because it seeks to re-assert the truth of science in detection (Leishman and Mason, 2003; Gever, 2005; Cavender and Deutsch, 2007).

The analysis of genre is an extremely useful way of understanding the relationships between media industries, textual properties, audience expectations and viewing competencies. This point is captured by Abercrombie when he explains that:

> Genres are a kind of complicity between producer and audience. The audience knows what it is getting. Indeed, part of the pleasure is knowing what the genre rules are, knowing that the programme has to solve problems in the genre framework, and wondering how it is going to do so. Audience members will wonder what is going to happen next, although much of what is bound to happen is known because of the genre conventions . . . The normality of genre conventions also makes it possible to put on programmes that break or stretch the conventions. (Abercrombie, 1996:43)

As this discussion of the police procedural genre has shown, there is considerable variation within the genre and the boundaries between different genres increasingly mutate (such as with medical dramas, soap operas and psychological horror).

Genres are socially organized sets of relations between texts that set up a kind of aesthetic contract between reader and text. Each text confirms the conventions of genre, while changing the rules slightly to introduce variation and surprise. Otherwise the work will disappoint audiences if it sticks too closely to a predictable generic formula and must offer some innovation to familiar ways of telling stories. At its best, genre theory enables us to ask what a text *means* as well as analyse how it *works* (Jameson, 1981/2000:169). But genres do not produce themselves and in the next chapter we turn to the realm of cultural production.

In her discussion of crime films Rafter (2000:63, emphasis in original) suggests that crime films perform a number of important ideological functions: 'assuring us that crime *can* be explained; identifying criminological authorities; defining the "crime problem"; and guiding our emotional reactions to crime'. Moreover, she demonstrates how many of the films endorse a particular criminological explanation of crime, whether this is derived from environmental, subcultural, pathological or rational choice theory.[6] In her most recent work she has attempted to pursue the question of how crime films relate to criminology. As we saw earlier in the chapter she draws a distinction between academic and popular criminology and suggests that the boundaries between them are beginning to blur with the rise of cultural criminology over the last decade (Rafter, 2007:415). Yet it remains the case that the analysis of representation in criminology is still an underdeveloped field and this chapter offers some important resources for improving the terrain.

PART III

Industries

7

Producing the News

While the last few chapters have concentrated on the representation of crime the focus of this part of the book shifts to the fields of cultural production. In particular, I will concentrate on the news media, in broadcasting, print, the Internet, and other new technologies conveying stories of crime, conflict and violence. It is now the convention to identify at least four different approaches seeking to explain what makes news the way it is (Schudson, 2005; Seaton, 2003). Each tends to foreground economic, political, social or cultural forces either separately or in tandem structuring quite complex processes of media production. Inevitably there are points of tension and dispute between these competing accounts, but each carries important implications for how the media select, shape and present news from the chaotic mass of events that happen 'out there' in the world at large.

In addition, there are different levels at which the production of news can be and has been studied, which ranges from specific texts (e.g. Brunsdon and Morley, 1978, on the current affairs programme *Nationwide*), genre production (e.g. Raphael, 2004, on reality TV crime programmes), investigating journalists at work (e.g. Schlesinger and Tumber, 1994, on crime reporters) and comparing different media (e.g. Ericson *et al.*, 1991, on how stories vary by medium) through to studies of entire media systems (e.g. Hallin and Mancini, 2004, distinguish three differing models of commercial broadcasting operating in the eighteen democracies they examined). The chapter begins by indicating how the different approaches each shed light on crucial aspects of news production and the best work captures something of the dynamics of news making that is ignored by others. These themes are then explored through an account of how sex crime is constructed in the mass media.

Perspectives on Media Production

Economic Organization

The critical theory of the Frankfurt School in the 1930s and 1940s has bequeathed a sceptical tradition of media research that concentrates on the economic organization of news production. In their scathing critique of the 'culture industry' Adorno and Horkheimer (1947/73) made it clear that the mass media contribute to the destruction of Enlightenment ideals as culture itself becomes consumed by processes of industrialization. Consequently a major issue is how the economic organization of media industries impacts on the production and circulation of meaning. Often this concern is situated in a broader context of profit maximization, class domination and ideological control, but there are also more detailed investigations of the struggles over the manufacturing of news. Overall, this approach maintains that economic dynamics play a pivotal role in shaping the broad context in which mediated communication takes place. The growing concentration of ownership, conglomeration and expansion of corporate giants like Microsoft, News Corporation and Sony suggest that the economic determination of cultural production continues to be a crucial force.

It has been argued that given these circumstances, the 'corporate priority of profit maximization is leading to increasingly superficial news formats where content becomes more uniform and the spaces available to report on controversial issues sharply reduced' (Allan, 2004:52). In America, for example, Fox News has overtaken CNN as the top-rated cable news channel, but many journalists have distanced themselves from it, criticizing 'the Fox effect' and deriding its mainstreaming 'opinionated news with an America-first flair' (Zelizer, 2005:202). Others have complained of commercial pressures leading to 'Ken and Barbie journalism' where the physical attractiveness of the 'anchor team' and the contrived 'happy talk' between the presenters is privileged over journalistic competence (van Zoonen, 1998:40).

For some the media have long been understood as an instrument of capitalist legitimation that stifles dissent; they point to how the news serves as 'a means of reinforcing' (Miliband, 1969:198) ruling-class interests. This instrumentalist view of class domination is taken further by Edward Herman and Noam Chomsky (1988:xi) in their 'propaganda model' of the American news media, where they insist that 'the powerful are able to fix the premises of discourse, to decide what the general populace is allowed to see, hear and think about, and to "manage" public opinion by regular propaganda campaigns'. Their provocative model is based on five related filters that in combination 'manufacture consent' for the official positions of economically and politically dominant elites. The first filter is the commercial basis of news organizations, which means that they are orientated to making profit and squeezing out competition. The second filter is the way advertisers are able to exert enormous power and influence by virtue of providing the main source of income for commercial news organizations. The reliance on government and corporate 'experts' is the third filter, while the fourth is government 'flak' directed to disciplining the media. The final filter is the role of anti-communism providing a national religion and control mechanism for the American news media. This was undoubtedly the case at the time they were writing in the 1980s, though now in the post 9/11 climate terrorism provides similar ideological work.

To be sure this argument is easily caricatured as a conspiracy theory which presents journalists and editors as little more than puppets manipulated by forces they cannot comprehend. Yet there is much in their argument that remains compelling:

> Government and business elites do have privileged access to the news; large advertisers do operate as a latter-day licensing authority, selectively supporting some newspapers and television programmes and not others; and media proprietors can determine the editorial line and cultural stance of the papers and broadcast stations they own. But by focusing solely on these kind strategic interventions they overlook the contradictions in the system. Owners, advertisers and key political personnel cannot always do as they would wish. They operate within structures that constrain as well as facilitate, imposing limits as well as offering opportunities. (Murdock and Golding, 2005:63)

It is significant that Graham Murdock and Peter Golding are emphasizing structural contradictions over instrumental agency, for in their analysis it is the economic determinants of the marketplace that ultimately shape media output. This position is also endorsed in a recent study of American television and print news which identified a clear shift towards 'soft news' as a result of organizational efforts to reach certain demographic groups attractive to advertisers – especially women aged eighteen to thirty-four (who have traditionally been only occasional news viewers) – in an effort to draw them in (Hamilton, 2004:189). Consequently, those without a suitable disposable income or who hold unconventional views will find themselves less likely to be addressed by media organizations chasing mainstream audiences. It is through the impersonal mechanisms of the marketplace, rather than the ideological scheming of the powerful, that news becomes a standardized commodity.

Critics point out that a strict economic explanation of news making can overgeneralize by ignoring the complexities of symbolic forms and the conflicts that surround the routine work of media organizations. There is a 'curious evacuation of the political at the heart of the propaganda model' in that the filters are held to be 'so effective, so overpowering, that the force-field of politics and power has become effectively stifled' (Cottle, 2006:19). The BBC and commercial broadcasters have come into conflict many times with the government of the day. Even though it is often said that truth is the first casualty of war, from the Munich crisis of 1938, through the Suez crisis, Falklands War, conflict in Northern Ireland, up to the controversies surrounding the second Gulf War (over weapons of mass destruction, war crimes, and so forth) journalists have found themselves fiercely at odds with politicians over the content of their coverage (while the *Sun* regarded *Newsnight*'s coverage of the Falklands War as 'Treason').[1] Consequently, to focus on the political aspects of representation is to emphasize the constructed and shifting nature of the national consensus as well as to acknowledge the space for dissenting voices to be heard in mainstream journalism.

Political Conflict

The question of political contestation lies at the heart of democratic principles. As Schlesinger and Tumber (1994:8) put it, arguments 'about media and democracy are at root about the relative openness and closure of communicative processes, both nationally and internationally, and the broader implications that these have for the conduct of political life'. In their analysis of crime reporting they invoke Habermas's influential account of the 'public sphere' as a normative ideal with which to grasp the obstacles that prevent genuinely open communication systems from forming in the universal interests of all. The significance of Habermas lies in his attempt to connect an ethical theory of communication to a substantive model of the public sphere, while making it clear that the democratic foundations of everyday life are far from being achieved in modernity. In contrast, it has been argued that democracy does not have a single form against which can be measured its actual manifestations, but is rather best understood as a promise that will always evade any particular effort at redemption (Derrida, 1994:64). Despite some fundamental differences in their positions, such as between Habermas's universalistic concerns and Derrida's postmodern deconstruction of communicative structures, they each address important ethical and moral problems confronting our current age.[2] There are some crucial issues here that can connect with the 'ethics of representation' discussed at the end of chapter 5 and to which we will return in the concluding chapter, but for now though the focus remains on the divided politics of news making.

In this regard the work of the Israeli scholar Gadi Wolfsfeld (1997, 2003, 2004) has been particularly influential through his 'political contest model' that challenges strict economic approaches. As he explains, the 'competition over the news media is a major element in modern political conflicts' with the Pro-Choice and Pro-Life movements in America, the Serbians and the Muslims in Bosnia, Amnesty International, Russia, Chechnya, Al-Qaida and the American government, among others, all competing 'for media attention as a means to achieve political influence' (Wolfsfeld, 1997:2). He recognizes that these are unequal political contests with antagonists competing over both access to the news media and how the media organize representation. The former calls for a structural analysis of the relationships between sources and the news media, while the latter involves a more cultural analysis of how norms, beliefs and routines guide interpretive frameworks – issues that are even more to the fore in the approaches outlined below. Nevertheless, problems remain. In his effort to prioritize 'the political' this is perversely at the expense of 'the economic' as he only makes fleeting reference to 'structures of media ownership, commercial imperatives and the general commoditization of culture' (Cottle, 2006:23).

In order to overcome some of these difficulties Murdock and Golding (2005:63) term their approach 'critical political economy'. Here they do not simply restrict themselves to analysing the economic structure of news organizations but also attend to the way that meaning is created through the concrete activities of producers and consumers. In doing so they seek to retain the basic Marxist insight that actors make choices, but only within the limits set by wider structural constraints. Moreover, the claim is that critical political economy is 'a necessary precursor to an adequate sociology of cultural production; it is not a substitute for it' (Murdock, 1995:92). Thus the key concern is with how media forms are shaped by wider economic and political processes. Two central concerns predominate. First is the emphasis on the ownership of media corporations and the consequences this has for potential abuses of power. Second is examining the relationship between states, markets and communications institutions. Clearly, these are broad questions of power and control but a question remains over whether such an approach can grasp the complexities of media production, which the following approaches explicitly set out to do.

Social Routine

The sociology of news production unsurprisingly emphasizes the social, collective and organizational dimensions of news making. As Paul Rock (1973:73) influentially put it, the 'news is the result of an organized response to routine bureaucratic problems', such as the need to produce material within strict limits on space and time in a predetermined form. This view contrasts with earlier accounts of 'gatekeepers' (White, 1950), which focused on the personal prejudices and preferences of editors in selecting the news, while larger studies found that the typical editor was 'concerned with goals of production, bureaucratic routine and interpersonal relations within the newsroom' (Gieber, 1964:175). The fundamental implication is that it is not politics or economics that structures news production, but the bureaucratic necessity of 'routine' regardless of the subjective inclinations of individual editors, journalists or proprietors.[3] This point is developed in Harvey Molotch and Marilyn Lester's (1974) typology of news stories where they classify stories according to whether the news 'occurrence' is a 'routine' news item, promoted as a 'scandal', or an unplanned 'accident'. However, it is arguably becoming increasingly evident that event-driven news is important and can oust even the most systematically planned institution-driven attempts to capture media space (Schudson, 2005:181). This is a crucial distinction as sociological studies have all emphasized the organizational character of news production.

A number of ethnographies have examined the institutional, bureaucratic and professional processes that shape the standardized form of news across many different outlets (examples include Tunstall, 1971; Epstein, 1973; Tuchman, 1978; Gans, 1979; Fishman, 1980; Ericson et al., 1987; Schlesinger and Tumber, 1994; Matthews, 2003). These studies are often based on years of newsroom observations and interviews to reveal how news is constrained by temporal routines and the spatial organization of newsroom layouts, with the newsroom division of labour, corporate hierarchy and professional cultural identities – all now regarded as the bedrock of analysis. Much has been made of how journalists have 'structured' access to official experts. For instance, the police and criminal justice system control much of the information on which crime reporters rely. These official sources are what Hall *et al.* (1978:58) term the 'primary definers' – those who provide the initial definition and primary interpretation of the topic in question.

Since news journalism routinely involves high levels of anxiety, as the pressures of daily deadlines arrive, a number of strategies have been devised to build certainty into the production process. One is to maintain stable relationships with these official sources, from government departments, accredited experts and other state agencies. These in turn are also aware of the importance of supplying material rich in news values. A second way to meet the organizational constraints of space and time is to turn to news agencies, like Agence France-Press, World Television News, Associated Press and Reuters which supply news as a commodity. These are the 'big four' agencies, which critics argue generate homogeneous news copy with very similar character-istics (Gurevitch *et al.*, 1991; Patterson, 1998). Third, news is planned as far as possible in advance through the use of a 'news diary', which 'allows journalists to be allocated to particular stories, the key news aspects of the event to be agreed, and item space or time provi-sionally allotted' (Manning, 2001:57). Taken together these bureau-cratic aspects of news production have considerable impact on the kind of news that is presented to audiences.

Although this institutionally driven social construction of news remains significant it is important to recognize that the growing acces-sibility of mobile video and photography has made some significant news stories possible – like the Rodney King beating in Los Angeles in 1991 to the American prison brutality at Abu Ghraib prison in Iraq in 2004. This has led to the claim that event-driven news coverage is increasing, which is held to be more dynamic and variable than the conventional institutionally produced news (Lawrence, 2000; Schudson, 2005). Certainly the controversies sparked by the jerky, hand-held video footage of Saddam Hussein's execution at the end of 2006 would endorse this view, as one journalist commented:

While CNN was running its Death of a Dictator special, Fox News Channel, the other leading purveyor of rolling news, preferred Date with Death. But neither could keep up with the news. And the debate about the niceties of showing the stark images of death had already been taken out of the Western media's hands. Like so much footage shot on the ubiquitous mobile phone, from acts of police brutality to misbehaving politicians, the raw information had circumvented the traditional instruments of control. First on Anwarweb.net and subsequently shown on Arabic television channels, the video soon spread to file-sharing websites such as Google Video, YouTube and Revver. (Glaister, 2007:3)

It is becoming clear that in today's news environment of digital, satellite and cable technologies with news coming in many different forms, including 'serious', 'soft', 'hard' and 'popular', delivered on-line as well as in traditional print, 24-hour and global broadcasting, with increasing concentration of media ownership, new approaches to 'the complex and more differentiated field of news production' (Cottle, 2003:16) will need to be developed. At the very least the institutional determinism of the early studies must be qualified if not overhauled.

Cultural Production

The fourth approach concentrates on cultures of news production to explain why certain images and stereotypes keep appearing. One starting point is to look to Émile Durkheim's sociological understanding of professional socialization that creates a journalistic 'news sense'. News content tends to be filtered through what reporters would define as 'newsworthiness'. In other words, journalists would argue that they can sense what makes a good story through their 'nose for news'. However, these news values are learnt as group norms and are a product of the 'newsroom culture' (Scraton et al., 1991:111). A number of elements have been identified that contribute to the newsworthiness of a story (Chibnall, 1977:22–45). The most central is immediacy. An event has to be new, before it becomes 'news', and thus contain an element of novelty. Journalists quickly learn the cliché: 'Dog bites man isn't news; man bites dog is.' Dramatization is another – for where an event is visible and spectacular it will be given more emphasis and space in consequence. Personalization refers to the ways in which leading individuals are emphasized at the expense of the context of the events. Titillation is also a prime news value, in which sexually related stories are emphasized or ordinary and mundane events become sexualized. 'Bad news' is favoured over 'good news' – as Marshall McLuhan once quipped, advertisements are the only 'good news' to be found in newspapers.

A related approach examines 'cultures of production' by following Howard Becker's (1982) pioneering account of 'art worlds'. The idea that art is a form of collective action is taken further in Pierre Bourdieu's (1993, 1996) understanding of artistic production where more structural concepts (like 'fields', 'positions' and 'habitus') are introduced to grasp the whole set of relationships between the artist and beyond to 'the whole set of agents engaged in the production of the work, or, at least, of the *social value* of the work (critics, gallery directors, patrons, etc.)' (Bourdieu, 1993/2003:97, emphasis in original). In a series of lectures Bourdieu (1998) set out to delineate the 'journalistic field' from other arenas of cultural production like the literary, artistic, scientific and juridical fields. He emphasizes how any form of serious political commentary loses out to sensational news coverage:

> To justify this policy of demagogic simplification (which is absolutely and utterly contrary to the democratic goal of informing or educating people by interesting them), journalists point to the public's expectations. But in fact they are projecting onto the public their own inclinations and their own views. Because they're so afraid of being boring, they opt for confrontations over debates, prefer polemics over rigorous argument, and in general, do whatever they can to promote conflict. (Bourdieu, 1998:3–4)

His intention is to identify the cultural conditions that turn news journalism into a collective activity that dispenses 'with sharp edges and anything that might divide or exclude readers' (Bourdieu, 1998:44).

These arguments were intended to be provocative and sparked a series of bitter public exchanges in France between Bourdieu and his critics (Marlière, 1998). Yet there is much in his overall approach that can be used in a more nuanced way to grasp the complexities of media production. Bourdieu (1998:70) characterizes journalism as a split field, which 'emerged as such during the nineteenth century around the opposition between newspapers offering "news", preferably "sensational" or better yet, capable of creating a sensation, and newspapers featuring analysis and "commentary", which marked their difference from the other group by loudly proclaiming the values of "objectivity" '. In Bourdieu the term field is used as a concept to grasp social structure and the increasingly specialized spheres of action characteristic of modernity. He explains that 'like the political and economic fields, and much more than the scientific, artistic, literary or juridical fields, the journalistic field is permanently subject to trial by market, whether directly, through advertisers, or indirectly, through audience ratings' (Bourdieu, 1998:71). Rather than encouraging originality and diversity, market competition produces a banal, worthless uniformity. The book thus provides a forceful condemnation of the degrading effects of television. As meaningful debate gives way to facile talkshow chatter where members of the pundit circuit – 'fast-thinkers' incapable of serious thought – go through the motions of comment in staged exchanges responding to complex (or irrelevant) questions in seconds with conventional, commonplace ideas.

In certain respects his diagnosis is close to Frankfurt School pessimism and some critics have dismissed the book as such, but this ignores what Bourdieu's larger sociological project has to offer (see the essays in Benson and Neveu, 2005, which variously pursue these questions). Yet his work does enable a consideration of the cultural production of news discourse. For example, it is possible to show that there are different ways of constructing a 'hard' news item from 'soft' news stories – Stuart Allan (2004:83–6) describes ten highly formalized properties inflecting newspaper 'objectivity', which further differentiate print from the expressive language of radio news and the fluid textuality of television presentation. Likewise Raymond Williams (1974/90:44–9) has shown how there are some significant ways in which broadcast news bulletins differ from newspaper items. The characteristic sequencing of the printed newspaper page is that of a mosaic, whereas television news is linear and this poses specific challenges for how editors prioritize and select stories in each medium.

These four approaches each provide conceptual frameworks with which to grasp the dynamics of news production. Each sheds light on significant aspects of news creation that would otherwise remain hidden. It is important to recognize how micro-level, face-to-face interactions between journalists, editors and sources are structured by bureaucratic routines, organizational cultures and corporate strategies which are themselves situated in broader political and economic contexts that are at once global in reach and local in character. For the remainder of the chapter the focus turns to the sexualization of the media and in particular the representation of sex crime in the news. While there is much truth in Bourdieu's (1998:17) claim that blood, sex, melodrama and crime have always been the staple fare of tabloid sensationalism, recent decades have seen some significant developments in the ways journalists report crimes of sexual violence. Since the 1970s, when tabloid content became more overtly sexualized and the 'quality' press began to print sex crime stories in earnest, there has not only been a marked increase in the quantity of stories but the reporting itself has become more explicit and gruesome in detail. At the same time, the problem of the sexual abuse of children has become a major source of public anxiety and concern.

Sexing Crime News

There is now a substantial literature on media representations of sex crime, with some important differences in theoretical and methodological approaches. One of the earliest and most influential studies is Keith Soothill and Sylvia Walby's (1991) *Sex Crime in the News*. The book was based on a longitudinal analysis of press reports from the 1950s through to the 1980s and revealed substantial increases in the reporting of rape and sexual assault over this period. Yet feminist critics took issue with 'the whole idea of "sex crime"' as conceptualized in Soothill and Walby's research for 'what counts as sex crime is taken as given . . . the sex of these apparently obvious sex crimes is never interrogated' (Howe, 1998:1–2). Instead Adrian Howe (1998) and the other contributors to her edited collection *Sexed Crime in the News* seek to challenge the conventional definitions of sex crime by problematizing the 'sex' of crimes of violence.

As she explains, 'sexed violence is not confined to rape or sexual assaults; it includes sexual harassment, "reckless" sex which risks the transmission of HIV/AIDS, and attacks on sexual minorities'; thus an understanding of 'violence as sexed helps to break down the arbitrary division which separates public from privatized forms of sexual violence' (Howe, 1998:6). One of the crucial issues tackled in the book is the extent to which the mass media have taken up child sexual abuse as a serious problem (Atmore, 1998). Although it bears some semblance to sexual violence against women, it is not the same. As Stan Cohen (2002:xiv) has pointed out, the 'term "child abuse" contains many different forms of cruelty against children – neglect, physical violence, sexual abuse – whether by their own parents, staff in residential institutions, "paedophile priests" or total strangers'. I now turn to how child abuse has been represented in the media, and then describe how sexual violence has been reported before giving an account of the sexualization of the popular press over the last few decades.

Representing Child Sexual Abuse

There are a number of distinct phases in the ways the issue of the sexual abuse of children has become a subject of public attention. From the 1950s to the 1970s the orthodox expert view was that the problem of child molestation was a rare crime committed by confused individuals, unlikely to repeat their offence or cause significant harm to children. Yet since the late 1970s this 'image of the rather pathetic child molester would be altered into a new and far more threatening stereotype: the sophisticated and well-organized paedophile' (Jenkins, 1992:71). According to Jenny Kitzinger (1999b:208) child sex abuse was 'discovered' by the modern media in the mid-1980s. In the UK, this 'discovery' began in 1986 when Esther Rantzen devoted an entire programme called *Childwatch* to the issue and launched the children's helpline 'Childline'. There then quickly followed a surge of coverage in the rest of the media. Her analysis of *The Times* reveals a four-fold increase in stories of child sexual abuse between 1985 and 1987 and it became a regular topic for documentaries like *Everyman*, *World in Action* and *Panorama*. By the early 1990s, the issue began to appear in chat shows and drama series like *The Bill* and *Casualty* as well as soap operas like *EastEnders* and *Brookside*.

Philip Jenkins (1992) also notes how in the 1980s paedophiles come to be associated with the organized abduction and murder of children. The launch of 'Operation Stranger' by the police in 1986 marked a national investigation into fourteen children murdered or missing since 1978, which was reinforced by a police operation against child sex rings in London in 1987. At the same time, the 'Cleveland affair' was widely reported in the media, which brought to public attention sexual abuse within families. But the press view was that innocent parents were the victims of meddling social workers and over-zealous feminist doctors obsessed with exposing a mythical evil (Nava, 1988). On closer inspection the reporting revealed an altogether more complicated picture, where few of the experts or key players in the drama could reach agreement on who, ultimately, was to blame for the abuse (McRobbie, 1994:208). Lurking behind this sustained media attention was the menacing figure of the paedophile, who would return as the 'monster among us' in the 1990s in a series of widely publicized cases.

Initial attention focused on Ireland where the controversies surrounding the failure of the government and the Roman Catholic Church to deal with the sexual abuse of children by priests were explored for several months in 1994. The rape and murder of four girls in Belgium in 1995 by Marc Dutroux, a released paedophile, amplified European media interest in the failure of authorities to punish predatory sex offenders – especially since it was revealed that high-ranking politicians and civil servants were involved in covering up the case while also being implicated in paedophile rings. These cases anticipated the gruesome discovery of the sexual murders carried out by Fred and Rosemary West as well as the Dunblane massacre in March 1996 (Critcher, 2003:103). Thomas Hamilton shot and killed sixteen children, their teacher and then himself in a Scottish primary school in the village of Dunblane. Hamilton had been banned from working with children following allegations of sexual abuse, while later in 1996 the government announced an inquiry into abuse in Welsh children's homes over the last two decades. Michael Howard (then Home Secretary) proposed legislation to monitor convicted sex offenders in the wake of these cases, which culminated in the Sex Offenders Act 1997.

Although it was perceived by some as a piece of political opportunism the idea of a national register of paedophiles had been around for some time among social work and policing circles (Thomas, 2000:106). There were also significant press crusades to 'out' sex offenders, with the *Sunday Express* among the first of the national titles to demand action with its 'Will your child be next?' campaign of May 1996. Subsequent headlines in the national press proclaimed: 'Parents in dark as paedophiles stalk schools' (*Guardian*, 24 November 1996), 'Paedophile out of prison "fearful for life and limb"' (*Observer*, 15 December 1996) and 'Stop hiding perverts say protest mums' (*Daily Mail*, 3 February 1997) (cited in Kitzinger, 1999b:209). The practice that came to be known as 'community notification' was fuelled by reports of 'Megan's Law' in the United States. This legislation was introduced in 1996 following the rape and murder of a seven-year-old girl, Megan Kanka from New Jersey, by a twice-convicted sex offender who lived on the same street. This law required all States to allow public access to and dissemination of sex offender registration information.

In Britain, the debate over whether paedophiles released from prison should be allowed to live anonymously in the community gathered force following the abduction and murder, in July 2000, of eight-year-old Sarah Payne by a previously convicted sex offender, Roy Whiting. The Sunday tabloid newspaper, the *News of the World*, launched a 'name and shame' campaign that promised to reveal the identity of every known child sex offender. The paper's vigilante journalism announced that the campaign was 'For Sarah' and sparked considerable controversy, not least as it seemed to be a cynical publicity attempt aimed to increase falling sales (Cross, 2005:288). The paper argued that it had captured the public mood. It also strove to maintain a distinction between the paper's vigilance and regrettable public acts of vigilantism (Bell, 2002).

The most infamous took place on the Paulsgrove estate in Portsmouth during August 2000. Crowds of up to three hundred gathered nightly to initially target the house of Victor Burnett (one of those 'named and shamed' by the *News of the World*), then cars were set alight, stones hurled through front-room windows and slogans daubed on houses of other alleged paedophiles. The broadsheet press condemned the 'lynch mob violence' for 'being irrational' and involving the 'wrong kind of mothers' (Lawler, 2002). It was very much a working-class protest and while pundits sought to draw ancient and modern parallels (from ethnic cleansing in Bosnia to witchcraft hysteria) a number of important issues were ignored: 'the mistaken idea that communities are safer when the "dirty old men" are driven out; the repercussions of failing to confront child sex abuse within families; the perceived indifference of officialdom to local concerns' (Silverman and Wilson, 2002:126).

However, it is important to recognize the crucial role played by the local press in alerting readers to the presence of paedophiles in their midst. The *News of the World* actually borrowed the naming and shaming idea from these intense local press crusades and had commissioned market research after Sarah Payne's murder and 'found that a strong campaign on the issue of paedophiles would play well among its four million readers' (Silverman and Wilson, 2002:150). Although they are often ignored in studies of the media, the local and regional press can significantly shape national news agendas. Since the 1990s Britain's local press has been energetically identifying the risks posed by convicted sex offenders in the local community. Kitzinger (1999b:209) has detailed how the theme of 'paedophiles within-the-community' attracted considerable coverage in the late 1990s 'across the UK from Aberdeen to Brighton, from Leicester to Belfast, from Teesside to Lancashire'. The local press has done much to construct a powerful, menacing figure of 'the paedophile' as the archetypal 'outsider' infiltrating the 'decent heart' of the community (Cross, 2005:290).

It would be a mistake to dismiss the anxieties provoked by the media coverage as a moral panic or simple sensationalism. There are complex issues behind the headlines. The communities felt besieged, fears of child abduction fill every parent with dread, policies over the monitoring of offenders were inconsistent if not incompetent[4] and housing inequalities compounded the crisis. Kitzinger (1999b:215) also found that where local residents failed to trust professionals or feared for their children's safety, these were often reasonable concerns. She also criticizes the way the term 'paedophile' is presented in media discourse. It casts sexual abusers as dangerous outsiders, when in fact most children are assaulted by men they know and trust. The concept of 'paedophilia' serves to distort the different forms of child sexual exploitation (Kelly, 1996).

This view is endorsed by Matthew Parris (1998) writing in *The Times*, where he poses the question: 'What is the act of paedophilia? The word describes an immense variety of possible acts, ranging from the most heinous to the venial . . . To describe all these as "paedophilia" lends the patina of science to a category so wide as to be meaningless.' It is a 'scary name . . . with a medical ring, but with just a hint of suppressed hysteria'. It also implies that the abuser cannot help themself and needs some kind of treatment. Indeed, it has been suggested that the concept only makes sense as a form of 'popular knowledge' that blends media discourses with community activism to powerful effect (Critcher, 2003:114–15). Kitzinger (2004) has subsequently coined the concept of 'media templates' to demonstrate how definitional complexities are dispensed with in favour of a shorthand terminology that journalists and the public use to make sense of troubling issues. The 'paedophile' provides one such template, while tapping into deep-seated anxieties over childhood and monstrous strangers.

Sexual Violence and the News

Representations of sexual violence are deeply engrained in Western culture. The popular press has long drawn on the potent mix of sex and violence to sell papers by selling certain images of women. A central point of much feminist research is that stories of sexual violence work on many different levels, but they each mark out the boundaries of what is 'acceptable' conduct for both men and women (Cameron and Frazer, 1987). The key contradiction here is that while violent sex crimes are widely regarded by the public as particularly abhorrent, reporting tends to focus on a very few disturbed serial rapists, rather than typical rape which tends to be committed by someone known to the victim. In other words, the construction of the 'sex beast' in popular national newspapers plays an important role in maintaining the threat of 'stranger danger' at the expense of representing 'intimate violence' as a serious social problem. In their examination of press reports of sex crime (mainly of rape and sexual assault) Soothill and Walby (1991:34) emphasize the central place that the 'sex fiend' occupies in the popular press, which while not being a gross misrepresentation of reality is rather 'a selective portrayal of specific facts'.

The contrast between national and local press coverage gives a telling insight into the dynamics of sex crime reporting. National newspapers tend only to retain an interest in a case 'if there is scope for the construction of a sex fiend who continues to wreak havoc on a community', whereas the local press are much less selective and 'on occasions will continue to maintain an interest in a case which seems unconnected with any other' (ibid.:35). The most obvious reason for tabloid interest in promoting connections between incidents of sexual assault lies in the fact that a sex beast will sell newspapers. Yet it is also the case that working on atrocious sex crime stories is the closest that most tabloid reporters will ever come to investigative journalism. However, while serious investigative journalism challenges official accounts of 'reality', the search for a major sex criminal rarely does so, as the press and the police use the same 'repertoire of scripts'. For instance, if an investigation is going unsuccessfully, the development of a sex-fiend theme can provide the police with the resources to sustain a particular line of investigation. Moreover, it is argued that the sex fiend conforms to the police's view of real sex crime. Walkowitz (1992:230) has shown how the investigation into the series of murders in Leeds and Bradford between 1975 and 1981 was seriously 'hampered by the investment of police themselves in the Ripper fantasy'. Peter Sutcliffe, who was eventually convicted of the murders, had been interviewed nine times by the police – but never as a serious suspect.

In Helen Benedict's (1992) *Virgin or Vamp: How the Press Covers Sex Crimes*, she provides a content analysis of the language US journalists used in their reporting of these stories during the 1970s and 1980s. Significantly she found that there is a tendency for the women themselves to be blamed for the violence perpetrated against them and to classify the women as 'virgins' or 'whores'. The analysis revealed that white, middle-class victims tend to be more favourably described as 'good' and 'innocent' than black or working-class women. From interviews with journalists it also became apparent that this cruel, insensitive and humiliating vocabulary was rarely due to individual prejudice but the much stronger influence of newsroom habits and broader, cultural 'rape myths' (Benedict, 1992:6). Similar conclusions are drawn in Lisa Cuklanz's (1996, 2000) analysis of the reporting of rape on prime-time US television news programming, where new stories were presented in individualistic and adversarial fashion (for example, 'her word against his' and a questioning of the victim's sexual history – was 'she asking for it?').

While these are studies of a handful of high-profile sex crimes that received extensive media coverage, Marion Meyers (1997:98) has analysed local news organizations and found the 'virgin–whore' dichotomy also influencing reporting: women who 'are battered, raped or even murdered appear to be journalistically unimportant unless they are white and middle-class – or if they can serve as a warning to other women'. These findings are not just restricted to the US. One study of the British tabloid the *Sun* examined how the language in sex crime stories conveys blame by constructing a contrast between dehumanized male attackers (variously described as 'beast', 'fiend', 'monster' and 'ripper') and those the paper regarded as 'normal' (where terms like 'hubby' and 'daddy' predominate), where female victims are held to blame for making these decent men violent (Clark, 1992).

At the same time the stories themselves have become a seemingly ordinary feature of the news – by the 1990s at least one sexual abuse story featured in every British tabloid for a week (Carter, 1998:220) and another study of the *Daily Mail*'s coverage of sexual abuse stories in 2000 identified an average of five such stories a week (Boyle, 2005:68). There are a number of ways in which these reports of sexual violence shape the 'normalization' of the harm represented. Crucial to the argument are the ways in which the discourses of 'normalcy' combine with those of the 'ideal', 'traditional', white, middle-class, nuclear family. Victims who are not from such 'good' families tend to be blamed for inviting sexual violence by transgressing the boundaries of 'decent' behaviour (Carter and Weaver, 2003:38). These stories are presenting a map of the normative order and expressing certain sensibilities about social relations.

One account argues that the news media address three fundamental aspects of order: moral evaluation, procedural justice and social hierarchy (Ericson *et al.*, 1991:5). As the authors go on to explain:

> A lot of news consists of moral-character portraits: of demon criminals, of responsible authorities, of crooked politicians, and so on. The emphasis on individual morality is not only a dramatic technique for presenting news stories as serial narratives involving leading actors but also a political means of allocating responsibility for actions and attributing accountability. (Ericson *et al.*, 1991:8)

In order to grasp why the media construct selective, sensational and frequently inaccurate stories calls for an understanding of how news organizations systematically privilege these particular classifications over others. As we have seen there are four distinctive approaches that explore the political, economic, social and cultural contexts of news making that shape how stories are produced and processed, but what has not yet been considered is the sexualization of the press – how news of sexual violence sits alongside pictures of 'topless' female bodies, pages of celebrity sex gossip, endless features on diets, fashion, cosmetic surgery and the like that each promise to make readers more sexually attractive.

The Sexualization of the Popular Press

In the first volume of his *History of Sexuality* Michel Foucault (1979) argued not only that the Victorian era was the opposite of what we suppose it to have been, that is a period when talk about sexuality was repressed, but also that our popular modern view that talking about sex is a form of liberation is mistaken. Instead he argues that the Victorian period was one in which a number of disciplines, such as medicine and psychiatry, developed their interrogations of sexuality. Moreover, this process of bringing sexuality under control through classification has continued to grow ever since and has nurtured a fascination with dangerous, forbidden sexualities. At the same time, the Victorian press sought to make visible the domestic, personal and intimate in order to reach an expanding and more diverse readership across the nation. As we saw in chapter 5 this 'new journalism' emphasized 'human interest' stories in order to appeal to the 'uneducated mass of all classes' (Carter *et al.*, 1998:1). To reach this audience, who had no intention of wading through the dense metaphors and classical allusions which then dominated newspaper prose, readers were now 'to be pampered and "tickled" rather than challenged or patronized' (Holland, 1998:19). A number of factors were responsible for this 'feminization of the press' in the last decades of the nineteenth century.

Among the most important is that news itself became gendered across a 'hard'/'soft' divide. This refers to not just the ways in which there is a hierarchical division between 'hard' news, considered to be serious and important (and to be covered by male journalists), and in stark contrast 'soft' news, regarded as trivial and insignificant (the province of female reporters). The latter came to 'be associated with a range of characteristics which were traditionally "feminine", especially its tendency towards sensation and the personalizing of information' (Beetham, 1996:118) in an effort to reach female readers. This process of feminization was a clear move to boost the circulation of newspapers, but it also opened up a more democratic, public space for the discussion of issues of concern to women.

A crucial turning point occurred in the 1970s when the meaning of 'popular' was pushed in a new direction – 'no longer feminized, but *sexualized*' (Holland, 1998:18, emphasis in original). Rupert Murdoch's takeover of the *Sun* in 1969 paved the way for popular tabloids to use explicit sexual material. The image of the 'Page Three' girl became its symbol, but sexualization has come to structure news stories as well as entertainment items. Patricia Holland (1998:24) details how 'the *Sun*'s assertive vulgarity became differently aligned to the cultural and political map of the day' as the years progressed. Thus in the 1980s the paper became fiercely associated with radical Conservative sympathies, and by the 1990s its sexual obsessiveness had been overtaken by the 'new lad' magazines like *Loaded, FHM* and *Maxim*.[5]

Despite frequent criticisms British tabloid editors still juxtapose stories of sexual violence alongside pictures of half-naked women. Arguably though, it is at the level of Page Three that 'the *Sun* seeks to dictate the terms by which issues of sexuality and lifestyle are to be normalized most clearly' (Allan, 2004:133). For in the 'daily mosaic of the newspaper, the image of the sexy woman continues to be laid against female demons like single mothers, lesbian teachers and ugly women' (Holland, 1998:25). Consequently, it has been argued that the sexualization of the news has marked the end of any genuine attempt to report sex crime as a serious social problem (Benedict, 1992:251). Instead the stories are presented as individual, bizarre or shocking case-histories that severely curtail public understanding of sexual violence.

Newswork itself is also characterized by a sexualized division of labour. The following summary of findings from an international range of studies conducted since the 1980s has found the same consistent pattern:

> daily journalism, whether it is print or broadcasting, is dominated by men; the higher up the hierarchy or the more prestigious a particular medium or section is, the less likely it is to find women; women tend to work in areas of journalism that can be considered an extension of their domestic responsibilities and their socially assigned qualities of care, nurturing and humanity; regardless of difference in years of experience, education level and other socio-economic factors, women are paid less for the same work. (van Zoonen, 1998:34)

Paula Skidmore (1998:207) has also suggested that among British newsworkers the predominance of men in journalism has produced a macho culture of newsgathering – aggressive and overbearing but also one of 'male camaraderie and "bonding" – which excludes women'. Female journalists are not only expected to adopt masculine forms of reporting, but also feel the pressure 'to write white' (Santos, 1997:123). I will deal with how the media construct race and racism in the next chapter; for now though it is important to emphasize that there is a gendered politics of 'objectivity' infusing news reporting.

Although there continue to be significant gender inequalities in news production processes it is crucial that the divisions are not simply reduced down to the gender of individual journalists. For example, the fetishization of factuality (which divorces facts from their social context) is an instance of how masculinized practices of reporting are mobilized and privileged, while the brutal competition to be first with the news (to 'scoop' rivals) point to the 'macho' culture of the newsroom (van Zoonen, 1998:35). Many studies of the gender politics of news sources reveal the extent to which news stories still privilege the authority of male sources and experts. In her interviews with British journalists Kitzinger (1998:198) found a further gendering of source dynamics: while 'both male and female journalists used their "gut feelings" in judging source credibility, some female journalists claimed that their "gut feelings" against alleged abusers were dismissed by male editors as "subjective" or "biased" whilst their male colleagues' "gut feelings" in favour of the same man were seen to constitute "common sense" or "professional instinct"'. Few though would insist that there is a distinctive 'woman's perspective' that female journalists inevitably bring to their reporting.

The overall point is that the reporting of sex crime must be situated in this broader shift in sexualization of the press. At the same time there were also important changes in understandings of sexuality rendered by the AIDS crisis, as the disease has come to be the symbolic bearer of a range of meanings in contemporary culture in what Jeffrey Weeks (1989/2006:78) has described as our 'post-permissive society'. As we will see in the next chapter much of the media AIDS commentary tends to draw on a wide range of concerns about childhood, sexuality, homosexuality, prostitution, pornography, drug use and so forth. At the same time the continual reporting of sexual assaults, murders, debates on sex education in schools and so on all speak to the larger question of sexuality itself, now understood as something intrinsically dangerous. The next chapter will examine in more detail the social uses of such threats and dangers.

8

Revisiting Moral Panics

The previous chapter provided an account of the various structural processes shaping news stories, and I now turn to the critical work that has attempted to grasp the social force of these media representations. The key concept here is that of moral panic and I have touched on it at various points in the book. The central assertion is that the hostile reaction to some activities is out of all proportion to the actual threat posed, while other more serious events are ignored, neglected or minimized by the mass media. The questions posed by moral panics relate directly to arguments over the possibility of rational debate in the public sphere, as well as fraught disputes over what now constitutes reality in a world saturated with media images, communication technologies and fabricated simulations. From its initial formulation in the heady cultural politics of the late 1960s the concept has been adapted, criticized and dismissed in equal measure by criminologists, sociologists and other commentators. Part of the task of this chapter will be to chart the intellectual origins, subsequent revisions and many objections against the study of moral panics. However, I want to insist that the concept remains a crucial one – even if it needs considerable updating and rescuing from simplistic, linear models of explanation that are unable to grasp the drama, energy and intensity of mediated interaction.

The concept of moral panic can be approached from a range of theoretical perspectives. These include the symbolic interactionism of the original definitions, ensuing Marxist revisions, various postmodern challenges and more orthodox attempts to tame the concept in American sociology through the study of collective behaviour. Here assorted claims-makers, professional associations, interest groups and social movements become the focus of attention. Yet what is lost in this migration is any sense of the urgent politics of anxiety that is crucial to the development of the concept in Britain. Indeed, all of the recent attempts to update the concept are drawn, in one way or another, to the risk society thesis (see Thompson, 1998; Jewkes, 1999; Ungar, 2001; Hier, 2003; Critcher, 2003). Few now dispute that we are living in times of high anxiety and that the mass media provide us with a daily diet of disasters from near and afar to continually remind us that we inhabit a world of crisis, danger and uncertainty. Yet the dry, probabilistic language that accompanies many of the discourses on risk has not replaced the distinctly moral framework through which modern hazards are understood. Instead, an emotional cultural politics of blame continues to inform moral panics.

The Sociology of Moral Panic

From the outset the concept of moral panic has been concerned with societal reaction. Explaining why there is a wildly disproportionate response to some perceived threat is the central motivation, but the interest in reaction was also to signal a radical shift in criminological emphasis. The critical thinking of the 1960s came to see 'objective' definitions of crime as problematic and the key melting pot for these new ideas was the National Deviancy Conference (NDC) held at York University. Established in July 1968 the NDC sought to challenge the old orthodoxies of mainstream criminology as represented by the Home Office and at the ancient universities. Among its founder members were Stanley Cohen, Laurie Taylor, Jock Young, Mary McIntosh and Ian Taylor – all were sociologists and the NDC quickly attracted a range of radical activists involved in student rebellion, penal reform, gay rights, anti-psychiatry and other social movements. The initial theoretical mix included anarchism, interactionism, Marxism, phenomenology and a little later feminism before ending in the late 1970s amid further divisions and schisms. In just over a decade criminology was transformed from a dull social science into the site of intense quarrels over the problems of crime, deviance and punishment.

While the study of crime became politicized and the question of which side you are on came to the fore these developments sought to radically expose how deviance is socially constructed, interpreted and judged. Thus signification has become an enduring feature of analysis. It is highly instructive to note that the first published reference to moral panic was made by Jock Young (1971b:37) when he asserted that the 'media can very quickly and effectively fan public indignation and engineer what one might call "a moral panic" about a certain type of deviancy' following a discussion of Marshall McLuhan and the 'implosive factor' of electronically mediated communication. Similarly, Stanley Cohen emphasized that much of our information about deviancy is received second hand and has already been processed by the mass media according to the commercial and political constraints identified in the previous chapter. In Cohen's systematic elaboration of the moral panic concept he emphasizes the importance of the sceptical revolution in criminology:

> The new tradition is sceptical in the sense that when it sees terms like 'deviant', it asks 'deviant to whom?' or 'deviant from what?'; when told that something is a social problem, it asks 'problematic to whom?'; when certain conditions or behaviour are described as dysfunctional, embarrassing, threatening or dangerous, it asks 'says who?' and 'why?' (Cohen, 1972/2002:12)

As he readily acknowledged, American developments in the sociology of deviance were crucial to this new criminology. In particular, the impact of symbolic interactionist ideas did much to unsettle orthodox thinking by insisting that deviance was not a property of the act committed, but is rather a category constructed in the course of interaction between the self and others. Howard Becker's (1963:9) famous studies of *Outsiders* popularized this approach by describing how deviance is a process created through the 'application by others of rules and sanctions to an "offender"'. This labelling process, as it soon became known, was by no means inevitable or irreversible, as Edwin Lemert's (1951, 1967) influential distinction between 'primary' and 'secondary' deviation emphasized.

Secondary deviation is more than simply a response to passing episodes of primary deviance. It is meant to describe the ways in which societal reaction (through stigma, punishment, myth and so on) can shape crime or deviance by obliging offenders to re-organize their self-identity in accordance with the public symbols, designations and interpretations of their conduct. Subsequent studies explored how drug users (Schur, 1963), homosexuality (Hooker, 1963) and mental illness (Goffman, 1962; Scheff, 1966) were constructed through labelling dynamics. Social problem construction also needs some form of individual and collective moral enterprise, as Becker (1963) recognized and Joseph Gusfield's (1963) account of 'symbolic crusades' makes clear.

Gusfield's discussion of the rise of the Temperance movement in the United States in the nineteenth century, which resulted in national alcohol Prohibition in 1919, reveals how the traditional middle classes viewed abstinence as a form of defence against their declining prestige and a vehicle of status protest in response to the world changing around them. Kai Ericson's (1966) study of deviance in seventeenth-century Massachusetts was another key text. The Salem witch trials, he argues, resulted from deep crises within Puritan society so that the witchcraft threat was created by the community to provide an outside enemy against whom society could unite as well as vividly demonstrating the shapes the devil could assume. Both Gusfield and Ericson crucially located deviance in broader social structures and community conflicts, rather than within specific individuals. This constructionist approach has been enormously influential and has led to intense debates between strict, contextual and objectivist proponents of social problem formation (see Jenkins, 1992:1–3). At the same time American subcultural theory, in particular the work on juvenile gangs (Cloward and Ohlin, 1961; Cohen, 1955), prison life (Clemmer, 1958; Sykes, 1958) and David Matza's (1964, 1969) pioneering account of delinquent drift provided some sense of the seductive, 'invitational edge' that transgression offers. Studies of labelling thus concentrated on social reaction, while subcultural theory focused on deviant action and it was the fusion of these two American traditions that would transform British criminology.

Amplification, Mystification and Projection

These developments in the American sociology of deviance combined with the British statistician Lesley Wilkins's (1964) understanding of 'deviancy amplification' laid the groundwork for analysing mediated moral panics. In both Cohen (1972/2002) and Young's (1971a and b) work there was an emphasis on the much-publicized conflicts between youth subcultures and Establishment forces in the 1960s. Cohen's study uses the notion of deviancy amplification to explain how the petty delinquencies of rival groups of mods and rockers at seaside resorts were blown up into serious threats to law and order. Understanding the role of the media is critical:

> The student of moral enterprise cannot but pay particular attention to the role of the mass media in defining and shaping social problems. The media have long operated as agents of moral indignation in their own right: even if they are not self-consciously engaged in crusading or muck-raking, their

very reporting of certain 'facts' can be sufficient to generate concern, anxiety, indignation or panic. (Cohen, 1972/2002:16)

Identifying a number of stages in the social reaction he divides the media inventory of the initial skirmishes into three phases: exaggeration, prediction and symbolization.

First, the media exaggerated the numbers involved, the extent of the violence and the damage caused. The seriousness of the events was further distorted by the use of sensational headlines, melodramatic reporting and unconfirmed rumours presented as fact. Second, predictions in the inventory period implicitly assumed that what had happened would inevitably happen again with even more devastating consequences. Third, the media coverage involved a form of symbolization where key symbols acquire semiotic power: 'a word (Mod) becomes symbolic of a certain status (delinquent or deviant); objects (hairstyle, clothing) symbolize the word; the objects themselves become symbolic of the status (and the emotions attached to the status)' (Cohen, 1972/2002:40). Drawing on arguments discussed in the last chapter he explains how the inventory works as manufactured news: 'the first is the institutionalized need to create news and the second is the selective and inferential structure of the newsmaking process' (Cohen, 1972/2002:45). One of the consequences of symbolization is that it leads to sensitization. Here, otherwise unconnected events are linked into a pattern by various moral entrepreneurs (judges, the police, politicians and so forth) and understood as symptomatic of the same underlying menace. Calls for action are stepped up, which leads to further marginalization and stigmatization in a deviancy amplification spiral, punitive legislation is rushed through parliament and new control measures proliferate.

Cohen goes to some length to situate the moral panic over mods and rockers in social context. In particular, the hostile reaction revealed much about how postwar social change was being experienced – the new affluence and sexual freedom of teenage youth cultures in the 1960s fuelled jealousy and resentment among a parental generation who had lived through hungry depression, world war and subsequent austerity. Although there is an implicit social psychology here that recognizes there are real problems at stake, the actual object of anxiety is displaced by a more diffuse fear or a mystification of the dangers posed. As Cohen (1972:192) puts it, the 'real Devil, whose shapes the early Puritans were trying to establish, was the same devil that the Mods and Rockers represented'. Thus he insists that moral panics are a product of 'boundary crises' (the term is Ericson's, 1966).

They occur when a society has some uncertainty about itself. This ambiguity is resolved through ritualistic confrontations between the deviant group and the community's official agents, whose duty it is to define where the boundaries lie and how much diversity can be tolerated. In effect they clarify the normative contours at times when the boundaries are blurred. In this way moral panics tend to occur when society is undergoing rapid change, when the need to define boundaries is particularly acute.

Young's (1971a, 1971b) argument was that in small-scale societies deviancy amplification was much less likely. In traditional societies everyone has at least some face-to-face contact with deviant members and the information about such members is rich and multidimensional, whereas modernity produces a significant drop in this sort of information. With severe social segregation there is a lack of direct information about those defined as different from the mainstream. Consequently there is a great reliance on the mass media for information. The media's need to give the public what it wants and maintain a circulation in competitive markets means that they constantly play on the normative worries of large sectors of the population, often employing outgroups on which collective fears and anxieties are projected. There is a strong Durkheimian theme here, in that the boundaries of normality and order are reinforced through the condemnation of the deviant – a point that lay at the heart of Ericson's (1966) study of *Wayward Puritans*. But what Cohen (1972) and Young (1971a and b) both were emphasizing was that this process only occurred in modernity through a considerable distortion of reality.

Mugging, Asylum and Disease

As we have seen in chapter 1, this emphasis on how the media distort the reality of social problems was developed by Stuart Hall and his colleagues at the Birmingham Centre for Contemporary Cultural Studies in their *Policing the Crisis: Mugging, the State, and Law and Order* (1978). In this book an explicitly Marxist account of crime is developed that stands in some contrast to this Durkheimian sociology of deviance tradition. It examines 'why and how the themes of *race, crime* and *youth* – condensed into the image of "mugging" – come to serve as the articulator of the crisis, as its ideological conductor' (Hall et al., 1978:viii, emphasis in original). The book thus draws together the Birmingham Centre's work on youth subcultures, media representation and ideological analysis in a magisterial account of the hegemonic crisis in Britain that began in the late 1960s and anticipates the

victory of Margaret Thatcher's authoritarian 'law and order' programme in the 1980s.[1] The book ostensibly explores the moral panic
that developed in Britain in the early 1970s over the phenomenon of
mugging. Hall and his colleagues demonstrate how the police, media
and judiciary interact to produce ideological closure around the issue
through a signification spiral. Through a process of convergence,
deviant activities from quite different sources (juvenile delinquency,
sexual permissiveness, trade union politics, Irish republicanism) coa-
lesce and create an escalating sense of disorder. Black youth is cast as
the folk devil in police and media portrayals of the archetypal mugger
– a scapegoat for all social anxieties produced by the changes to an
affluent, but destabilized society.

In many respects, the real strength of the book lies in the way it
attempts to deconstruct the politics of representation in such an
extended fashion. It also paved the way for more nuanced accounts of
the 'social production of news' than discussed in the last chapter and,
crucially, placed race on the intellectual agenda. Paul Gilroy, a col-
league at the Birmingham Centre, would draw from these arguments
and go on to criticize the implicit nationalism, ethnic absolutism and
'morbid celebration of England' in the cultural studies project (Gilroy,
1987:228). The discursive construction of race and racism revolves
around a black/white dualism that is most readily apparent in media
representations of crime. In the North American context, Fiske
(1996:80) has explained how underlying much of the crime reporting
is a deep-rooted white hysteria about the 'power of the black male
body' that by its very presence constitutes a turbulent, sexualized
danger to the fragile white social order.

Over the last decade or so, and across Europe, questions of asylum
and immigration have increasingly taken centre stage, with the figure
of the asylum seeker receiving an almost constant barrage of mediated
hostility. The metaphors cluster around three dominant images invok-
ing biblical disaster of flood, wave, tide and deluge, as well as criminal
activity involving fraud, scrounging, thieving and bogus presence, and
finally an invading army swamping the streets bringing terror and violence to host communities. It has been argued that these kind of 'dehumanized depictions of asylum-seekers (i.e. as a tide threatening to
breach national borders) play an increasingly pivotal role in structuring the national imaginary' (Tyler, 2006:192), a view confirmed in a
recent study of the British news media produced by the Information
Centre about Asylum and Refugees (ICAR). Combining detailed
content analysis with focus group findings, the research shows how
the reporting of asylum forms a 'communications spiral' where the

'rhetoric of "floods" and "waves" of immigrants is the signal for official endorsement of "tough" action' (ICAR, 2004:25). This action includes a series of punitive laws that have increasingly refused to recognize asylum seekers as political refugees, deprived of rights and existing in a sub-human state of identity cards, electronic tagging, indefinite detention and all the while living with the constant threat of deportation. Such work demonstrates how moral panic discourse prevents any ethical form of recognition while politically subjecting asylum seekers to the barest of lives.

Moral panic theory has also proven influential in studies of sexuality and disease. Susan Sontag's (1983) *Illness and Metaphor* describes how illnesses are given moral meaning through stigmatizing the victim as pariah or deviant, a view developed by Jeffrey Weeks in an essay on AIDS where he explains in a much-cited passage how moral panic mechanisms 'are well known':

> The definition of a threat to a particular event (a youthful "riot", a sexual scandal); the stereotyping of the main characters in the mass media as particular species of monsters (the prostitute as "fallen woman", the paedophile as "child molester"); a spiralling escalation of the perceived threat, leading to a taking up of absolutist positions and the manning of moral barricades; the emergence of an imaginary solution – in tougher laws, moral isolation, a symbolic court action; followed by the subsidence of the anxiety, with its victims left to endure the new proscription, social climate and legal penalties. (Weeks, 1985:45)

His overall argument is that a devastating disease that seemed to disproportionately affect black people and gay men symbolized much wider anxieties over shifting personal moralities and drew on longstanding tensions over race and sexual diversity. Yet this position was quickly criticized. As Simon Watney (1987/97:40) argued, the 'problem for anyone trying to analyse the representation of homosexuality in terms of available theories of moral panic' is that the 'entire subject is historically constituted as "scandal" '. Watney's critique is one of the earliest and most incisive demonstrations of the limits of moral panic theory and I will cover it in more detail below.

Some Criticisms

In mainstream criminology the concept has received extensive criticism. Some – who took issue with the empirical evidence presented in *Policing the Crisis*, arguing that, contrary to the view of Hall and his colleagues, the incidence of mugging was increasing (Waddington, 1986) – have accused the authors of ignoring the impact of crime on the working class (Young, 1987) and of overstating the extent to which the criminality crisis was contrived by elites for dominant interests (Goode and Ben-Yehuda, 1994). Others have warned against the dangers of eliding all anxieties under a single heading 'of some (hypothetically universal, endlessly cyclical) feature of social life, namely panickyness' (Sparks, 1992:65). In his recent review of the concept Cohen acknowledges that the term 'panic' has caused much trouble:

> The term is unfortunate, though, because of its connotation with irrationality and being out of control. It also evokes the image of a frenzied crowd or mob: atavistic, driven by contagion and delirium, susceptible to control by demagogues and, in turn, controlling others by 'mob rule' . . . After being at first apologetic and accepting the downgrade of 'panic' to a mere metaphor, I remain convinced that the analogy works. (Cohen, 2002:xxvii)

The term does still convey well the drama, urgency and energy of certain media narratives, though problems remain with the contrast between an 'irrational' panic and the supposedly 'rational' analysis of it.

It is this last difficulty that lies at the centre of Watney's critique. He argued that the gradual and staged creation of folk devils as described in classic moral panic theory was not capable of grasping how the entire field of sexuality is saturated with 'monstrous' representations. It cannot distinguish between different degrees of anxiety or explain how sexuality is regulated through a multiplicity of overlapping institutions with competing understandings of the world. As he explains:

> the theory of moral panic is unable to conceptualize the mass media as an industry which is intrinsically involved with *excess*, with a voracious appetite and capacity for substitutions, displacements, repetitions and signifying absences. Moral panic theory is always obliged in the final instance to refer and contrast 'representation' to the arbitration of 'the real', and is hence unable to develop a full theory concerning the operations of ideology within all representational systems. Moral panics seem to appear and disappear, as if representation were not the site of *permanent* ideological struggle over the meaning of signs. (Watney, 1987/97:41–2, emphasis in original)

In making this criticism, Watney is emphasizing that the policing of desire does not emanate from one or two sites of social control, but constantly surrounds us and suggests that we need to understand the puzzled indifference, insatiable fascination and even obsession exhibited by moral guardians for the objects of their anxiety. Consequently, his position is one that brings fresh psychoanalytical insights to the concept of moral panic by revealing how indignation is often structured by deep and contradictory desires that saturate the field of representation.

Some of these ideas have been developed by Angela McRobbie and Sarah Thornton in their respective attempts to revamp moral panic theory in the light of contemporary multi-mediated social worlds (McRobbie, 1994; McRobbie and Thornton, 1995; Thornton, 1994). The central themes in their critique can be summarized as follows. First, there is frequency – moral panics have an extremely short shelf life and a rapid rate of turnover, making it extremely difficult to cling to a model that emphasizes their episodic quality, spirals and flows. On their reckoning, moral panics have become 'a standard response, a familiar, sometimes weary, even ridiculous rhetoric rather than an exceptional emergency intervention'; used 'by politicians to orchestrate consent, by business to promote sales in certain niche markets, and by media to make home and social affairs newsworthy, moral panics are constructed on a daily basis' (McRobbie and Thornton, 1995:560). Second, moral panics are contested. There has been a growth of interest groups and pressure groups who respond to and question media demonization of various social issues and the categorization of people as problems. The influence of such groups allows the media to portray reporting as responsible and providing 'balance'. The third point concerns reflexivity. The notion of moral panics now pervades media and political rhetoric. It is now a question directly aimed at politicians when, for example, they are perceived as deliberately trying to whip up a moral panic over an issue, and they live in a world of press release, spin doctors and being on message.

Fourth, moral panics have become vital marketing strategies. Thornton (1994:183) provides a detailed account of the ways in which disapproving 'tabloid coverage legitimates and authenticates youth cultures'. They welcome adult condemnation and disapproval. Fifth, the media can no longer be treated as something separate from society. Echoing Watney they state that when 'sociologists call for an account which tells how life actually is, and which deals with the real issues rather than the spectacular and exaggerated ones, the point is that these accounts of reality are already representations and sets of meanings about what they perceive the "real" issues to be' (McRobbie and Thornton, 1995:570–1). Their final point highlights diversity. In an increasingly culturally cosmopolitan world the 'hard and fast boundaries between "normal" and "deviant" would seem to be less common' (McRobbie and Thornton, 1995:572–3). On their reckoning these changes result from the vast expansion and diversification of the mass media.

More than any other critique their position is one that points to the datedness of the classic moral panic models. What they are less clear about is precisely how the concept can be developed for contemporary conditions. For, while it is clear there has been a proliferation of communication technologies bringing new spaces for diverse niche interests, there has also been a broader tendency towards the merging of news and entertainment. Jock Young (1999, 2007), for example, has warmly endorsed the key features of their argument but departs from their account in this crucial respect:

> their notion of 'multi-mediated world' would suggest a greater diversity of representations than actually occurs. Or, to put it another way, diversity, of course, occurs from speciality magazines to Internet chat circles, but the main thrust of representation hinges around the major media chains and their ever-increasing oligopolization. Panics and scapegoating would seem to me to focus upon the socially excluded: in particular, the triptych of welfare scrounger, immigrant and drug addict, frequently elided and racialized, and to which after 9/11, a further refracting mirror has been added: that of actual and imaginary terrorist. (Young, 2007:63)

Yet there have also arisen new sites of social anxiety fed by specific risks generated by the pace and scale of industrial advances in Western societies. Since the mid-1980s particular fears have built up around nuclear, chemical, biological, environmental, genetic and medical hazards. Some well-known examples include global warming, nuclear fallout, toxic pollution, BSE, bird flu and other food scares that have made us acutely aware of the catastrophic potential of scientific and technological developments.

In order to grasp the significance of these changes for moral panic theory a number of authors have turned to the concept of 'risk society', as formulated by the theorist Ulrich Beck (1986), to understand the anxieties provoked by these transitions from modern to late modern social formations. For instance, it has been argued that the increased frequency of dramatic moral narratives in the mass media over the last decade or so is partly a response to the increased pressures of market competition, but is also a key means by which 'the at-risk character of modern society is magnified and is particularly inclined to take the form of moral panics in modern Britain due to factors such as the loss of authority of traditional elites, anxieties about national identity in the face of increasing external influences and internal diversity' (Thompson, 1998:141).

While this is an important effort to bring moral panic theory into line with the risk society thesis, others have questioned the utility of such an approach. Sheldon Ungar (2001) argues that the new sites of techno-anxiety that cluster around the apocalyptic potential of risk society leave the concept of moral panic incapable of grasping the unpredictable roulette dynamics of environmental disasters. Indeed the term 'amoral panic' has recently been coined in an effort to describe how society today is in a permanent state of anxiety due to the collapse of traditional politics and morality, as well as their radical alternatives, so that new 'vulnerable publics' emerge (Waiton, 2007). Others have suggested that there are not changing, but converging sites of social anxiety and, moreover, that the language of risk is infused with morality (Hier, 2003). What is missing though from all these accounts is the implosive character of the mass media – the sheer speed, intense impact and barrage of information that propels contemporary media spectacles.

Postmodern Media Spectacles

Both Jock Young and Stan Cohen made clear their indebtedness to the famous Canadian media theorist Marshall McLuhan in their respective formulations of the concept. In a footnote to his recent introduction to *Folk Devils and Moral Panics* Cohen explains how they 'both probably picked it up from Marshall McLuhan's *Understanding Media* published in 1964'. As we have seen, this is undoubtedly the case as they both cite McLuhan's account of the 'implosive factor' of the electronic media pointing to the 'continual bombardment by images of phenomena that otherwise could conveniently be forgotten' (Cohen and Young, 1973b:340). McLuhan had initially trained as a Shakespearean literary scholar, but had become by the 1960s a popular culture guru through coining terms like 'the medium is the message', 'global village' and 'information age' and drawing distinctions between 'hot' and 'cool' media. As he traded provincial academic status for international fame his ideas were increasingly criticized so that his thinking was either rejected for its technological determinism, boundless optimism, and inadequate political analysis or else ignored completely. There has however been a resurgence of interest in his work. This is partly due to his influence on Continental social theory in Jean Baudrillard, Friedrich Kittler and Paul Virilio, among others identified with postmodernism. It is also seen as providing prophetic insights that have been picked up in studies of new media, cyber culture and the emerging digital age (Levinson, 1999; Lister *et al.*, 2003; MacDonald, 2006). His idea of a 'global village' arguably makes more sense today, in the age of the World Wide Web, than when he initially coined the phrase.

Although McLuhan remains a controversial figure his overall position is one that emphasizes how different media fundamentally change social life. This point is captured in his famous soundbite 'the medium is the message'. The real message is not the actual content of a message, but the distinctive ways in which each medium extends our senses and perceptions of the world. As he put it, 'the "message" of any medium or technology is the change of scale or pace or pattern that it introduces into human affairs' (McLuhan, 1964:8). For McLuhan the shift from oral to print communication altered the balance of our senses, isolating some and privileging others. Print intensified the visual and shortened memory, since information can be stored in the form of the book and encouraged linear, sequential and rational forms of thinking. The later shift from print to electronic media extends acoustic and tactile sensations while bringing people affectively closer together in a 'global village'. As just suggested these arguments were quickly challenged. Guy Debord (1967/77:29) maintained that far from unifying humanity in a network of communication the global village marks the triumph of capitalism as a 'global spectacle' that shatters the 'unity of the world'. Raymond Williams (1974/90:127–9) took McLuhan's technological determinism to task and criticized his 'idealist model of human history'.

Ever since his 1967 review of *Understanding Media* Jean Baudrillard has been regarded as both heir and postmodern proponent of McLuhan's vision. In doing so he rejects McLuhan's optimistic neo-tribal future while taking the idea that the 'medium is the message' beyond anything envisaged by McLuhan. Baudrillard (2001:42) follows McLuhan by seeing the message of television as lying not in its content, but in 'the new modes of relations and perceptions that it imposes' and its destructive replacement of lived relations with semiotic relations. In a now famous move he argued that representation has moved through successive stages where modern society has moved from copying the real object (the Renaissance) to reproducing it (industrial capitalism) to copying the process of copying that is more real than reality (contemporary hyperreality). Reality is not hidden by simulation, it is hijacked. Too much is seen obscenely fast. As he puts it:

> the entire universe comes to unfold arbitrarily on your domestic screen (all the useless information that comes to you from the entire world, like a microscopic pornography of the universe, useless, excessive, just like the sexual close-up in a porno film) . . . We are no longer a part of the drama of alienation; we live in the ecstasy of communication. And this ecstasy is obscene. (Baudrillard, 1985:130)

Despite its later adoption, simplification and vilification in debates around postmodernism, his theory of 'the orders of simulacra' and of simulation makes an important contribution. It historically and philosophically grounds a critique of the contemporary processes of consumer and media society through the ancient concept of the 'simulacrum' – the way in which the image has always been understood as a powerful force and moral threat to the real (Baudrillard, 1988:170). Of course, he also achieved notoriety for claiming that the first 'Gulf War did not take place' in a series of essays (later collected in Baudrillard, 1995). This provocative assertion met with a fierce backlash and was attacked for its postmodern absurdity (Norris, 1992), but there is something in his thinking here that does get at how the media create non-events – points forcefully made in his later writings on 9/11 and the subsequent Afghan and Iraq Wars to argue that the West is engaged in a global contest for semiotic and symbolic control (Baudrillard, 2002 and 2005).

Baudrillard's is clearly a hyperbolic voice, but in developing his media theory he draws on the work of American historian Daniel Boorstin and his 1961 book *The Image*. Now largely negelected the book is full of contemporary resonance. For instance, he is the source of one of the most widely quoted aphorisms about celebrity: '*the celebrity is a person who is well-known for their well-knownness . . .* fabricated on purposed to satisfy our exaggerated expectations of human greatness' (Boorstin, 1961/87:57–8, emphasis in original). Boorstin also coined the term 'pseudo-event' to describe events which are created for the sole purpose of being reported or reproduced, like press conferences and presidential debates, which are then judged for their success on how widely they are reported. Writing over forty-five years ago he claimed that the torrent of 'pseudo-events' has flushed away the distinction between 'hard' and 'soft' news (Boorstin, 1961/

87:23) to the extent that one of the few exceptions remains the reporting of crime. He explains:

> The world of crime, even more than that of sports, is a last refuge of
> the authentic, uncorrupted spontaneous event. Of course there are
> rare exceptions . . . But, generally speaking, crimes are not pseudo-
> events, however industriously they may be exploited by the press . . .
> Only seldom are they committed for the purpose of being reported.
> Quite the contrary, a man who commits a murder or a rape, who robs
> a bank or embezzles from his employer, hopes to get away with it. Our
> hunger for crime news and sports news, then, far from showing we
> have lost our sense of reality, actually suggests that even in a world so
> flooded by pseudo-events and images of all kinds, we still know (and
> are intrigued by) a spontaneous event when we see one. (Boorstin,
> 1961/77:252–5)

In important respects both Baudrillard and Boorstin rework
Frankfurt School-style pessimism, as they both share 'the belief that
something is lost in the social and technical advance of the contemporary media, and that the latter do not merely transform experience
but *kill* it' (Merrin, 2005:55, emphasis in original). The crucial point
though is that mediated communication fundamentally alters our
experience of reality and it is here that much more work needs to be
done to develop these insights. Yet the unexpected and the exceptional still happen and it remains the job of the media to translate
these spontaneous anomalies into neat and tidy stories. Occasionally
though these events can produce an electrifying force that unleashes
cultural change and quite profound social transformations.

Mediatized Public Crises

The most influential theorization of 'mediatized public crises' lies in
Jeffrey Alexander and Ronald Jacobs's (1998) account of the contested and disruptive dynamics of exceptional news stories. In doing
so, they emphasize the importance of ritual, symbolism and emotional
appeals as well as narrative, drama and performance to the unfolding
sense of crisis. Theirs is certainly a more optimistic vision, for when
these 'mediatized public crises' occur they suggest that

> the media create public narratives that emphasize not only the tragic
> distance between is and ought but the possibility of heroically overcom-
> ing it. Such narratives prescribe struggles to make 'real' institutional

relationships more consistent with the normative standards of the
utopian civil society discourse. (Alexander and Jacobs, 1998:28)

In their analysis they show how the Watergate crisis of 1972 and the
Rodney King beating of 1991 both disturbed the moral order and
became catalysts for social change, largely through the communicative power of the media.

These elements are picked up in Simon Cottle's (2005, 2006)
recent attempts to develop these insights. Drawing on Victor Turner's
(1974) anthropology, this framework shows how 'social dramas can
generate emotional intensity, mobilize moral solidarity and encourage
social reflexivity in precipitous moments that reside, on occasion,
outside of "normal" space and time' (Cottle, 2005:53). The particular case he uses to build his argument is the racist murder of Stephen
Lawrence and its gradual transformation into a 'mediatized public
crisis' that challenged the normative contours of British society.

There have been many racist murders in Britain, yet the killing of
Stephen Lawrence in Southeast London in April 1993 became an
exceptional case and eventually prompted widespread criticism of
powerful state institutions. Initially, though, the murder received scant
attention in the British news media. While the parents and their sup-
porters campaigned for justice it was not until the Crown Prosecution
Service decided not to prosecute the prime suspects that a crucial
'breach' occurred that paved the way for a period of 'mounting crisis'
during which time there were further failures of institutional redress:

> Now, three years later with the opening of the private prosecution of 19
> April 1996, it was prominently replayed in terms that emphasized its
> racist brutality: 'Hacked to Death Just for Being Black' (*Sun*), 'Race-
> hate Led to Boy's Knife Killing' (*Daily Mirror*), 'Black "Murdered" by
> Race-hate Gang', *The Times* (1996) described Stephen's last hours and
> included eye-witness statements and graphic accounts of both the attack
> and the knife that caused his fatal injuries. Press reporting, then, was
> giving full vent to the racist nature of the attack and its appalling vio-
> lence. Through this relived violence, readerships were being invited to
> bear witness and see and feel the hurt that this had caused. (Cottle,
> 2005:58)

Less than a week later the case controversially collapsed[2] and the subsequent coroner's inquest was reported in detail. Here was revealed
for the first time the damaging extent of police mistakes, while various
police claims were also challenged by the Lawrences' legal team, and
the refusal by the five suspects to answer questions in the witness box

provoked universal press denunciation. The *Daily Mail* (14 February 1997) famously led the front page with the one-word headline 'Murderers' above a photograph of the five acquitted men. In the wake of the inquest the press produced further detailed analyses and damning commentaries on the failures of the criminal justice system.

Only once the public inquiry opened in March 1998 could a phase of judicial and symbolic redress begin. The subsequent publication of the Macpherson report in February 1999 marked the peak of this activity, where 'the political centre of society came together to publicly demonstrate its support for the Lawrences, acknowledge a collective sense of shame and lend support to symbolic processes of redress' (Cottle, 2005:62). As time passed divisions appeared in the press coverage – some newspapers sought to halt if not reverse the institutional reforms, others argued the changes were too slow in appearing. There is an important issue here in that these public rituals need not automatically produce moral solidarity, but are often contested. It could hardly be otherwise, given the material inequalities structuring the field of 'race', racism and British identity. Cottle (2005:68) too draws further attention to the way the case 'continues to hold charge partly because the issues and identities that surfaced through its cognitive and affective mapping of society remain contested terrains, but also because it accrued to itself symbolic power that burnt accusingly in the glare of the media'. Some fifteen years after the murder the case still holds a moral force and like the killing of James Bulger in February 1993, remains etched in the collective memory.

In contrast, though, the horror provoked by the Bulger case was immediate. Here a couple of ten-year-old boys abducted a toddler from a Liverpool shopping centre and walked him two-and-a-half miles to a railway line where they battered him to death with bricks and an iron bar. The poet Blake Morrison was among many who painfully struggled to make sense of the crime:

> In that spring of cold fear, it was as if there'd been a breach in nature: the tides frozen; stars nailed to the sky; the moon weeping far from sight. Those nameless boys had killed not just a child but the idea of childhood, all its happy first associations . . . It was the video footage from a security camera, jumpy and poignant as a cine film, that made the case famous. The little boy could be seen at loose among the shoppers, then following two older boys, then disappearing with them – the beginning of the long march to his death. Since then, there've been other killings by children. In France, as the Bulger trial opened, three boys, one of them only ten, kicked and beat a tramp to death. In

Norway, a five-year-old girl was battered and left to die in the snow by three boys of six. In Chicago, two boys aged ten and eleven dropped a five-year old boy fourteen storeys to his death, after he'd refused to give them sweets. There weren't public trials in these cases; the killers weren't treated as adults in an adult court: only the Bulger case has that distinction. (Morrison, 1997:21–2)

Yet long before the trial began in November a significant proportion of media space was filled with images of lawless youth 'joyriding' or else 'rioting' on out of town council estates, descriptions of the mounting wickedness of ever younger children, and persistent young offenders – into which underclass landscape walk Robert Thompson, Jon Venables and James Bulger (see Brown, 2005:58–65 for a more detailed account of press coverage in the months leading up to the Bulger murder).

The story clearly stands as a 'mediatized public crisis' and involves all the elements of 'breach', 'mounting crisis', 'redress' and 'reintegration/schism', but instead of 'race' it is adult Britain's troubled relationship with childhood that lies at the centre of the narrative. The Bulger case prompted considerable unease, shame and guilt, not least as most of us have done 'something terrible – something serious and adult, but performed in a childish, first-time daze' when we were young and, as Morrison (1997:241) goes on to write, with luck 'it isn't rape or murder, and no one gets badly hurt'. His point is that children can be cruel, selfish and do awful things. Without looking within ourselves we will never really understand what the boys did nor grasp why exceptional cases like this, and the slower burn of Stephen Lawrence's murder, fundamentally threaten the moral order and become part of our collective memory. Of course, the press sought to locate the malaise elsewhere, in demonized 'others', while repressing these inner feelings of guilt.

Shameless underclass families became one of the prime targets. In reaction to the murder of James Bulger, Lynda Lee Potter, a columnist for the *Daily Mail*, warned readers in an article entitled 'Horror as our worst fears now become sickening reality' that if society continued to allow women to have many children by different fathers and to devalue marriage, then:

we are doomed to live in an increasing maelstrom of horror. More children will die. There will be more young murderers . . . We have a world where children are growing up virtually as savages. Through video shops they have recourse to scenes of evil and black magic. (*Daily Mail*, 23 November 1993, cited in Thompson, 1998:98)

In this passage absent fathers, feckless mothers and video nasties combine to produce a new breed of murderous, feral children. The importance of video violence to the case arose largely from police speculation that the boys had copied scenes from *Child's Play 3* (1991), a film rented by one of the boy's fathers a month before the murder. The judge thought that 'violent video films may in part be an explanation' (cited in Schubart, 1995:222) and the *Sun* launched a campaign to burn all copies of the film – even though it was never actually established whether either boy had ever seen the video.

Conclusion

This chapter has concentrated on exceptional media events and has covered classic moral panic theory, postmodern simulated spectacles and mediatized public crises. Each has tended to follow Freud by implicitly insisting that studying the pathological, or rather the exaggerated, will reveal much about the contours of normality. Such phenomena are seen as symptoms of underlying structural changes and ideological conflicts as well as efforts to contain, or at least make sense of, disorder and danger through a cultural politics of substitution. To echo the Durkheimian theme that underpins much of the old moral panic theory, the most basic social classification is between the sacred and profane and that is still one of the most powerful binary oppositions that structures communication and enables a common code for evaluating events, relationships and people (Alexander and Jacobs, 1998:30). Yet to concentrate solely on the exceptional will render inevitable misunderstandings. As previous chapters have suggested and as Roger Silverstone (1999:143) has put it, the power of the media lies in 'the drip, drip, drip of ideology as well as the shock of the luminous event'. His overall argument is that it is in the familiar, mundane world that the media operate most significantly.

But now the normal background is as much characterized by insecurity and risk as it is by stability and security. Malcolm Feeley and Jonathan Simon (2007) have recently argued that in the US moral panics have now become an institutionalized part of social life and are a routine part of governing through crime. One of the examples they give is the AMBER alert system that was initially developed by the Dallas Police Department and Texas area broadcasters following the abduction and murder of nine-year-old Amber Hagerman in 1996. In essence, the system is that should the police become aware of a child abduction in progress, broadcasters would provide an early warning system alerting the general public to the fact and provide details useful in identifying the child or the abductors. In 2002, congress enacted the AMBER alert system and implemented it nationally. As it now operates the system automatically notifies broadcasters, special announcements interrupt regular radio and television programming, text messages are sent to mobile phones, notices are flashed on highway bulletin boards as well as distributed across the Internet and messages are instantly printed on lottery tickets. Their overall point is that at some point this case stopped being a moral panic and instead became institutionalized – a background norm for understanding concerns over safety and security while at the same time encouraging a new kind of political subjectivity that sees danger and menace everywhere.

In our current age of rapid information delivery via the World Wide Web and the sensory bombardment brought by e-mails, mobile phones, instant messaging, and the hundreds of television channels that can be accessed on cable and satellite, it is becoming increasingly likely that we will forget or ignore far more than we will ever know – a point made by Paul Virilio (1986) over twenty years ago when he argued that the 'speed' of modern communication is hardly the positive and politically neutral occurrence that it is often held up to be. Yet it is the dynamic between spectacle and routine that ultimately shapes the relationships between media audiences, textual structure and cultural production – points to which we now turn.

Conclusion

This book has explored the many relationships between crime, culture and the media. To organize the discussion it has divided the material into accounts of audiences, representations and industries. It is an approach that emphasizes the internal complexities of each of these domains, while suggesting that the relations between them are complicated and need unravelling. In his account of popular music Brian Longhurst (2007b:264) has usefully summarized the framework by insisting that we 'need to consider the production of texts, the nature of texts themselves, the "readings" that have and can be made of such texts and the way in which such readings take place in the context of the "lived cultures" of everyday social relations'. There are, however, some fundamental differences over how these dimensions should be studied. Here I will address these difficulties by revisiting examples drawn from previous chapters but emphasize that these remain open arguments rather than settled conclusions.

At this point it is worth identifying the substance of the disputes (Denzin and Lincoln, 2000:157; Cottle, 2003:7). At root the differences are five-fold and concern ontology (the nature of social reality), epistemology (what is valid knowledge of this social reality), methodology (what is the best way of researching it), politics (how to change the social reality for the better) and ethics (what is morally just). These philosophical terms capture something of the issues at stake and caution against a superficial synthesis of incompatible, or even irreconcilable, approaches. Ontological disputes are among the most essential and question whether society has an independent reality in its own right (a 'reality *sui generis*' in Durkheim's famous formulation), or can only be understood through the symbolic and cultural meanings with which social actors colour the world.

Epistemological questions are bound up with theories of knowledge and rival ways of knowing the world (empiricism, rationalism and interpretivism are among the competing philosophical positions). Methodological issues stem from what procedures (content analysis, questionnaire survey, focus groups or textual exegesis) are thought best equipped to gain knowledge of the world. Politics and political philosophy are at the heart of debates over media power, democratic principles and conflicting understandings of what is the 'good' society. Ethics and morality present themselves as preconditions for social life and part of the rich diversity of human experience is a diversity of cultures, practices and values. Inevitably this leads to antagonisms and calls for a just way of adjudicating between these differences.

The book began with the audience and the debates surrounding media 'effects'. Many of the studies, particularly in the United States, were informed by the empiricist assumptions of behavioural psychology and sociological functionalism (using quantitative methods like questionnaire surveys or laboratory experiments) to produce decidedly mixed, if not contradictory, results. This tradition gave rise to two polarized positions, one characterized by an all-powerful understanding of the media as a source of 'mass manipulation', the other a more pluralistic 'laissez-faire' model which suggests that the media have little or no effect in changing public understandings of social problems (Cohen and Young, 1973:10–11). Although more sophisticated approaches have developed, this mass communications tradition remains allied to a linear model of communication, which can be contrasted with more semiotic understandings of meaning exchange that had their origins in European cultural theory and the developments in criminology described in the last chapter.[1]

One response to these events was the turn to fear of crime, where ontological and epistemological difficulties soon surfaced – for example, over how conventional approaches could not grasp the emotional complexity of fear nor situate these experiences in broader social context. Feminists were early critics and argued that the conceptual thinking and methodological preferences of orthodox criminology failed to comprehend women's encounters with sexual danger (Stanko, 1988), while advocating more nuanced understandings of fear, reason and emotion (Walklate, 1998). Since it proved difficult to establish a straightforward relationship between the media and fear other factors were explored to explore the place of crime and anxiety in people's daily lives. This new direction has produced much work excavating how the 'fear of crime' condenses broader worries over the pace of socio-economic change, while revealing much about our increased risk consciousness and susceptibility to scaremongering.

At the same time characterizations of a passive, easily manipulated mass audience were challenged from two directions. One was influenced by semiotic/psychoanalytic film theory and Marxist understandings of ideological structures, which came to be associated with extreme forms of textual determinism, but nevertheless pointed to hidden desires in the spectator. In contrast, ethnographic studies of television audiences attempted to grasp the active, conscious ways in which viewers interpret the medium in domestic settings. It is here that tensions between text-centred approaches to audience interpretation and the culturalist emphasis on lived experience are at their most apparent. But it is important not to reify experience, as we 'still need to understand how media enter into the worlds of everyday life, how their poetry reaches and touches and enables us to make sense and manage and get on' (Silverstone, 1999:45–6). There are many links yet to be made between the formal, structural analysis of narrative and socially situated, practical understanding. One that I touched on in chapter 3 is how cultural criticism always involves questions of morality and politics.

Indeed, elitist aesthetic standards are often used to condemn popular cultural forms while reinforcing class inequalities. This is not an argument for relativizing aesthetic worth, but a way of distinguishing what is 'good' and 'bad' from the 'posh' and 'common' (Sayer, 2005). It is a strategy that while

> recognizing the inadequacies of the erstwhile academic pieties about intrinsic literary merit and the eternal verities of the text, one may yet defend the fairly obvious literary merits of Hardy or Dostoevsky over James Herriot or Jeffrey Archer; of how to present a given text or artwork as more or less progressive from a feminist or post-colonial point of view if all conceptions of the good life are deemed to be on a par. (Soper, 1999:70)

In this passage Kate Soper is seeking to preserve elements of Adorno's *Ideologiekritik* (a form of ideological criticism that seeks to demystify social processes and is linked to human emancipation), which I suggest can then be used to make explicit the classed judgements of moral worth that lie behind assertions of cultural value. Adorno's bleak claim that the 'world wants to be deceived' is often caricatured, but both he and Horkheimer (Adorno and Horkheimer, 1947/73:167) were keenly aware that the 'triumph of advertising in the culture industry is that consumers feel compelled to buy and use its products even though they see through them'. Adorno develops this possibility of seeing through yet obeying in a study of the astrology column of the *Los Angeles Times* in the 1950s (later published as 'The Stars Down to Earth' (1975/94), which is an excellent example of the rich subtlety of his thinking.[2]

The book then turned to representation, beginning with the texts themselves and the rise of the print media from the 1500s. The overall argument is that history matters and I wanted to give a sense of the diversity of criminal narratives in the early modern period, not least since many of our contemporary representations bear traces from this past. Yet there are also important differences. One crucial distinction is that between replication and representation. From antiquity up to the Renaissance producing a perfect simulacrum of the world as it is seen was the very ambition of the visual arts,[3] yet the arrival of the novel and its playful approach to truth and fiction provoked considerable debate over 'realist' forms of representation in the nineteenth century. These debates have continued in arguments over photography, radio, film and television up to the present day. For example, debates over the epistemological status of documentary programmes over 'reality' television are one recent instance of this preoccupation. From the late nineteenth century a distinction is increasingly made between realistic detail (realism as method), realism as an ontological disposition towards reality (the search for a larger reality beyond surface details) and realistic subject matter (Williams, 1988:257). It is these realist conventions that modernist and postmodernist forms of representation often subvert and parody, as we saw in chapters 5 and 6.

One of literary realism's defining characteristics is the way it claims to provide faithful representations of the world by concealing the signs of its fabrication (Barthes, 1953/77). Likewise, Richard Dyer (1997) has argued that photography and the cinema are 'media of light' that lend themselves to privileging whiteness. He explains:

> the photographic media are centerpieces in a whole culture of light that is founded on two particular notions, namely that reality can be represented as being on a ground of white, and that light comes from above; these notions have the effect not only of advantaging white people in representation and of discriminating between and within them, but also of suggesting a special affinity between them and the light. (Dyer, 1997:84, cited in Turner, 2001:180)

As an example he details the technical difficulties facing the cine-matographer working on *The Color Purple*, a film with an all-black cast, which meant that all the set interiors and decorations had to be made darker than 'normal' to allow the actors to be clearly seen.

Work like this can connect to an ethics of representation I touched on chapter 5. Here I was concerned to introduce an account of how we ought to respond to the images of suffering routinely paraded before us. Elsewhere, I have described how Emmanuel Lévinas's (1969) ethics of unconditional responsibility towards the Other have been particularly influential on postmodern moral reasoning (Carrabine, 2006). Liberal ethics are based on recognizing the essen-tial similarity between the self and others, and it is precisely this understanding of shared intersubjectivity and reciprocity with which postmodern thinkers take issue by emphasizing the singular, particu-lar and local. The appeal of Lévinas lies in his insistence that there can be no shared agreement as there is always something about the Other that escapes comprehension and it is this ethical opening to alterity that must be acknowledged.

This moral responsibility towards difference goes much further than the contingency of liberal tolerance, which is dependent on the disposition of the superior tolerator and can be granted or abandoned, since the Other is placed in relations of inferiority. For Derrida (2003:127) tolerance involves a 'condescending condescension' and he advances the notion of unconditional hospitality to deconstruct the apparent neutrality of tolerance. In Lévinas there is a radical reversal of modern liberal ethics by giving priority to the negative Other 'which was once unquestionably assigned to the self' (Bauman, 1993:85). It is also a view that is 'based on the assumption that we can somehow learn to understand each other and on this basis conduct a global politics so as to minimize catastrophe and conflict' (McRobbie, 2006:85). This 'politics of humility' is not without problems (see Carrabine, 2006:197–8), but it does offer the prospect of a more inclusive vision of cosmopolitanism than the 'hegemonic liberal' one currently being aggressively waged in the 'war against terror' (Habermas, 2006). I would also suggest that such an ethics of repre-sentation can get to grips with the issues raised by alterity in chapters 7 and 8.

Feminist struggles for rights and recognition have long sought to expose how abstract universal norms are in fact partial male con-structs. For instance, Simone de Beauvoir (1949) explained how women are oppressed by being a secondary Other to man's pri-mary Self, whose existence is determined by being unlike men. The patriarchal subordination of the feminine is discussed further by Luce Irigaray (1985) who argues that the polis, from Plato's ideal republic to Hegel's universal sphere, is founded on exclusion through which women are forced to resemble men and reject their specificity in order to participate in civic life. Imogen Tyler (2006:187) has also shown how the dehumanizing detention of asylum seekers is the 'underside of the cosmopolitan face of Britain' and she describes how there is a legitimation crisis in the very idea of 'rights' and 'citizenship'. Even in highly unequal societies media coverage can be a critical force leading to social change, as we saw in the Stephen Lawrence case. Powerful institutions can be pressurized to act in line with widely accepted norms rather than from narrow private interest – broadcasting a 'politics of shame' and in doing so broadening democratic principles where there are widespread structural inequalities and systematic discrimination (Barnett, 2003:65). For all its faults Habermas's (1992) normative ideal of the public sphere remains a vital touchstone for considering the obstacles that prevent genuinely democratic communication systems.

A final theme I will touch on here is the tension between popular criminology and academic criminology. The following passage nicely describes the differences between the two:

> Popular criminology covers a wide range of apparently factual material, but is, usually, concerned with a particular crime or criminal and the process of detection. It is aimed at a non-specialist market, is cheap, easily available and easy to read. Popular criminologists use techniques familiar to journalists and crime novelists to heighten the tension and to get the pages turning . . . Unlike popular criminology, the main concerns [of academic criminology] are crime and criminals in bulk. Not only is there an ethical injunction against identifying individuals, but also the single crime or criminal is regarded as too limited a sample from which to make the sort of generalizations that are assumed to be the objective of academic criminology . . . Academic criminology regards itself as scientific: presenting facts, theories and conclusions in a dispassionate and undramatic manner. It avoids the accessibility which popular criminology craves through the used of obfuscatory language and footnotes, and by burying itself in the catacombs of conferences, journals and books. (Rawlings, 1998:1–2)

Rawlings also points out that while popular criminology (especially the 'true crime' type) offers a great deal of poor-quality work, it can also lay claim to books like Truman Capote's *In Cold Blood*, Norman Mailer's *The Executioner's Song* and Blake Morrison's *As If*, to which list can be added documentaries like Spike Lee's (2006) film, *When the Levees Broke*, on the devastation New Orleans suffered in the wake of Hurricane Katrina and the shameful governmental response.

A similar point is made by Rafter (2007) in her discussion of the ethical and philosophical issues raised by her close reading of a small sample of sex crime films:

> Popular criminology's audience is bigger (even a cinematic flop will reach a larger audience than this article). And its social significance is greater, for academic criminology cannot offer so wide a range of criminological wares . . . The two types of criminology, popular and academic, complement one another, each contributing in its own way to understandings of crime. (Rafter, 2007:415)

But the two are not equally valued. To echo arguments just rehearsed, it is crucial to identify 'good' and 'bad' kinds of each type of criminology. Consequently, one of the implications of the book is that the texts, audiences and industries involved in producing popular criminology ought to become targets for academic research. Not least since these forms of representation powerfully shape how crime is understood.

This is not an exhaustive summary of all the arguments in the book, nor is it a comprehensive signpost of where future work might best be directed, but despite some of the serious and difficult issues just outlined the study of crime, culture and the media is also a lot of fun. By enabling us to make better sense of the world around us it allows us to examine the 'ways we are manipulated into taking some things too seriously and other things not seriously enough' (Cohen, 2002:xxxv). What I hope to have shown is that important dynamics, like pleasure and fear, spectacle and routine, normal and pathological and so on, structure the field. The media do not just provide us with endless, worrying accounts of social problems or distract us with unchallenging diversions, but are fundamentally involved in how existence is organized in the contemporary world. It is for this reason that I have drawn attention here to big issues like ontology and epistemology, politics and ethics, for in media analysis the devil lies anywhere but in the detail. This is also a methodological point – we need occasionally to step away from the minutiae of character, content and technology to consider issues of structure, discourse and form. Here we will find how the exceptional, catastrophic and unique becomes domesticated, exploited and sensationalized. In doing so we will want 'to know what we want to do about it besides change channels' (Gitlin, 2002:210). Clearly, this is a political project as much as a cultural one and it remains a task for future work to push this argument considerably further.

Notes

Chapter 1   Media Effects

1   The definition of violence used in the studies is 'only clear, unambiguous, overt physical violence. To be recorded at all, a violent incident must be plausible and credible. It must be directed against human or human-like beings, and it must hurt or kill, or threaten to do so, as part of the script's plot' (Gerbner *et al.*, 1978). Significantly, Gerbner argues that it is the cumulative effect of watching the torrent of violence on television over time, rather than a particular film or programme, that is responsible for producing misinformed understandings of the world. The assumption is that it is more important to concentrate on the common messages that permeate television as a whole, rather than examine differences between specific texts.

2   Umberto Eco (1959/79:51) had too argued that 'every sentence and every trope is "open" to a multiplicity of meanings', but this 'openness' is not the same as suggesting there are 'infinite' possibilities of reading. He goes on to explain how in the Middle Ages there developed a theory of allegory which maintained that there were a number of possible ways to read the Scriptures (and later extended to poetry, painting, sculpture and the arts generally) beyond the literal sense, but also in three others: the moral, the allegorical, and the analogical sense that came to govern textual interpretation.

3   The shift in direction is partly explained by other theoretical developments. In particular, Jacques Derrida's deconstruction of the stable binaries of structuralism and his insistence that meaning is continually deferred is a clear influence. Julie Kristeva's concept of intertextuality is another influence on Barthes's post-structuralism. Barthes's (1970/75) most ambitious analysis is the exhaustive commentary on Balzac's short story 'Sarrasine' where he breaks the text down into small units to explain how they carry many different meanings simultaneously.

4   E. P. Thompson (1978) was an extremely vocal opponent of structuralism. For instance, he recognized that the law can function ideologically

to legitimate the existing order, but he went on to explain that 'people are not as stupid as some structural philosophers suppose them to be. They will not be mystified by the first man who puts on a wig . . . If the law is evidently partial and unjust, then it will mask nothing, legitimize nothing, contribute nothing to any class's hegemony' (Thompson, 1977:262–3).

5   The bridge did not last long – see Cohen's (1980) scathing critique of the Centre's work, in the introduction to the second edition of *Folk Devils and Moral Panics*. In particular, Hebdige's (1979) structuralist, textual reading of punk is given short shrift 'for being unconcerned with "real" political issues or for being too literary, too instinctive a mode of analysis for any "real" social scientist' (McRobbie, 1994:207). To be fair to Cohen, he was not totally antagonistic towards developments in French social theory and his *Visions of Social Control* is strongly influenced by Foucault.

Chapter 2   Fearing Crime

1   A Home Office working party report, published in 1989 and chaired by the then Channel 4 chief executive and head of ITV, Michael Grade, recommended that 'all criminal statistics should carry a prominent "health warning" as the quarterly crime statistics for England and Wales are currently fed to the media by the Home Office in a form that is hard to digest and therefore easily distorted' (cited in Schlesinger and Tumber, 1994:183).

2   This study has been held up as 'a good example of poor research strategy: two questionnaires were sent to each of 500 households, with a resulting 29 per cent response rate . . . and effects were not controlled for the influence of other variables, even for such important ones as gender' (Ditton *et al.*, 2004:597). The problem is that such an approach cannot grasp how the newspapers are actually read nor examine the play of meanings in the texts themselves.

3   Jo Goodey (2005:82) argues that the 1988 British Crime Survey also revealed high levels of respondent 'anger' to victimization; it is therefore not a new phenomenon, but 'the political convenience of remaining with an image of the passive and therefore compliant victim is undoubtedly of greatest benefit to those government and non-government institutions with a remit to serve a certain "image" of the victim'.

4   Ancient epics like *The Iliad* and *Beowulf*, the medieval literature of Dante's *Inferno* and Chaucer's *Canterbury Tales*, through to Shakespeare's *Titus Andronicus* and Goya's painting *Woman with her Throat Cut* are among the examples usually cited. Little produced in the twentieth century can compare to the horrors of *Titus Andronicus*. Here the hero's daughter Lavinia is raped and has her hands chopped off and her tongue cut out by her assailants, who are later butchered by Titus (with their blood running into a basin held by Lavinia with what remains of her arms), and their dismembered body parts are then baked into a pie and later fed to the perpetrators' unsuspecting mother.

Chapter 3   Making Meaning

1   Lacan identifies three different psychic realms (the 'imaginary', the 'symbolic' and the 'real') that constitute the human subject. For Lacan, the 'imaginary' is the stage when the young infant has no sense of itself as a separate being, so there is no distinction between self and Other. However, the 'mirror phase' of a child's development (after six to eighteen months) begins when the infant sees an image of self in a mirror or through another person. This image is fascinating as it is the first time a child sees themselves as a subject to identify with and as a separate human being. But this recognition is also a 'misrecognition'. For the image is really precisely that, a powerful illusion. This development crucially distinguishes Lacan's approach from other psychoanalytical schools as 'it is a profoundly alienating act', yet it is 'a necessary illusion as without it it is difficult to see how the infant could gain any sense of itself at all' (Craib, 2001:157). But the longing for the 'imaginary' unity is never lost and produces a sense of lack that characterizes human consciousness, while establishing the unconscious as the seat of these unfulfilled desires. All desire springs from a lack, which provokes the subject into an endless search to fill that absence of unity. To enter language, as a child must to become an adult, is to be cut off from the realm of the 'real'. For Lacan, the 'real' should not be confused with what we represent to ourselves as 'reality'; it is a domain of the unknowable that lies beyond signification.

2   Other recent criminological studies include Marie Gillespie's and Eugene McLaughlin's (2005) focus group research on public perceptions of crime and punishment and the Cambridge University Public Opinion Project carried out by Anna King and Shadd Maruna (2006), which explores how punitive views shape personal identity.

Chapter 4   The Print Revolution

1   Various elements of the carnivalesque and grotesque realism persist in many contemporary cultural forms. Examples include James Joyce's (1922) *Ulysses*, an epic modernist parody of Homer's *Odyssey*, which over some 900 pages details a day in the life of an unsuccessful advertising salesman's obsessions with sex and bodily functions on his travels around Dublin, to his eventual return home to a miserable wife. More recently, David Cronenburg's films have explored the sinister implications of developments in science and technology on the human mind, body and sexuality. His remake of *The Fly* (1986) is perhaps the best example, though *Videodrome* (1983), *Dead Ringers* (1988), *Crash* (1996) and *Existenz* (1999) pursue similar ideas in bizarre and monstrous fashion. Angela Carter's fiction subversively parodies fairy tales (such as a bawdy Puss-in-Boots, strange Beauty and the Beast transformations, and the labyrinth mysteries of sado-masochistic desire) in the *Bloody Chamber*

(1979b) collection of short stories, each of which revels in the unsettling power of grotesque reversal.

2   None of the concerns about crime that figured prominently in the late fourteenth and early fifteenth centuries were new. Crimes like vagrancy, gambling, prostitution, blasphemy and sodomy were outlawed in the thirteenth century (Dean, 2001:68–9).

3   When the *Index* was eventually abandoned in 1966 it contained not only hundreds of theological works regarded as dangerous to Catholic faith but also hundreds of others by secular writers like Voltaire, Diderot and Graham Greene (Manguel, 1996:287).

4   It has been estimated, for instance, that some 27 publications addressed the Northumberland rebellion of 1569–70. All supporting the state, as in this ballad entitled 'A godly ditty or prayer to be sung unto God for the preservation of his Church, our Queene and Realme, against all Traytors, Rebels and papisticall enemies' (Chibnall, 1980:210 footnote 15). Throughout the early modern period riots were common, and were seen by the participants as defences of traditional rights and customs (Thompson, 1991).

5   In 1811 Lord Dudley caught the mood of the times, when he proclaimed in the House of Lords (after a particularly gruesome serial killing) that he would rather see 'half-a-dozen people's throats cut . . . every three of four years' than have to put up with professional policeman (cited in Wilson, 2007:261). For the English the word 'police' meant a French system of paid state spies who informed on their neighbours and interfered in private life – indeed parliamentary committees considered and rejected the idea of a 'standing police force' for the capital no fewer than five times (Carrabine *et al.*, 2004:271)!

Chapter 5   Entertaining the Nation

1   The Romantic celebration of nature over technology achieves its most popular expression in Mary Shelley's (1818) account of scientific interventions into life, death and the body in her novel *Frankenstein*. Written under the inspiration of conversations with Byron in a villa on the shores of Lake Geneva, the monster and vampire are born together one night out of a party game among friends (each agreed to write a new ghost story to while away a wet summer). Shelley's monster remains a noble creature to the end, while Polidori's vampire is still a petty feudal lord forced to wander Europe strangling young women in order to survive. By the time Bram Stoker (1897) writes *Dracula* the vampire is a monopoly capitalist who wants to buy the City of London and intends to keep his victims *for ever* (Moretti, 1983:92) by breeding a new race of mindless, bloodsucking demons enslaved to the Count. Whether the novel is read as an allegory of Empire, study of class conflict, anatomy of sexual desire or account of charismatic power, the key contrast structuring the text is that between a bright, modern, rational world and the nocturnal, dangerous, primitive forces that threaten to destroy it.

2 The novella also presents a striking metaphor for the duality of human nature and the urban experience in the early chapters, which anticipates Freud's ideas on the divide between the unconscious and conscious by some three decades. It opens with the 'Story of the Door', where a lawyer charged with the custody of Jekyll's will seeks to find Jekyll's heir, Edward Hyde, who happens to live behind Jekyll's elegant townhouse in a busy quarter of London. As the celebrated horror writer Stephen King (1981:90) nicely summarizes it: 'Here is one large block of buildings. On Jekyll's side, the side presented to the public eye, it seems a lovely, graceful building, inhabited by one of London's most respected physicians. On the other side – but still part of the same building – we find rubbish and squalor, people abroad on questionable errands at three in the morning, and that "blistered and disdained door" set in "a blind forehead of discoloured wall". On Jekyll's side, all things are in order and life goes its steady Apollonian round. On the other side, Dionysus prances unfettered. Enter Jekyll here, exit Hyde there.' King's *Danse Macabre* is, as one might have expected, one of the best analyses of the delights of horror, terror and the supernatural.

3 Stephen Knight (2004:10) highlights the 'sheer difficulty of conceiving of someone who, on his own, could inquire into crime and justice'. As we saw in the last chapter there was considerable opposition to the idea of official detectives (they were often regarded as government spies) well into the nineteenth century.

4 A theme initially explored by Wilkie Collins in *The Moonstone*, originally published in 1868, which can lay a claim to being the first full-length detective novel. The mystery here is not a murder but the theft of an Indian diamond, which was originally set in a Hindu idol; its connection to 'the East gives it a mystic, religious significance that is represented as inferior and the opposite of Western rationality' (McCracken, 1998:53).

5 Angela McRobbie (2005:173), for example, offers an extended commentary on the film and concludes that it 'postmodernizes psychoanalysis by drawing dream-type materials and fantasies up from underneath, right onto the surface and interspersing these segments with the twists and turns of the fragments of narrative'.

Chapter 6 Telling Stories

1 It is important to note that while the British police procedural has mostly treated the fictional detective kindly, documentary makers have taken a much more critical approach: *World in Action* (1985) ran a series of programmes exposing the framing of the Birmingham Six by the West Midlands Serious Crime Squad and, more recently, Mark Daly's *The Secret Policeman* (2003) covertly filmed racist recruits training to join the force.

2 Indeed, he details fourteen thematic differences, including the level of action, crime, violence, status, chronology and so forth, that distinguish 'media' cops from their 'real' counterparts (Perlmutter, 2000:41–52).

3 Eugene McLaughlin (2005b) has explored the deep cultural work that
   Ealing Studios undertook to develop the iconic image of Dixon in his first
   appearance on screen in the film *The Blue Lamp* (1950), which also
   offered audiences the young, violent 'cop killer' played by a menacing
   Dirk Bogarde in the immediate postwar period.
4 Of course, these were not the only films these directors made but they
   each, in different ways, set new standards for on-screen violence – bringing an operatic, apocalyptic quality to the carnage by using slow-motion
   action to convey the time caught between life and death, described as a
   "ballet of death" by those critics who saw not gratuitous bloodshed but a
   new poetic aesthetic in the ways these films constructed the relationships
   between action, music and tragedy.
5 A further series, *Ashes to Ashes* (2008) has recently been broadcast.
6 Likewise Ruggiero (2003:6) analyses literary classics like Cervantes's
   Rinconete and Cortadilo, John Gay's *The Beggar's Opera* and Brecht's *The
   Threepenny Opera* to show how many criminological theories appear in
   these works, where 'crime is associated with relative deprivation and
   Mertonian "innovation", but also with lack of control . . . and theories of
   organized crime'.

Chapter 7   Producing the News

1 The war in Vietnam was the first televised war and never before had the
   horrors of armed conflict been presented to media audiences in such
   graphic and relentless fashion. Susan Sontag (2003:58) describes how
   photojournalism came to provide normative criticism of the Vietnam war.
   The 1972 photograph of a naked Vietnamese girl running away from a
   village just napalmed by US planes is one the most distressing images
   from the era and brought home the terror of the indiscriminate killing.
   Since Vietnam many governments have learnt how to manage press coverage of armed conflict. In the 1982 British campaign in the Falklands,
   the prime minister Margaret Thatcher allowed only two pre-selected photographers access to the combat, with no direct television coverage per-
   mitted whatsoever – restrictions on press reporting that had not been seen
   since the Crimean War. Similar lessons from Vietnam had been learnt by
   the American military during the Gulf War in 1991, where the US authorities manipulated coverage to present images of a 'techno war' which
   depicted the combat as a video-game conflict where human casualties
   appeared only as animated explosions on computer screens, while
   euphemisms like 'surgical strike' and 'collateral damage' dominated press
   briefings. Since then American and British operations in Afghanistan and
   Iraq have been off limits to news photographers. That said, the Internet
   phenomenon of warblogging offers a very different kind of 'embedded'
   reporting – as in the case of the Baghdad Blogger – than conventional war
   journalism (see Allan, 2006:109–12).

2   It is significant that Derrida co-signed Habermas's (2006:48) essay 'February 15, or: What Binds Europeans' which invited a number of intellectuals to urgently respond to the US government's intention to attack Iraq in 2003 by repudiating Eurocentrism and reviving the Kantian memory of 'the moral foundations of politics'.

3   Robert Park (1923), a leading figure at the famous Department of Sociology at the University of Chicago was a former journalist and had pointed to the discipline's neglect of the newspaper as a social and cultural force in his article 'The Natural History of the Newspaper'. For Park the newspaper was an institution whose output and influence resulted from a complex interaction between readers and producers, where news is more than information but a means of securing social cohesion and is closely tied to the daily routines of urban life – a defining feature of his sociology.

4   The police had regularly visited the Wests' home in Cromwell Street before the discovery of the murders; while there were extensive records of the children's abuse at hospitals and social services, the 'veneer of the traditional family had actually hidden years of terrible sexual violence' (Wykes, 2001:178). Similarly the abduction and murder of ten-year-olds Holly Wells and Jessica Chapman – the dreadful story that dominated the British news media during August 2002 – reveals further problems with the dominant image of the paedophile. Ian Huntley, who was convicted of their murder, was known to the girls and the picture that has emerged after his conviction is 'of a man with a history of trying to control young women' (Boyle, 2005:73).

5   These mass-market monthly magazines have themselves been losing readers to *Zoo* and *Nuts* (both launched in 2004), which offer a weekly downmarket diet of 'topical gags', 'football coverage' and 'a bevy of big-breasted babes' (Turner, 2007:11).

Chapter 8   Revisiting Moral Panics

1   *Policing the Crisis* would lead Hall (1989) into a confrontation with the politics of Thatcherism over the next decade and he coined the term 'authoritarian populism' to describe the distinctive combination of popular social conservatism and free market economics that the Thatcher project aggressively invoked.

2   The judge ruled that covert video evidence of the prime suspects acting out racist attacks was inadmissible – a decision that drew further outraged headlines.

Conclusion

1   This led to heated debates between those who defined themselves as 'left realists' against the 'left idealists' (Young, 1986). Those identified as

'idealists' were quick to reject the label and argued that theirs was a 'criminology from below', critical of the authoritarian state developing under Thatcherism; they did produce interventionist work around controversial issues in prisons, policing, domestic violence and Northern Ireland on behalf of the marginalized. As one important collection put it: '[W]e are not saying that crime is not a problem for working-class people or that, contrary to the innuendo in some new realist writing, the terrible brutality suffered by many women is not a problem for them. Neither are we saying that the state cannot be reformed . . . What we are saying is that the new realist position on law and order is theoretically flawed and, from a socialist perspective, it remains politically conservative in its conclusions about what can be done about the state' (Sim *et al.*, 1987:59). This quote conveys well the close relationships between ontological dispute, political orientation and ethical responsibility.

2   Rather than dismissing astrology as simply irrational, he argued that the instrumental rationality of capitalist societies gives astrology a degree of coherence with which to provide the readers of columns the means of living with conditions beyond their apparent control. Yet for Adorno, astrology avoids fatalism. The reader of horoscope columns is continually exhorted to make choices, but in the end this is an empty autonomy as it produces social conformity. The column's implicit rule is that the reader must adjust to the command of the stars, while appealing to the narcissism of the individual by portraying the reader as someone able to change their circumstances through their personal "assets" (such as deploying "charm", "magnetism" or "intuition" in particular situations). The result is that individuality 'itself is submerged in the process of transformation of ends into means' (Adorno, 1975/94:83).

3   Baudrillard (1988:166) notes how 'the finest allegory of simulation' is 'the Borges tale where the cartographers of the Empire draw up a map so detailed that it ends up exactly covering the territory' and there are ancient accounts of painting, by the elder Pliny and others, which have 'stories of paintings of fruit which deceived birds into pecking at that fruit' (Brewster, 1987:145). We have also seen in chapter 6 how Aristotle's account of mimetic representation emphasized reflective emulation as the pinnacle of writing.

References

Abercrombie, N. (1996) *Television and Society*, Cambridge: Polity.

Abercrombie, N. and B. Longhurst (1998) *Audiences: A Sociological Theory of Performance and Imagination*, London: Sage.

Adorno, T. (1975/94) *The Stars Down to Earth and other Essays on the Irrational in Culture*, London: Routledge.

Adorno, T. and M. Horkheimer (1947/73) *Dialectic of Enlightenment*, London: Allen Lane.

Alexander, J. and R. Jacobs (1998) 'Mass Communication, Ritual and Civil Society', in Liebes, T. and J. Curran (eds) *Media, Ritual and Identity*, London: Routledge.

Allan, S. (2004) *News Culture*, Buckingham: Open University Press.

Allan, S. (2006) *Online News: Journalism and the Internet*, Maidenhead: Open University Press.

Allen, J., S. Livingstone and R. Reiner (1998) 'True Lies: Changing Images of Crime in British Postwar Cinema', in *European Journal of Communication*, Vol. 47, No. 4, pp. 1–13.

Allen, R. (2004) 'Psychoanalytic Film Theory', in Miller, T. and R. Stam (eds) *A Companion to Film Theory*, Oxford: Blackwell.

Altheide, D. (2002) *Creating Fear: News and the Construction of Crisis*, New York: Aldine de Gruyter.

Althusser, L. (1971) 'Ideological State Apparatuses', in Althusser, L. *Lenin and Philosophy*, London: New Left Books.

Anderson, B. (1991) *Imagined Communities: Reflections on the Origin and Spread of Nationalism*, London: Verso.

Anderson, P. (1991) *The Printed Image and the Transformation of Popular Culture, 1790–1860*, Oxford: Clarendon Press.

Ang, I. (1985) *Watching Dallas: Soap Opera and the Melodramatic Imagination*, London: Methuen.

Ang, I. (1991) *Desperately Seeking the Audience*, London: Routledge.

Aristotle (1996) *Poetics*, London: Penguin.

Arnold, M. (1869/1960) *Culture and Anarchy*, Cambridge: Cambridge University Press.

Atmore, C. (1998) 'Towards 2000: Child Sex Abuse and the Media', in Howe, A. (ed.) *Sexed Crime in the News*, Sydney: Federation Press.

Attwood, F. (2002) 'A Very British Carnival: Women, Sex and Transgression in *Fiesta* Magazine', in *Cultural Studies*, Vol. 5, No. 1, pp. 91–105.

Bakhtin, M. (1984) *Rabelais and His World*, Bloomington, IN: Indiana University Press.

Bandura, A. (1965) 'Influence of Models' Reinforcement Contingencies on the Acquisition of Imitative Responses', in *Journal of Personality and Social Psychology*, Vol. 1 pp. 589–95.

Bandura, A., D. Ross, and S. Ross (1961) 'Transmission of Aggression through Imitation of Aggressive Models', in *Journal of Abnormal and Social Psychology*, Vol. 63, pp. 575–82.

Bandura, A., D. Ross, and S. Ross (1963) 'Imitation of Film-Mediated Aggressive Models', in *Journal of Abnormal and Social Psychology*, Vol. 66, pp. 3–11.

Banks, M. (2005) 'Spaces of (in)security: Media and Fear of Crime in a Local Context', in *Crime, Media, Culture*, Vol. 1, No. 2, pp. 169–87.

Bannister, J. and N. Fyfe (2001) 'Introduction: Fear and the City', in *Urban Studies*, Vol. 38, Nos. 5–6, pp. 807–13.

Barker, M. (1997) 'The Newson Report: A Case Study in "Common Sense"', in Barker, M. and J. Petley (eds) *Ill Effects: The Media/Violence Debate*, London: Routledge.

Barker, M. and J. Petley (1997) 'Introduction', in Barker, M. and J. Petley (eds) (1997) *Ill Effects: The Media/Violence Debate*, London: Routledge.

Barnett, C. (2003) *Culture and Democracy: Media, Space and Representation*, Edinburgh: Edinburgh University Press.

Barrett, A. and C. Harrison (eds) (1999) *Crime and Punishment in England: A Sourcebook*, London: University College of London Press.

Barthes, R. (1953/77) *Writing Degree Zero*, New York: Hill and Wang.

Barthes, R. (1957/93) *Mythologies*, London: Village.

Barthes, R. (1966/77) 'Introduction to the Structural Analysis of Narrative', in *Image-Music-Text*, London: Fontana.

Barthes, R. (1968/77) 'Death of the Author', in *Image-Music-Text*, London: Fontana.

Barthes, R. (1970/5) *S/Z*, London: Jonathan Cape.

Barthes, R. (1973/5) *The Pleasure of the Text*, New York: Hill and Wang.

Barthes, R. (1977/90) *A Lover's Discourse: Fragments*, Harmondsworth: Penguin.

Baudrillard, J. (1985) 'The Ecstasy of Communication', in Foster, H. (ed.) *Postmodern Culture*, London: Pluto Press.

Baudrillard, J. (1988) *Jean Baudrillard: Selected Writings*, ed. M. Poster, Cambridge: Polity.

Baudrillard, J. (1995) *The Gulf War Did Not Take Place*, Sydney: Power Publications.

Baudrillard, J. (2001) *The Uncollected Baudrillard*, (ed.) G. Genosko, London: Sage.

Baudrillard, J. (2002) *The Spirit of Terrorism*, London: Verso.

Baudrillard, J. (2005) *The Intelligence of Evil*, Oxford: Berg.

Baudry, J.-L. (1974/92) 'Ideological Effects of the Basic Cinematographic Apparatus', in Mast, G., M. Cohen, and L. Braudy (eds) *Film Theory and Criticism: Introductory Readings*, 4th edn, Oxford: Oxford University Press.

Bauman, Z. (1993) *Postmodern Ethics*, Oxford: Blackwell.

Bauman, Z. (1994) *Life in Fragments: Essays in Postmodern Morality*, London: Blackwell.

Bauman, Z. (1998) *Globalization: The Human Consequences*, Cambridge: Polity.

Bauman, Z. (2006) *Liquid Fear*, Cambridge: Polity.

Beck, U. (1986) *The Risk Society: Towards a New Modernity*, London: Sage.

Becker, H. (1963) *Outsiders*, New York: Free Press.

Becker, H. (1982) *Art Worlds*, Berkeley: University of California Press.

Beetham, M. (1996) *A Magazine of Her Own?: Domesticity and Desire in the Woman's Magazine, 1800–1914*, London: Routledge.

Bell, I. (1992) *Literature and Crime in Augustan England*, London: Routledge.

Bell, V. (2002) 'The Vigilant(e) Parent and the Paedophile: The *News of the World* Campaign 2000 and the Contemporary Governmentality of Child Sexual Abuse', in *Feminist Theory*, Vol. 3, No. 1, pp. 83–102.

Benedict, H. (1992) *Virgin or Vamp: How the Press Covers Sex Crimes*, Oxford: Oxford University Press.

Benjamin, Walter (1983) *Charles Baudelaire: A Lyric Poet in the Era of High Capitalism*, London: Verso.

Bennett, T. (1981) *Popular Culture: Themes and Issues*, Milton Keynes: Open University Press.

Bennett, T. and J. Woollacott (1987) *Bond and Beyond: The Political Career of a Popular Hero*, Basingstoke: Macmillan.

Benson, R. and E. Neveu (2005) *Bourdieu and the Journalistic Field*, Cambridge: Polity.

Bertrand, I. and P. Hughes (2005) *Media Research Methods: Audiences, Institutions, Texts*, Basingstoke: Palgrave Macmillan.

Biressi, A. (2001) *Crime, Fear and the Law in True Crime Stories*, Basingstoke: Palgrave.

Black, J. (1987) *The English Press in the Eighteenth Century*, London: Croom Helm.

Bloch, E. (1965/96) *The Utopian Function of Art and Literature: Selected Essays*, Cambridge, MA: MIT Press.

Bondebjerg, I. (1996) 'Public Discourse/Private Fascination: Hybridization in "True-Life-Story" Genres', in *Media, Culture and Society*, Vol. 18, pp. 27–45.

Booker, C. (2004) *The Seven Basic Plots: Why We Tell Stories*, London: Continuum.

Boorstin, D. (1961/87) *The Image: A Guide to Pseudo-Events in America*, New York: Vintage Books.

Bourdieu, P. (1993) *The Field of Cultural Production*, Cambridge: Polity.

Bourdieu, P. (1993/2003) 'But Who Created the "Creators"?', in Tanner, J. (ed.) *The Sociology of Art: A Reader*, London: Routledge.

Bourdicu, P. (1996) *The Rules of Art*, Cambridge: Polity.

Bourdieu, P. (1998) *On Television and Journalism*, London: Pluto.

Box, S., C. Hale and G. Andrews (1988) 'Explaining Fear of Crime', in *British Journal of Criminology*, Vol. 28, pp. 340–56.

Boyle, K. (2005) *Media and Violence: Gendering the Debates*, London: Sage.

Brand, D. (1991) *The Spectator and the City in Nineteenth Century Literature*, Cambridge: Cambridge University Press.

Brewster, B. (1987) 'Film' in Cohn-Sherbok, D. and M. Irwin (eds) *Exploring Reality*, London: Unwin Hyman.

Briggs, A. and P. Burke (2005) *A Social History of the Media: From Gutenberg to the Internet*, 2nd edn. Cambridge: Polity.

Briggs, R. (1996) *Witches and Neighbours: The Social and Cultural Context of European Witchcraft*, London: HarperCollins.

Brown, S. (2003) *Crime and Law in Media Culture*, Buckingham: Open University Press.

Brown, S. (2005) *Understanding Youth and Crime: Listening to Youth?* 2nd edn. Buckingham: Open University Press.

Brownmiller, S. (1976) *Against Our Will: Men, Women and Rape*, London: Penguin.

Brunsdon, C. (1997) *Screen Tastes: Soap Opera to Satellite Dishes*, London: Routledge.

Brunsdon, C. (1998) 'Structure of Anxiety: Recent British Television Crime Fiction', in *Screen*, Vol. 39, No. 3, pp. 223–43.

Brunsdon, C., C. Johnson, R. Moseley and H. Wheatley (2001) 'Factual Entertainment on British Television: The Midlands TV Research Group's "8–9 Project"', in *European Journal of Cultural Studies*, Vol. 4, No. 1, pp. 29–62.

Brunsdon, C. and D. Morley (1978) *Everyday Television: Nationwide*, London: BFI.

Buckingham, D. (1987) *Public Secrets: EastEnders and its Audience*, London: BFI.

Buckingham, D. (2003) 'Children and Television: A Critical Overview of the Research', in Nightingale, V. and K. Ross (eds) *Critical Readings: Media and Audiences*, Maidenhead: Open University Press.

Cameron, D. and E. Frazer (1987) *The Lust to Kill: A Feminist Investigation of Sexual Murder*, Cambridge: Polity.

Campbell, A. (2005) 'Keeping the "Lady" Safe: The Regulation of Femininity through Crime Prevention Literature', in *Critical Criminology*, Vol. 13, pp. 119–40.

Campbell, J. (2005) *Film and Cinema Spectatorship*, Cambridge: Polity.

Carrabine, E. (2006) 'Punishment, Rights and Justice', in Morris, L. (ed.) *Rights: Sociological Perspectives*, London: Routledge.

Carrabine, E., P. Cox, M. Lee and N. South (2002) *Crime in Modern Britain*, Oxford: Oxford University Press.

Carrabine, E., P. Iganski, M. Lee, K. Plummer and N. South (2004) *Criminology: A Sociological Introduction*, London: Routledge.

Carter, A. (1979a) *The Sadeian Woman: An Exercise in Cultural History*, London: Virago.

Carter, A. (1979b) *The Bloody Chamber*, London: Penguin.

Carter, C. (1998) 'When the "Extraordinary" Becomes "Ordinary": Everyday News of Sexual Violence', in Carter, C., G. Branston and S. Allan (eds) *News, Gender and Power*, London: Routledge.

Carter, C., G. Branston and S. Allan (1998) 'Setting New(s) Agendas: An Introduction', in Carter, C., G. Branston and S. Allan (eds) *News, Gender and Power*, London: Routledge.

Carter, C. and K. Weaver (2003) *Violence and the Media*, Buckingham: Open University Press.

Castel, R. (2003) *L'Insécurité sociale. Qu'est-ce qu'être protégé*. Paris: Seuil.

Cavender, G. and S. Deutsch (2007) '*CSI* and Moral Authority: The Police and Science', in *Crime, Media, Culture*, Vol. 3, No. 1, pp. 67–81.

Cawelti, J. (1971) *The Six-Gun Mystique*, Bowling Green, OH: Bowling Green University Popular Press.

Charters, W. (1933) *Motion Pictures and Youth: A Summary*, New York: Macmillan.

Chaytor, H. (1945) *From Script to Print: An Introduction to Medieval Vernacular Literature*, London: Sidgwick and Jackson.

Chibnall, S. (1977) *Law and Order News*, London: Tavistock.

Chibnall, S. (1980) 'Chronicles of the Gallows: The Social History of Crime Reporting', in Christian, H. (ed.) *The Sociology of Journalism and the Press*, Sociological Review Monograph, 29, Keele: University of Keele.

Chiricos, T., S. Eschholz and M. Gertz (1997) 'Crime, News and Fear of Crime: Toward an Identification of Audience Effects', in *Social Problems*, Vol. 44, No. 3, pp. 342–57.

Chodorow, N. (1989) 'Toward a Relational Individualism: The Mediation of Self through Psychoanalysis', in *Feminism and Psychoanalytical Theory*, Cambridge: Polity Press.

Clark, K. (1992) 'The Linguistics of Blame: Representations of Women in *The Sun's* Reporting of Crimes of Sexual Violence', in Toolan, M. (ed.) *Language, Text and Context: Essays in Stylistics*, London: Routledge

Clark, S. (1997) *Thinking with Demons: The Idea of Witchcraft in Early Modern Europe*, Oxford: Clarendon Press.

Clarke, A. (1983) 'Holding the Blue Lamp: Television and the Police in Britain', in *Crime and Social Justice*, Vol. 19, pp. 44–51.

Clarke, A. (1986) ' "This is not the Boy Scouts": Television Police Series and Definitions of Law and Order', in Bennett, T., C. Mercer and J. Woollacott (eds) *Popular Culture and Social Relations*, Buckingham: Open University Press.

Clarke, J. (1996) 'Crime and Social Order: Interrogating the Detective Story', in Muncie, J. and E. McLaughlin (eds) *The Problem of Crime*, 1st edn. London: Sage.

Clarke, J. (2001) 'The Pleasures of Crime: Interrogating the Detective Story', in Muncie, J. and E. McLaughlin (eds) *The Problem of Crime*, 2nd edn. London: Sage.

Clemmer, D. (1958) *The Prison Community*. New York: Rinehart and Co.

Cloward, R. and L. Ohlin (1961) *Delinquency and Opportunity*, London: Routledge and Kegan Paul.

Cohen, A. (1955) *Delinquent Boys: The Culture of the Gang*, New York: Free Press.

Cohen, S. (ed.) (1971) *Images of Deviance*, Harmondsworth: Penguin Books.

Cohen, S. (1972/2002) *Folk Devils and Moral Panics: The Creation of the Mods and Rockers*, London: McGibbon and Kee.

Cohen, S. (1973) 'Mods and Rockers: the Inventory as Manufactured News', in Cohen and Young (1973b).

Cohen, S. (1980) 'Symbols of Trouble: Introduction to the New Edition', in *Folk Devils and Moral Panics*, 2nd edn. Oxford: Blackwell.

Cohen, S. (1985) *Visions of Social Control: Crime, Punishment and Classification*, Cambridge: Polity.

Cohen, S. (1996) 'Crime and Politics: Spot the Difference', in *British Journal of Sociology*, Vol. 47, No. 1, pp. 1–21.

Cohen, S. (2001) *States of Denial: Knowing about Atrocities and Suffering*, Cambridge: Polity.

Cohen, S. (2002) 'Moral Panics as Cultural Politics: Introduction to the Third Edition', in *Folk Devils and Moral Panics*, 3rd edn. London: Routledge.

Cohen, S. and Seu, B. (2002) 'Knowing Enough Not to Feel too Much: Emotional Thinking about Human Rights Appeals', in Bradley, P. and P. Petro (eds) *Truth Claims: Representation and Human Rights*, New Brunswick, NJ: Rutgers University Press.

Cohen, S. and Young, J. (1973a) 'Effects and Consequences' in Cohen and Young (1973b).

Cohen, S. and J. Young, (eds) (1973b) *The Manufacture of News*, London: Constable.

Coleman, C. (1993) 'The Influence of Mass Media and Interpersonal Communication on Societal and Personal Risk Judgements', in *Communication Research*, Vol. 20, No. 4, pp. 611–28.

Connell, I. (1985) 'Fabulous Powers: Blaming the Media', in Masterton, L. (ed.) *Television Mythologies*, London: Comedia.

Corner, J. (1991) 'Meaning, Genre and Context', in Curran, J. and M. Gurevitch (eds) *Mass Media and Society*, London: Edward Arnold.

Cottle, S. (2003) 'Media Organization and Production: Mapping the Field', in Cottle, S. (ed.) *Media Organization and Production*, London: Sage.

Cottle, S. (2004) *Media Performance and Public Transformation: The Racist Murder of Stephen Lawrence*, Westport, CT: Praeger.

Cottle, S. (2005) 'Mediatized Public Crisis and Civil Society Renewal: The Racist Murder of Stephen Lawrence', in *Crime, Media, Culture*, Vol. 1, No. 1, pp. 49–71.

Cottle, S. (2006) *Mediatized Conflict*, Maidenhead: Open University Press.

Craib, I. (2001) *Psychoanalysis: A Critical Introduction*, Cambridge: Polity Press.

Crawford, A., T. Jones and J. Young (1990) *The Second Islington Crime Survey*, London: Middlesex Polytechnic Centre for Criminology.

Cressy, D. (2000) *Travesties and Transgressions in Tudor and Stuart England: Tales of Discord and Dissension*, Oxford: Oxford University Press.

Critcher, C. (2003) *Moral Panics and the Media*, Buckingham: Open University Press.

Cross, S. (2005) 'Paedophiles in the Community: Inter-agency Conflict, News Leaks and the Local Press', in *Crime, Media, Culture*, Vol. 1, No. 3, pp. 284–300.

Cuklanz, L. (1996) *Rape on Trial: How the Mass Media Construct Legal Reform and Social Change*, Philadelphia: University of Pennsylvania Press.

Cuklanz, L. (2000) *Rape on Prime Time: Television, Masculinity and Sexual Violence*, Philadelphia, PA: University of Pennsylvania Press.

Culler, J. (1981) 'Story and Discourse in the Analysis of Narrative', in *The Pursuit of Signs: Semiotics, Literature, Deconstruction*, London: Routledge and Kegan Paul.

Culler, J. (1983) *Roland Barthes*, London: Fontana.

Cumberbatch, G., Woods, S., and Maguire, A. (1995) *Crime in the News: Television, Radio and Newspapers: A Report for BBC Broadcasting Research*, Birmingham: Aston University, Communications Research Group.

Curran, J. (1990) 'The "New Revisionism" in Mass Communication Research – a Reappraisal', in *European Journal of Communications*, Vol. 5, Nos 2–3, pp. 130–64.

Curran, J. (2003) 'Press History', in Curran, J. and J. Seaton (eds) *Power without Responsibility*, 6th edn. London: Routledge.

Davis, L. (1980) 'A Social History of Fact and Fiction: Authorial Disavowal in the Early English Novel', in Said, E. W. (ed.) *Literature and Society: Selected Papers from the English Institute*, Baltimore: Johns Hopkins University Press.

Davis, L. (1983) *Factual Fictions: The Origins of the English Novel*, New York: Columbia University Press.

De Beauvoir, S. (1949) *Le Deuxième Sexe*, Paris: Gallimard.

Dean, T. (2001) *Crime in Medieval Europe: 1200–1500*, Harlow: Pearson.

Debord, G. (1967/77) *Society of the Spectacle*, Detroit, MI: Black and Red Books.

Defoe, D. (1722/1989) *Moll Flanders*, London: Penguin Classics.

Deleuze, G. and F. Guattari (1972/1984) *Anti-Oedipus: Capitalism and Schizophrenia*, London: Athlone Press.

Denzin, N. and Y. Lincoln (eds) (2000) *Handbook of Qualitative Research*, London: Sage.

Derrida, J. (1980/2000) 'The Law of Genre', in Duff, D. (ed.) *Modern Genre Theory*, Harlow: Longman.

Derrida, J. (1994) *Specters of Marx*, London: Routledge.

Derrida, J. (2003) 'Autoimmunity: Real and Symbolic Suicides', in Borradori, G. (ed.) *Philosophy in a Time of Terror*, Chicago: University of Chicago Press.

Ditton, J. and J. Duffy (1983) 'Bias in the Newspaper Reporting of Crime', in *British Journal of Criminology*, Vol. 23, No. 2, pp. 159–65.

Ditton, J., J. Bannister, E. Gilchrist and S. Farrall (1999) 'Afraid or Angry? Recalibrating the "Fear" of Crime', in *International Review of Victimology*, Vol. 6, pp. 83–99.

Ditton, J., D. Chadee, S. Farrall, E. Gilchrist and J. Bannister (2004) 'From Imitation to Intimidation: A Note on the Curious and Changing Relationship between the Media, Crime and Fear of Crime', in *British Journal of Criminology*, Vol. 44, pp. 595–610.

Dobash, R. E., P. Schlesinger, R. Dobash and C. Weaver (1998) 'Crimewatch UK: Women's Interpretations of Televised Violence', in Fishman, M. and G. Cavender (eds) *Entertaining Crime: Television Reality Programs*, New York: Aldine du Gruyter.

Doob, A. and G. MacDonald (1979) 'Television Viewing and Fear of Victimisation', in *Journal of Personality and Social Psychology*, Vol. 37, No. 2, pp. 170–9.

Douglas, M. (1966) *Purity and Danger: an Analysis of Concepts of Pollution and Taboo*, London: Routledge and Kegan Paul.

Douglas, M. (1985) *Risk Acceptability According to the Social Sciences*, New York: Russell Sage Foundation.

Douglas, M. (1992) *Risk and Blame: Essays in Cultural Theory*, London: Routledge.

Du Gay, P., S. Hall, L. Janes, H. Mackay and K. Negus (1997) *Doing Cultural Studies: The Story of the Sony Walkman*, London: Sage.

Dyer, R. (1997) *White*, London: Routledge.

Eagleton, T. (1984) *The Function of Criticism*, London: Verso.

Eagleton, T. (1996) *Literary Theory: An Introduction*, Oxford: Blackwell.

Eaton, M. (1995) 'A Fair Cop? Viewing the Effects of the Canteen Culture in *Prime Suspect* and *Between the Lines*', in Kidd-Hewitt, D. and R. Osborne (eds) *Crime and the Media: the Post-modern Spectacle*, London: Pluto Press.

Eco, U. (1959/79) 'The Poetics of the Open Work', in *The Role of the Reader: Explorations in the Semiotics of Texts*, Bloomington: Indiana University Press.

Eco, U. (1979) 'Narrative Structures in Fleming', in *The Role of the Reader*, Bloomington: Indiana University Press.

Eco, U. (1990/2006) 'The *Poetics* and Us', in *On Literature*, London: Vintage.

Eisenstein, E. (1979) *The Printing Press as an Agent of Change*, 2 Volumes, Cambridge: Cambridge University Press.

Ellis, J. (1982) *Visible Fictions*, London: Routledge and Kegan Paul.

Epstein, E. (1973) *News from Nowhere: Television and the News*, New York: Random House.

Ericson, K. (1966) *Wayward Puritans*, New York: Wiley.

Ericson, R. (1991) 'Mass Media, Crime, Law, and Justice: An Institutional Approach', in *British Journal of Criminology*, Vol. 13, No. 3, pp. 219–49.

Erikson, R., P. Baranek and J. Chan (1987) *Visualizing Deviance: A Study of News Organization*, Milton Keynes: Open University Press.

Erikson, R., P. Baranek and J. Chan (1991) *Representing Order: Crime, Law, and Justice in the News Media*, Toronto: Toronto University Press.

Faller, L. (1987) *Turned to Account: The Forms and Functions of Criminal Biography in Late Seventeenth- and Early Eighteenth-century England*, Cambridge: Cambridge University Press.

Farrall, S. and D. Gadd (2004) 'Research Note: The Frequency of the Fear of Crime', in *British Journal of Criminology*, Vol. 44, pp. 127–32.

Featherstone, M. (1992) 'Postmodernism and the Aestheticization of Everyday Life', in Lash, S. and J. Freedman (eds) *Modernity and Identity*, Oxford: Blackwell.

Feeley, M. and J. Simon (2007) '*Folk Devils and Moral Panics*: An Appreciation from North America', in Downes, D. *et al.* (eds) *Crime, Social Control and Human Rights: From Moral Panics to States of Denial. Essays in Honour of Stanley Cohen*, Cullompton: Willan.

Fielder, L. (1982) *What was Literature?: Class Culture and Mass Society*, New York: Simon and Schuster.

Firestone, S. (1970) *The Dialectic of Sex: The Case for Feminist Revolution*, New York: Bantam.

Fishman, M. (1980) *Manufacturing the News*, Austin: University of Texas Press.

Fiske, J. (1982) *Introduction to Communication Studies*, London: Methuen.

Fiske, J. (1987) *Television Culture*, London: Methuen.

Fiske, J. (1989) 'Moments of Television: Neither the Text Nor the Audience', in Seiter, E., H. Borchers, G. Kreutzner and E. Warth (eds) *Remote Control*, London: Routledge.

Fiske, J. (1992) 'Popularity and the Politics of Information', in Dahlgren, P. and C. Sparks (eds) *Journalism and Popular Culture*, London: Sage.

Fiske, J. (1996) *Media Matters: Race and Gender in US Politics*, Minneapolis: University of Minnesota Press.

Fiske, J. and J. Hartley (1978) *Reading Television*, London: Methuen.

Foucault, M. (1966/94) *The Order of Things: An Archaeology of the Human Sciences*, New York: Vintage Books.

Foucault, M. (1977) *Discipline and Punish: The Birth of the Prison*, London: Allen Lane.

Foucault, M. (1979) *The History of Sexuality, Volume One: An Introduction*, London: Allen Lane.

Freedman, J. (2002) *Media Violence and Its Effect on Aggression: Assessing the Scientific Evidence*, Toronto: University of Toronto Press.

Fuery, P. (2000) *New Developments in Film Theory*, London: Macmillan.

Furedi, F. (1997) *The Culture of Fear: Risk Taking and the Morality of Low Expectations*, London: Cassell.

Furedi, F. (2001) *Paranoid Parenting: Abandon your Anxieties and Be a Good Parent*, Harmondsworth: Penguin

Furedi, F. (2007) 'The Only Thing we Have to Fear is the "Culture of Fear" Itself', in *Spiked* online, 4 April 2007, URL (accessed July 2007): http://www.spiked-online.com/index.php?/site/article/3053/.

Gans, H. (1979) *Deciding What's News*, New York: Pantheon.

Garafalo, J. (1979) 'Victimisation and the Fear of Crime', in *Journal of Research in Crime and Delinquency*, Vol. 16, pp. 80–97.

Gauntlett, D. (1995) *Moving Experiences: Understanding Television's Influences and Effects*, London: John Libbey.

Gauntlett, D. and A. Hill (1999) *TV Living: Television, Culture and Everyday Life*, London: Routledge.

Gerbner, G. (1970) 'Cultural Indicators: The Case of Violence in Television Drama', in *Annals of the American Association of Political and Social Science*, Vol. 338, pp. 69–81.

Gerbner, G. and L. Gross (1976) 'Living with Television: The Violence Profile', in *Journal of Communication*, Vol. 26, pp. 172–99.

Gerbner, G., L. Gross, M. Jackson-Beeck, S. Jeffries-Fox and N. Signorelli (1978) 'Cultural Indicators: Violence Profile no. 9', in *Journal of Communication*, Vol. 28, No. 3, pp. 176–207.

Gerbner, G., L. Gross, M. Morgan and N. Signorelli (1980) 'The Mainstreaming of America: Violence Profile no. 11', in *Journal of Communication*, Vol. 30, No. 3 pp. 10–29.

Gerbner, G., L. Gross, M. Morgan and N. Signorelli (1994) 'Growing Up with Television: The Cultivation Perspective', in Bryant, J. and D. Zillmann (eds) *Media Effects: Advances in Theory and Research*, Hillsdale, NJ: Lawrence Erlbaum Associates.

Gever, M. (2005) 'The Spectacle of Crime, Digitized: *CSI: Crime Scene Investigation* and Social Anatomy', in *European Journal of Cultural Studies*, Vol. 8, No. 4, pp. 445–63.

Giddens, A. (1990) *The Consequences of Modernity*, Cambridge: Polity Press.

Giddens, A. (1991) *Modernity and Self-Identity: Self and Society in the Late Modern Age*, Cambridge: Polity Press.

Gieber, W. (1964) 'News is what Newspapermen make it', in Dexter, L. and D. Manning (eds) *People, Society, and Mass Communications*, New York: Free Press.

Gilchrist, E., J. Bannister, J. Ditton and S. Farrall (1998) 'Women and the "Fear of Crime": Challenging the Accepted Stereotype', in *British Journal of Criminology*, Vol. 38, No. 2, pp. 283–98.

Gillespie, M. (1995) *Television, Ethnicity and Cultural Change*, London: Routledge.

Gillespie, M. and E. McLaughlin (2005) 'Consuming Crime and Avoiding Punishment: Media Influence in the Shaping of Public Perceptions of Crime and Sentencing', in Emsley, C. (ed.) *The Persistent Prison: Problems, Images and Alternatives*, London: Francis Boutle Publishers.

Gilroy, P. (1987) *There Ain't No Black in the Union Jack*, London: Hutchinson.

Girard, R. (1979) *Violence and the Sacred*, Baltimore: Johns Hopkins University.

Girard, R. (1986) *The Scapegoat*, Baltimore: Johns Hopkins University.

Girling, E., I. Loader and R. Sparks (2000) *Crime and Social Change in Middle England: Questions of Order in an English Town*, London: Routledge.

Gitlin, T. (2002) *Media Unlimited: How the Torrent of Images and Sounds Overwhelms our Lives*, New York: Henry Holt.

Gladfelder, H. (2001) *Criminality and Narrative in Eighteenth-Century England: Beyond the Law*, Baltimore: Johns Hopkins University Press.

Glaister, D. (2007) 'The Power of the Mobile Phone with its Shaky, Hand-held Video Footage', in *The Guardian*, 1 January 2007.

Glasgow Media Group (1976) *Bad News*, London: Routledge.

Glasgow Media Group (1980) *More Bad News*, London: Routledge.

Glasgow Media Group (1985) *War and Peace News*, London: Open University Press.

Goffman, E. (1962) *Asylums: Essays on the Social Situation of Mental Patients and other Inmates*, Harmondsworth: Penguin.

Goffman, E. (1986) *Frame Analysis: An Essay on the Organization of Experience*, Boston: Northeastern University Press.

Gomme, I. (1986) 'Fear of Crime among Canadians: A Multi-Variate Analysis', in *Journal of Criminal Justice*, Vol. 14, pp. 249–58.

Goode, E. and N. Ben-Yehuda (1994) *Moral Panics: The Social Construction of Deviance*, Oxford: Blackwell.

Goodey, J. (1997) 'Boys Don't Cry: Masculinities, Fear of Crime and Fearlessness', in *British Journal of Criminology*, Vol. 47, No. 3, pp. 401–18.

Goodey, J. (2005) *Victims and Victimology: Research, Policy and Practice*, Harlow: Pearson.

Gordon, M. and L. Heath (1981) 'The News Business, Crime, and Fear', in Lewis, D. (ed.) *Reactions to Crime*, London: Sage.

Gray, A. (1992) *Video Playtime: The Gendering of a Leisure Technology*, London: Routledge.

Greer, G. (1971) *The Female Eunuch*, London: Paladin.

Grella, G. (1988) 'The Formal Detective Novel', in Winks, R. (ed.) *Detective Fiction: A Collection of Critical Essays*, Woodstock, VT: Countryman Press.

Gunter, B. (1985) *Dimensions of Television Violence*, Aldershot: Gower.

Gurevitch, M., M. Levy and I. Roeh (1991) 'The Global News Room: Convergences and Divergences in the Globalization of Television News', in Dahlgren, P. and C. Sparks (eds) *Communication and Citizenship: Journalism and the Public Sphere in the New Media Age*, London: Routledge.

Gusfield, J. (1963) *Symbolic Crusade: Status Politics and the American Temperance Movement*, Urbana: University of Illinois Press.

Habermas, J. (1962/89) *The Structural Transformation of the Public Sphere*, Cambridge: Polity Press.

Habermas, J. (1985) 'Modernity – An Incomplete Project', in Foster, H. (ed.) *Postmodern Culture*, London: Pluto.

Habermas, J. (1989/2006) 'The Public Sphere: An Encyclopaedia Article', in Durham, M. and D. Kellner (eds) *Media and Cultural Studies: Keyworks*, Oxford: Blackwell.

Habermas, J. (1992) *The Structural Transformation of the Public Sphere: An Inquiry into a Category of Bourgeois Society*, Cambridge: Polity Press.

Habermas, J. (2006) *The Divided West*, Cambridge: Polity. Edited and translated by Ciarin Cronin.

Hale, C. (1996) 'Fear of Crime: A Review of the Literature', in *International Review of Victimology*, Vol. 4, pp. 79–150.

Hall, S. (1980a) 'Cultural Studies: Two Paradigms', in *Media, Culture and Society*, Vol. 2, pp. 57–72.

Hall, S. (1980b/2003) 'Encoding/Decoding', in Nightingale, V. and K. Ross (eds) *Critical Readings: Media and Audiences*, Maidenhead: Open University Press.

Hall, S. (1982) 'The Rediscovery of Ideology: Return of the Repressed in Media Studies', in Gurevitch, M., T. Bennett, J. Curran and J. Woollacott (eds) *Culture, Society and the Media*, London: Methuen.

Hall, S. (1989) 'Authoritarian Populism', in Jessop, B. *et al.* (eds) *Thatcherism*, Cambridge: Polity.

Hall, S., I. Connell and L. Curti (1976) 'The "Unity" of Current Affairs Television', CCCS, University of Birmingham, *Working Papers in Cultural Studies*, Spring (9), pp. 51–95.

Hall, S., C. Critcher, T. Jefferson, J. Clarke and B. Roberts (1978) *Policing the Crisis: Mugging, the State and Law and Order*, London: Macmillan.

Hallin, D. and P. Mancini (2004) *Comparing Media Systems: Three Models of Media and Politics*, Cambridge: Cambridge University Press.

Hamilton, J. (2004) *All the News that's Fit to Sell*, Princeton, NJ: Princeton University Press.

Hardy, S. (1998) *The Reader, The Author, His Woman and Her Lover: Soft-Core Pornography and Heterosexual Men*, London: Cassell.

Hartley, J. (1987) 'Invisible Fictions: Television Audiences, Paedocracy, Pleasure', in *Textual Practice*, Vol. 1, No. 2, pp. 121–38.

Hartley, J. (1999) *Uses of Television*, London: Routledge.

Hawkes, T. (1977) *Structuralism and Semiotics*, London: Methuen.

Heath, L. (1984) 'Impact of Newspaper Crime Reports on Fear of Crime: Multimethodological Investigation', in *Journal of Personality and Social Psychology*, Vol. 47, No. 2, pp. 263–76.

Heath, L. and K. Gilbert (1996) 'Mass Media and Fear of Crime', in *American Behavioural Scientist*, Vol. 39, No. 4, pp. 379–86.

Heath, L. and J. Petraitis (1987) 'Television Viewing and Fear of Crime: Where is the Mean World?', *Basic and Applied Social Psychology*, Vol. 8, Nos. 1–2, pp. 97–123.

Hebdige, D. (1979) *Subculture: The Meaning of Style*, London: Methuen.

Herman, E. and N. Chomsky (1988) *Manufacturing Consent: The Political Economy of the Mass Media*, New York: Pantheon.

Hermes, J. (1995) *Reading Women's Magazines*, Oxford: Polity.

Hermes, J. (2000) 'Of Irritation, Texts and Men: Feminist Audience Studies and Cultural Citizenship', in *International Journal of Cultural Studies*, Vol. 3, No. 3, pp. 351–67.

Hermes, J. (2005) *Re-reading Popular Culture*, Oxford: Blackwell.

Hermes, J. with C. Stello (2000) 'Cultural Citizenship and Crime Fiction: Politics and the Interpretive Community', in *European Journal of Cultural Studies*, Vol. 3, No. 2, pp. 215–32.

Hier, S. (2003) 'Risk and Panic in Late Modernity: Implications of the Converging Sites of Social Anxiety', in *British Journal of Sociology*, Vol. 54, no. 1, pp. 3–20.

Hirsch, F. (1999) *Detours and Lost Highways: A Map of Neo-Noir*, New York: Limelight Editions.

Hirsch, P. (1980) 'The "Scary World" of the Nonviewer and other Anomalies: A Reanalysis of Gerbner *et al.*'s Findings on the Cultivation Analysis, Part I', in *Communication Research*, Vol. 7, pp. 403–56.

Hirsch, P. (1981) 'On Not Learning from One's Mistakes: A Reanalysis of Gerbner *et al.*'s Findings on the Cultivation Analysis, Part II', in *Communication Research,*Vol. 8, pp. 3–37.

Hobsbawm, E. (1969/2001) *Bandits*, London: Abacus.

Hobson, D. (1982) *Crossroads: The Drama of a Soap Opera*, London: Hutchinson.

Hoggart, R. (1958) *The Uses of Literacy*, London: Penguin.

Hohendahl, P. (1982) *The Institution of Criticism*, Ithaca, NY: Cornell University Press.

Holland, P. (1998) 'The Politics of the Smile: "Soft News" and the Sexualisation of the Press', in Carter, C., G. Branston and S. Allan (eds) *News, Gender and Power*, London: Routledge.

Hollway, W. and T. Jefferson (1997) 'The Risk Society in an Age of Anxiety: Situating Fear of Crime', in *British Journal of Sociology*, Vol. 48, No. 2, pp. 255–66.

Hollway, W. and T. Jefferson (2000) 'The Role of Anxiety in Fear of Crime', in Hope, T. and R. Sparks (eds) *Crime, Risk and Insecurity*, London: Routledge.

Holohan, S. (2005) *The Search for Justice in a Media Age: Reading Stephen Lawrence and Louise Woodward*, Aldershot: Ashgate.

Hooker, E. (1963) 'Male Homosexuality', in Farberow, N. (ed.) *Taboo Topics*, New York: Prentice Hall.

Hope, T. and R. Sparks (2000) 'Introduction: Risk, Insecurity and the Politics of Law and Order', in Hope, T. and R. Sparks (eds) *Crime, Risk and Insecurity*, London: Routledge.

Hough, M. (1995) *Anxiety about Crime: Findings from the 1994 British Crime Survey*, Home Office Research Study 147, London: Home Office.

Howe, A. (ed.) (1998) *Sexed Crime in the News*, Sydney: Federation Press.

Hubbard, P. (2003) 'Fear and Loathing at the Multiplex: Everyday Anxiety in the Post-Industrial City', in *Capital and Class*, 80: 51–75.

Hughes, M. (1980) 'The Fruits of the Cultivation Analysis: A Reexamination of some Effects of Television Viewing', in *Public Opinion Quarterly*, Vol. 44, pp. 287–302.

Hunt, A. (1999) 'Anxiety and Social Explanation: Some Anxieties about Anxiety', in *Journal of Social History*, Vol. 32, No. 3, pp. 509–28.

Hurd, G. (1979) 'The Television Presentation of the Police', in Holdaway, S. (ed.) *The British Police*, London: Edward Arnold.

Hutchings, P. (2001) *The Criminal Spectre in Law, Literature and Aesthetics: Incriminating Subjects*, London: Routledge.

Information Centre about Asylum and Refugees in the UK (ICAR) Project Team (2004) *Media Image, Community Impact: Assessing the Impact of Media and Political Images of Refugees and Asylum-Seekers on Community Relations in London*, London: Information Centre About Asylum and Refugees in the UK, International Policy Institute, King's College London.

Innes, M. (2003) ' "Signal Crimes": Detective Work, Mass Media and Constructing Collective Memory', in Mason, P. (ed.) *Criminal Visions: Media Representations of Crime and Justice*, Cullompton: Willan.

Irigaray, L. (1985) *Speculum of the Other Woman*, Ithaca, NY: Cornell University Press.

Jameson, F. (1981/2000) 'Magical Narratives: On the Dialectical Use of Genre Criticism', in Duff, D. (ed.) *Modern Genre Theory*, Harlow: Longman.

Jancovich, M. (1995) 'Screen Theory', in Hollows, J. and M. Jancovich (eds) *Approaches to Popular Film*, Manchester: Manchester University Press.

Jancovich, M. and L. Faire with S. Stubbings (2003) *The Place of the Audience: Cultural Geographies of Film Consumption*, London: BFI.

Jenkins, P. (1992) *Intimate Enemies: Moral Panics in Contemporary Britain*, New York: Aldine de Gruyter.

Jenkins, P. (1998) *Moral Panic: Changing Concepts of the Child Molester in Modern America*, New Haven, CT: Yale University Press.

Jenkins, P. (2002) *Beyond Tolerance: Child Pornography on the Internet*, New York: New York University Press.

Jensen, K. B. and K. E. Rosengren (1990) 'Five Traditions in Search of the Audience', *European Journal of Communication* V, nos 2–3, pp. 207–38.

Jewkes, Y. (1999) 'Moral Panics in a Risk Society: A Critical Evaluation', *Crime, Order and Policing. Occasional Paper Series* No. 15, Scarman Centre, Leicester: University of Leicester.

Jewkes, Y. (2002) *Captive Audience: Media, Masculinity and Power in Prisons*, Cullompton: Willan.

Katz, E. and P. Lazarsfield (1955/2003) 'Movie Leaders', in Nightingale, V. and K. Ross (eds) *Critical Readings: Media and Audiences*, Maidenhead: Open University Press.

Katz, J. (1987) 'What Makes Crime "News"?', in *Media, Culture and Society*, Vol. 9, pp. 47–75

Kay, S. (2003) *Žižek: A Critical Introduction*, Cambridge: Polity.

Keane, J. (1996) *Reflections on Violence*, London: Verso.

Kelly, L. (1996) 'Weasel Words: Paedophiles and the Cycle of Abuse', in *Trouble and Strife*, Vol. 33: 44–9.

Kilborn, R. (1992) *Television Soaps*, London: Batsford.

Killias, M. and C. Clerici (2000) 'Different Measures of Vulnerability in their Relation to Different Dimensions of Fear of Crime', in *British Journal of Criminology*, Vol. 40, pp. 437–50.

King. A. and S. Maruna (2006) 'The Function of Fiction for a Punitive Public', in Mason, P. (ed.) *Captured by the Media: Prison Discourse in Popular Culture*, Cullompton: Willan.

King, S. (1981) *Danse Macabre*, London: Futura.

Kitzinger, J. (1993) 'Understanding AIDS: Researching Audience Perceptions of Acquired Immune Deficiency Syndrome', in Glasgow Media Group (eds) *Getting the Message: News, Truth and Power*, London: Routledge.

Kitzinger, J. (1998) 'The Gender-Politics of News Production: Silenced Voices and False Memories', in Carter, C., G. Branston and S. Allan (eds) *News, Gender and Power*, London: Routledge.

Kitzinger, J. (1999a) 'A Sociology of Media Power: Key Issues in Audience Reception Research', in Philo, G. (ed) *Message Received: Glasgow Media Group Research 1993–1998*, London: Longman.

Kitzinger, J. (1999b) 'The Ultimate Neighbour from Hell? The Media Representation of Paedophilia', in Franklin, B. (ed.) *Social Policy, the Media and Misrepresentation*, London: Routledge.

Kitzinger, J. (2004) *Framing Abuse: Media Influence and Public Understanding of Sexual Violence Against Children*, London: Pluto Press.

Knelman, J. (1998) *Twisting in the Wind: The Murderess and the English Press*, Toronto: University of Toronto Press.

Knight, S. (2004) *Crime Fiction, 1800–2000: Detection, Death, Diversity*, Basingstoke: Palgrave Macmillan.

Kornhauser, W. (1959) *The Politics of Mass Society*, New York: Free Press.

Kuhn, A. (1982) *Women's Pictures*, London: Routledge and Kegan Paul.

Lacan, J. (1977) *Ecrits: A Selection*, London: Tavistock.

Lacey, N. (2000) *Narrative and Genre: Key Concepts in Media Studies*, London: Macmillan.

Lake, P. (1993) 'Deeds against Nature: Cheap Print, Protestantism and Murder in Early Seventeenth Century England', in Sharpe, K. and P. Lake (eds) *Culture and Politics in Early Stuart England*, Basingstoke: Macmillan.

Langbein, J. H. (1983) 'Shaping the Eighteenth-Century Criminal Trial: A View from the Ryder Sources', *University of Chicago Law Review*, Vol. 5, No. 1, pp. 1–136.

Lauer, J. (2005) 'Driven to Extremes: Fear of Crime and the Rise of the Sport Utility Vehicle in the United States', in *Crime, Media, Culture*, Vol. 1, No. 2, pp. 149–68.

Law, A. and W. McNeish (2007) 'Contesting the New Irrational Actor Model: A Case Study of Mobile Phone Mast Protest', in *Sociology*, Vol. 41, No. 3, pp. 439–56.

Lawler, S. (2002) 'Mobs and Monsters: Independent Man Meets Paulsgrove Woman', in *Feminist Theory*, Vol. 3, No. 1, pp. 103–13.

Lawrence, G. (2000) *The Politics of Force: Media and the Construction of Police Brutality*, Berkeley: University of California Press.

Lazarsfeld, P., B. Berelson and H. Gaudet (1948) *The People's Choice*, New York: Columbia University Press.

Lee, M. (2001) 'The Genesis of "Fear of Crime"', in *Theoretical Criminology*, Vol. 5, No. 4, pp. 467–85.

Leishman, F. and P. Mason (2003) *Policing and the Media: Facts, Fictions and Factions*, Devon: Willan.

Leitch, T. (2002) *Crime Films*, Cambridge: Cambridge University Press.

Lemert, E. (1951) *Social Pathology*, New York: McGraw-Hill.

Lemert, E. (1967) *Human Deviance, Social Problems and Social Control*, Englewood Cliffs, NJ: Prentice Hall.

Leps, M.C. (1992) *Apprehending the Criminal: The Production of Deviance in Nineteenth-Century Discourse*, London: Duke University Press.

Lévi-Strauss, C. (1950/68) *Structural Anthropology*, Vol. 1, Harmondsworth: Penguin.

Lévi-Strauss, C. (1955/73) *Triste Tropiques*, London: Jonathan Cape.

Lévi-Strauss, C. (1964/92) *The Raw and the Cooked: Introduction to the Study of Mythology*, Harmondsworth: Penguin.

Lévi-Strauss, C. (1966) *The Savage Mind*, London: Weidenfield and Nicolson.

Lévi-Strauss, C. (1977) *Structural Anthropology*, Vol. 2, London: Allen Lane.

Lévinas, E. (1969) *Totality and Infinity: An Essay on Exteriority*, Pittsburgh, PA: Duquesne University Press.

Levinson, P. (1999) *Digital McLuhan: A Guide to the Information Millenium*, London: Routledge.

Liebes, T. (2005) 'Viewing and Reviewing the Audience: Fashions in Communication Research', in Curran, J. and M. Gurevitch (eds) *Mass Media and Society*, London: Hodder Arnold.

Liebes, T. and E. Katz (1993) *The Export of Meaning: Cross-Cultural Readings of Dallas*, Cambridge: Polity Press.

Linebaugh, P. (1977) 'The Ordinary of Newgate and his *Account*', in Cockburn, J. (ed.) *Crime in England 1550–1800*, London.

Linebaugh, P. (2003) *The London Hanged: Crime and Civil Society in the Eighteenth Century*, London: Verso.

Liska, A. and W. Baccaglini (1990) 'Feeling Safe by Comparison: Crime in the Newspapers', in *Social Problems*, Vol. 37, no. 3, pp. 360–74.

Lister, M., J. Dovey, S. Giddings, I. Grant, K. Kelly (2003) *New Media: A Critical Introduction*, London: Routledge.

Livingstone, S. (1996) 'On the Continuing Problem of Media Effects', in Curran, J. and M. Gurevitch (eds) *Mass Media and Society*, London: Arnold.

Livingstone, S. (2002) *Young People and New Media*, London: Sage.

Livingstone, S., J. Allen and R. Reiner (2001) 'Audiences for Crime Media 1946–91: A Historical Approach to Reception Studies', *The Communication Review*, Vol. 4, No. 2, pp. 165–92.

Longhurst, B. (2007a) *Cultural Change and Ordinary Life*, Berkshire: Open University Press.

Longhurst, B. (2007b) *Popular Music and Society*, Cambridge: Polity. 2nd edn.

Lotz, A. (2000) 'Assessing Qualitative Television Audience Research: Incorporating Feminist and Anthropological Innovation', in *Communication Theory* X, no. 4, pp. 447–67.

Lull, J. (1990) *Inside Family Viewing*, London: Routledge.

Lupton, D. (1999) 'Introduction: Risk and Sociocultural Theory', in Lupton, D. (ed.) *Risk and Sociolcultural Theory: New Directions and Perspectives*, Cambridge: Cambridge University Press.

Lupton, D. and J. Tulloch (1999) 'Theorizing Fear of Crime: Beyond the Rational/Irrational Opposition', in *British Journal of Sociology*, Vol. 50, No. 3, pp. 507–23.

Lury, K. (2005) *Interpreting Television*, London: Hodder Arnold.

MacDonald, M. (2006) 'Empire and Communication: the Media Wars of Marshall McLuhan', in *Media, Culture and Society*, Vol. 28, No. 4. pp. 505–20.

Mace, J. (1992) 'Television and Metaphors of Literacy', in *Studies in the Education of Adults*, Vol. 24, No. 2, pp. 176–87.

Mandel, E. (1984) *Delightful Murder*, London: Pluto.

Manguel, A. (1996) *A History of Reading*, New York: Viking.

Manning, P. (2001) *News and News Sources: A Critical Introduction*, London: Sage.

Marcuse, H. (1972) *One Dimensional Man*, London: Abacus.

Marlière, P. (1998) 'The Rules of the Journalistic Field', in *European Journal of Communication*, Vol. 13, No. 2, pp. 219–34.

Mathiesen, T. (1997) 'The Viewer Society: Michel Foucault's "Panopticon" Revisited', in *Theoretical Criminology*, Vol. 1, No. 2, pp. 215–34.

Matthews, J. (2003) 'Cultures of Production: The Making of Children's News', in Cottle, S. (ed.) *Media Organization and Production*, London: Sage.

Matza, D. (1964) *Delinquency and Drift*. New York: Wiley.

Matza, D. (1969) *Becoming Deviant*, Englewood Cliffs, NJ: Prentice Hall.

Mawby, R. (2003) 'Completing the "Half-formed Picture"? Media Images of Policing', in Mason, P. (ed.) *Criminal Visions: Media Representations of Crime and Justice*, Cullompton: Willan.

Maxfield, M. (1984) *Fear of Crime in England and Wales*, London: HMSO.

Mayhew, P. (1989) *The 1988 British Crime Survey*, Home Office Research Study no. 111, London: HMSO.

Mayhew, P. and M. Hough (1988) 'The British Crime Survey: Origins and Impact', in Maguire, M. and J. Pointing (eds) *Victims of Crime: A New Deal?*, Milton Keynes: Open University Press.

Mayne, J. (1993) *Cinema and Spectatorship*, London: Routledge.

McCahill, M. (2003) 'Media Representations of Visual Surveillance', in Mason, P. (ed.) *Criminal Visions: Media Representations of Crime and Justice*, Cullompton: Willan.

McCall, A. (2004) *The Medieval Underworld*, Stroud: Sutton.

McCracken, S. (1998) *Pulp: Reading Popular Fiction*, Manchester: Manchester University Press.

McGuigan, J. (1992) *Cultural Populism*, London: Routledge.

McIntosh, M. (1971) 'Changes in the Organization of Thieving', in Cohen, S. (ed.) *Images of Deviance*, Hardmonsworth: Penguin Books.

McKeon, M. (1987) *The Origins of the English Novel, 1600–1740*, Baltimore: Johns Hopkins University.

McLaughlin, E. (2005a) 'Recovering Blackness – Repudiating Whiteness: The *Daily Mail*'s Construction of the Five White Suspects Accused of the Racist Murder of Stephen Lawrence', in Murji, K. and J. Solomos (eds) *Racialization: Studies in Theory and Practice*, Oxford: Oxford University Press.

McLaughlin, E. (2005b) 'From Reel to Ideal: *The Blue Lamp* and the Popular Cultural Construction of the English "Bobby" ', in *Crime, Media, Culture*, Vol. 1, No. 1, pp. 11–30.

McLuhan, M. (1964) *Understanding Media: The Extensions of Man*, New York: Signet.

McNamee, S. (1998) 'Youth, Gender and Video Games: Power and Control in the Home', in Skelton, T. and G. Valentine (eds) *Cool Places: Geographies of Youth Cultures*, London: Routledge.

McRobbie, A. (1994) *Postmodernism and Popular Culture*, London: Routledge.

McRobbie, A. (2005) *The Uses of Cultural Studies*, London: Sage.

McRobbie, A. (2006) 'Vulnerability, Violence and (Cosmopolitan) Ethics: Butler's *Precarious Life*', in *The British Journal of Sociology*, Vol. 57, No. 1, pp. 69–86.

McRobbie, A. and S. Thornton (1995) 'Rethinking "Moral Panic" for Multi-mediated Social Worlds', in *British Journal of Sociology*, Vol. 46, No. 4, pp. 559–74.

Merrin, W. (2005) *Baudrillard and the Media*, Cambridge: Polity.

Messent, P. (1997) 'Introduction: From Private Eye to Police Procedural – The Logic of Contemporary Crime Fiction', in Messent, P. (ed.) *Criminal Proceedings: The Contemporary American Crime Novel*, London: Pluto.

Metz, C. (1982) *Psychoanalysis and Cinema: The Imaginary Signifier*, Bloomington: Indiana University Press.

Meyers, M. (1997) *News Coverage of Violence Against Women: Engendering Blame*, London: Sage.

Miliband, R. (1969) *The State in Capitalist Society: The Analysis of the Western System of Power*, London: Quartet.

Miller, D. (1994) *Don't Mention the War: Northern Ireland, Propaganda and the Media*, London: Pluto Press.

Miller, D. and G. Philo (1999) 'The Effective Media', in Philo, G. (ed.) *Message Received: Glasgow Media Group Research 1993–1998*, Harlow: Longman.

Millett, K. (1969) *Sexual Politics*, New York: Doubleday.

Modleski, T. (1988) *The Woman Who Knew Too Much: Hitchcock and Feminist Film Theory*, New York: Methuen.

Molotch, H. and M. Lester (1974) 'News as Purposive Behaviour: On the Strategic Use of Routine Events, Accidents and Scandals', in *American Sociological Review*, Vol. 39, pp. 101–12.

Monk, C. (1999) 'From Underworld to Underclass: Crime and British Cinema in the 1990s', in Chibnall, S. and R. Murphy (eds) *British Crime Cinema*, London: Routledge.

Moretti, F. (1983) *Signs Taken for Wonders: On the Sociology of Literary Forms*, London: Verso.

Morgan, M. and N. Signorelli (1990) 'Cultivation Analysis: Conceptualization and Methodology', in Signorelli, N. and M. Morgan (eds) *Cultivation Analysis: New Directions in Media Effects Research*, London: Sage.

Morgan, R. (1980) 'Theory and Practice: Pornography and Rape', in Lederer, L. (ed.) *Take Back the Night: Women on Pornography*, New York: William Morrow.

Morley, D. (1980) *The Nationwide Audience: Structure and Decoding*, London: BFI.

Morley, D. (1986) *Family Television: Cultural Power and Domestic Leisure*, London: Camedia.

Morley, D. (1992) *Television, Audiences and Cultural Studies*, London: Routledge.

Morley, D. (1996) 'Theories of Consumption in Media Studies', in Miller, D. (ed.) *Acknowledging Consumption*, London: Routledge.

Morris, M. (1990) 'The Banality of Cultural Studies', in Mellenkamp, P. (ed.) *Logics of Television: Essays in Cultural Criticism*, London: BFI.

Morrison, B. (1997) *As If*, London: Granta.

Mulvey, L. (1975/1992) 'Visual Pleasure and Narrative Cinema', in Mast, G., M. Cohen and L. Braudy (eds) *Film Theory and Criticism: Introductory Readings*, 4th edn, Oxford: Oxford University Press.

Mulvey, L. (1990) 'Afterthoughts on "Visual Pleasure and Narrative Cinema" inspired by *Duel in the Sun*', in Bennett, T. (ed.) *Popular Fiction: Technology, Ideology, Production, Reading*, London: Routledge.

Murdock, G. (1995) 'Across the Great Divide: Cultural Analysis and the Condition of Democracy', in *Critical Studies in Mass Communications*, Vol. 12, pp. 89–95.

Murdock, G. (1997) 'Reservoirs of Dogma: an Archaeology of Popular Anxieties', in Barker, M. and J. Petley (eds) *Ill Effects: The Media/Violence Debate*, London: Routledge.

Murdock, G. and P. Golding (2005) 'Culture, Communication and Political Economy', in Curran, J. and M. Gurevitch (eds) *Mass Media and Society*, 4th edn. Oxford: Oxford University Press.

Nava, M. (1988) 'Cleveland and the Press: Outrage and Anxiety in the Reporting of Child Sexual Abuse', in *Feminist Review*, Vol. 28, pp. 103–22.

Neale, S. (1993) 'Masculinity as Spectacle: Reflections on Men and Mainstream Cinema', in Cohan, S. and I. Hark (eds) *Screening the Male: Exploring Masculinities in Hollywood Cinema*, London: Routledge.

Nelson, W. (1973) *Fact or Fiction: The Dilemma of the Renaissance Storyteller*, Cambridge, MA: Harvard University Press.

Nightingale, V. (1996) *Studying Audiences: The Shock of the Real*, London: Routledge.

Nightingale, V. and K. Ross (2003) 'Introduction', in Nightingale, V. and K. Ross (eds) *Critical Readings: Media and Audiences*, Maidenhead: Open University Press.

Norris, C. (1992) *Uncritical Theory: Postmodernism, Intellectuals, and the Gulf War*, London: Lawrence and Wishart.

Norton, R. (1992) *Mother Clap's Molly House: The Gay Subculture in England, 1700–1830*, London: Chalford Press.

O'Donnell, I. and C. Milner (2007) *Child Pornography: Crime, Computers and Society*, Cullompton: Willan.

O'Keefe, G. and K. Reid-Nash (1987) 'Crime News and Real-World Blues: The Effects of the Media on Social Reality', in *Communication Research*, Vol. 14, No. 2, pp. 147–63.

O'Mahony, D. and K. Quinn (1999) 'Fear of Crime and Locale: The Impact of Community Related Factors upon Fear of Crime', in *International Review of Victimology*, Vol. 6, pp. 231–51.

O'Toole, L. (1998) *Pornocopia: Porn, Sex, Technology and Desire*, London: Serpent's Tail.

Palmer, G. (1998) 'The New Spectacle of Crime', in *Information, Communication and Society*, Vol. 1, No. 4, pp. 361–81.

Palmer, G. (2000) 'Governing Through Crime: Surveillance, the Community and Local Crime Programming', in *Policing and Society*, Vol. 10, pp. 321–42.

Pantazis, C. (2000) ' "Fear of Crime", Vulnerability and Poverty: Evidence from the British Crime Survey', in *British Journal of Criminology*, Vol. 40, pp. 414–36.

Park, R. (1923) 'The Natural History of the Newspaper', in *American Journal of Sociology*, Vol. 29, No. 3, pp. 273–89.

Parkin, F. (1973) *Class Inequality and Political Order*, London: Paladin.

Parris, M. (1998) 'Call Off the Lynch Mob', in *The Times*, 10 April.

Patterson, C. (1998) 'Global Battlefields', in Boyd-Barrett, O. and T. Rantanen (eds) *The Globalization of News*, London: Sage.

Pearson, G. (1983) *Hooligan: A History of Respectable Fears*, London: Macmillan.

Perlmutter, D. (2000) *Policing the Media: Street Cops and Public Perceptions of Law Enforcement*, London: Sage.

Philo, G. (1990) *Seeing and Believing*, London: Routledge.

Philo, G. (1996) 'The Media and Public Belief', in Philo, G. (ed.) *Media and Mental Distress*, London: Longman.

Philo, G. and M. Berry (2004) *Bad News from Israel*, London: Pluto Press.

Picard, L. (2003) *Elizabeth's London: Everyday Life in Elizabethan London*, London: Orion.

Picard, R. (1965) *Nouvelle critique ou nouvelle imposture*, Paris: Pauvert.

Plummer, K. (1995) *Telling Sexual Stories: Power, Change and Social Worlds*, London: Routledge.

Postman, N. (1986) *Amusing Ourselves to Death: Public Discourse in the Age of Showbusiness*, London: Methuen.

Pribram, D. (2004) 'Spectatorship and Subjectivity', in Miller, T. and R. Stam (eds) *A Companion to Film Theory*, Oxford: Blackwell.

Propp, V. (1928/1968) *The Morphology of the Folktale*, Austin: University of Texas Press.

Radway, J. (1988) 'Reception Study: Ethnography and the Problems of Dispersed Audiences and Nomadic Subjects', in *Cultural Studies*, Vol. 2, No. 3, pp. 359–76.

Rafter, N. (2000) *Shots in the Mirror: Crime Films and Society*, Oxford: Oxford University Press.

Rafter, N. (2007) 'Crime, Film and Criminology: Recent Sex-Crime Movies', in *Theoretical Criminology*, Vol. 11, No. 3, pp. 403–20.

Raphael, C. (2004) 'The Political Origins of Reali-TV', in Murray, S. and L. Ouellette (eds) *Reality TV: Remaking TV Culture*, New York: New York University Press.

Rawlings, P. (1992) *Drunks, Whores and Idle Apprentices: Criminal Biographies of the Eighteenth Century*, London: Routledge.

Rawlings, P. (1998) 'True Crime' in *British Criminology Conferences*, Vol. 1. www.britsoccrim.org/volume1/010.pdf. Accessed 09/06/08.

Reiner, R. (1985, 1992) *The Politics of the Police*, 1st and 2nd edns, Hemel Hempstead: Wheatsheaf.

Reiner, R. (2002) 'Media Made Criminality: The Representation of Crime in the Mass Media', in Maguire, M., R. Morgan, and R. Reiner (eds) *The Oxford Handbook of Criminology*, 3rd edn. Oxford: Oxford University Press.

Reiner, R. (2007) 'Media-Made Criminality: The Representation of Crime in the Mass Media', in Maguire, M., R. Morgan and R. Reiner (eds) *The Oxford Handbook of Criminology*, 4th edn. Oxford: Oxford University Press.

Reiner, R., S. Livingstone and J. Allen (2000) 'No More Happy Endings? The Media and Popular Concern about Crime since the Second World War', in Hope, T. and R. Sparks (eds) *Crime, Risk and Insecurity*, London: Routledge.

Reiner, R., S. Livingstone and J. Allen (2001) 'Casino Culture: Media and Crime in a Winner-Loser Society', in Stenson, K. and R. R. Sullivan (eds) *Crime, Risk and Justice: The Politics of Crime Control in Liberal Democracies*, Cullompton: Willan.

Reiner, R., S. Livingstone and J. Allen (2003) 'From Law and Order to Lynch Mobs: Crime News since the Second World War', in Mason, P. (ed.) *Criminal Visions: Media Representations of Crime and Justice*, Cullompton: Willan.

Reisman, D. (1953) *The Lonely Crowd*, Garden City, NY: Doubleday.

Richetti, J. (1996) 'Introduction', in Richetti, J. (ed.) *The Cambridge Companion to the Eighteenth Century Novel*, Cambridge: University of Cambridge Press.

Rixon, P. (2003) 'The Changing Face of American Television Programmes on British Screens', in Jancovich, M. and J. Lyons (eds) *Quality Popular Television*, London: BFI.

Robertson, G. (2000) *Crimes against Humanity: The Struggle for Global Justice*, London: Penguin.

Rock, P. (1973) 'News as Eternal Recurrence', in Cohen, S. and J. Young (eds) *The Manufacture of News: Deviance, Social Problems and the Mass Media*, London: Constable.

Rogers, P. (1972) *Grub Street: Studies in a Subculture*, London: Methuen.

Root, J. (1986) *Open the Box*, London: Comedia.

Ross, K. and V. Nightingale (2003) *Media and Audiences: New Perspectives*, Buckingham: Open University Press.

Ruddock, A. (2001) *Understanding Audiences:Theory and Method*, London: Sage.

Ruggiero, V. (2003) *Crime in Literature: Sociology of Deviance and Fiction*, London: Verso.

Ryall, T. (1975) 'Teaching through Genre', *Screen Education*, no. 17, pp. 25–35.

Sacco, V. (1982) 'The Effects of Mass Media on Perceptions of Crime: A Reanalysis of the Issues', in *Pacific Sociological Review*, Vol. 25, No. 4, pp. 475–93.

Sacco, V. (1995) 'Media Constructions of Crime', in *Annals of the American Academy of Political and Social Science*, Vol. 39, pp. 141–55.

Santos, J. (1997) '(Re)imagining America', in Dennis, E. and E. Pease (eds) *The Media in Black and White*, Brunswick, NJ: Transaction.

Sayer, A. (2005) *The Moral Significance of Class*, Cambridge: Cambridge University Press.

Schechter, H. (2005) *Savage Pastimes: A Cultural History of Violent Entertainment*, New York: St Martins Press.

Scheff, T. (1966) *Being Mentally Ill*, London: Weidenfeld and Nicolson.

Schlesinger, P. and H. Tumber (1994) *Reporting Crime:The Media Politics of Criminal Justice*, Oxford: Clarendon Press.

Schlesinger, P., H. Tumber and G. Murdock (1991) 'The Media Politics of Crime and Criminal Justice', in *British Journal of Sociology*, Vol. 41, No. 3, pp. 397–420.

Schmid, D. (2005) *Natural Born Killers: Serial Killers in American Culture*, Chicago, IL: University of Chicago Press.

Schubart, R. (1995) 'From Desire to Deconstruction: Horror Films and Audience Reactions', in Kidd-Hewitt, D. and R. Osborne (eds) *Crime and the Media:The Post-Modern Spectacle*, London: Pluto Press.

Schudson, M. (2005) 'Four Approaches to the Sociology of News', in Curran, J. and M. Gurevitch (eds) *Mass Media and Society*, 4th edn. Oxford: Oxford University Press.

Schur, E. (1963) *Narcotic Addiction in Britain and America*, London: Tavistock.

Scraton, P., J. Sim and P. Skidmore (1991) *Prisons Under Protest*, Milton Keynes: Open University Press.

Seaman, W. (1992) 'Active Audience Theory: Pointless Populism', in *Media, Culture and Society*, Vol. 14, No. 2, pp. 301–12.

Seaton, J. (2003) 'The Sociology of the Mass Media', in Curran, J. and J. Seaton (eds) *Power without Responsibility*, 6th edn. London: Routledge.

Segal, L. (1992) 'Introduction', in Segal, L. and M. McIntosh (eds) *Sex Exposed: Sexuality and the Pornography Debate*, London: Virago Press.

Seiter, E. (1999) *Television and New Media Audiences*, Oxford: Oxford University Press.

Sennett, R. (1990) *The Conscience of the Eye*, London: Faber.

Shaaber, M. (1922) *Some Forerunners of the Newspaper in England 1476–1622*, Philadelphia: University of Pennsylvania Press.

Shapland, J. and J. Vagg (1988) *Social Control and Policing in Rural and Urban Areas*, Oxford: University of Oxford Centre for Criminological Research.

Sharpe, J. A. (1984) *Crime in Early Modern England*, London: Longman.

Sharpe, J. A. (1987) ' "Last Dying Speeches": Religion, Ideology and Public Execution in Seventeenth Century England', in *Past and Present*, Vol. 107, pp. 144–67.

Shepherd, L. (1972) *The History of Street Literature*, Newton Abbot: David and Charles.

Shields, R. (1991) *Places on the Margin: Alternative Geographies of Modernity*, London: Routledge.

Sigel, L. (2002) *Governing Pleasures: Pornography and Social Change in England, 1815–1914*, London: Rutgers University Press.

Silverman, J. and D. Wilson (2002) *Innocence Betrayed: Paedophilia, the Media and Society*, Cambridge: Polity.

Silverstone, R. (1994) *Television and Everyday Life*, London: Routledge.

Silverstone, R. (1999) *Why Study the Media?*, London: Sage.

Sim, J., P. Scraton and P. Gordon (1987) 'Introduction: Crime, the State and Critical Analysis', in Scraton, P. (ed.) *Law, Order and the Authoritarian State*, Milton Keynes: Open University Press.

Simpson, P. (2000) *Psycho Paths: Tracking the Serial Killer Through Contemporary American Film and Fiction*, Carbondale, IL: Southern Illinois University Press.

Sindall, R. (1990) *Street Violence in the Nineteenth Century: Media Panic or Real Danger?*, Leicester: Leicester University Press.

Skidmore, P. (1995) 'Telling Tales: Media Power, Ideology and the Reporting of Child Sexual Abuse', in D. Kidd-Hewitt and R. Osborne (eds) *Crime and the Media: The Post-Modern Spectacle*, London: Pluto Press.

Skidmore, P. (1998) 'Gender and the Agenda: News Reporting of Child Sexual Abuse', in Carter, C., G. Branston and S. Allan (eds) *News, Gender and Power*, London: Routledge.

Skogan, W. and M. Maxfield (1981) *Coping with Crime: Individual and Neighbourhood Reactions*, London: Sage.

Smith, S. (1984) 'Crime in the News', in *British Journal of Criminology*, Vol. 24, No. 3, pp. 289–95.

Smith, S. (1986) *Crime, Space and Society*, Cambridge: Cambridge University Press.

Sontag, S. (1983) *Illness as Metaphor*, London: Penguin.

Sontag, S. (2003) *Regarding the Pain of Others*, London: Penguin.

Soothill, K. and S. Walby (1991) *Sex Crime in the News*, London: Routledge.

Soper, K. (1999) 'Relativism and Utopianism: Critical Theory and Cultural Studies', in Aldred, N. and M. Ryle (eds) *Teaching Culture: The Long Revolution in Cultural Studies*, London: NIACE.

Sparks, R. (1992) *Television and the Drama of Crime: Moral Tales and the Place of Crime in Public Life*, Buckingham: Open University Press.

Sparks, R. (1993) 'Inspector Morse: "The Last Enemy"', in G. Brandt (ed.) *British Television Drama in the 1980s*, Cambridge: Cambridge University Press.

Sparks, R. (1996) 'Masculinity and Heroism in the Hollywood "Blockbuster": The Culture Industry and Contemporary Images of Crime and Law Enforcement', in *British Journal of Criminology*, Vol. 36, No. 3, pp. 348–60.

Sparks, R. (2001) 'Degrees of Estrangement: The Cultural Theory of Risk and Comparative Penology', in *Theoretical Criminology*, Vol. 5, No. 2, pp. 159–76.

Stallybrass, P. and A. White (1986) *The Politics and Poetics of Transgression*, London: Methuen.

Stanko, B. (1987) 'Typical Violence, Normal Precaution: Men, Women, and Interpersonal Violence in England, Wales and the USA', in Hanmer, J. and M. Maynard (eds) *Women, Violence and Social Control*, Basingstoke: Macmillan.

Stanko, B. (1988) 'Fear of Crime and the Myth of the Safe Home: A Feminist Critique of Criminology', in Yllo, K. and M. Bograd (eds) *Feminist Perspectives on Wife Abuse*, London: Sage.

Stanko, B. (1990) *Everyday Violence*, London: Pandora.

Stanko, B. (1997) 'Safety Talk: Conceptualising Women's Risk Assessment as a "Technology of the Soul"', in *Theoretical Criminology*, Vol. 1, No. 4, pp. 479–99.

Stedman Jones, G. (1971) *Outcast London: A Study in the Relationship Between Classes in Victorian Society*, Oxford: Oxford University Press.

Stevenson, N. (1999) *The Transformation of the Media: Globalisation, Morality and Ethics*, Harlow: Longman.

Stones, R. (2002) 'Social Theory, the Civic Imagination and Documentary Film: A Past-modern Critique of the "Bloody Bosnia" Season's *The Roots of War*', in *Sociology* 36(2): 355–75.

Studlar, G. (1985/1992) 'Masochism and the Perverse Pleasures of the Cinema', in Mast, G., M. Cohen, and L. Braudy (eds) *Film Theory and Criticism: Introductory Readings*, 4th edn, Oxford: Oxford University Press.

Surette, R. (1998) *Media, Crime and Criminal Justice: Images and Realities*, Belmont, CA: Wadsworth.

Sutton, R. and S. Farrall (2005) 'Gender, Socially Desirable Responding and the Fear of Crime: Are Women Really More Anxious about Crime?', in *British Journal of Criminology*, Vol. 45, No. 2, pp. 212–24.

Swift, J. (1726/1994) *Gulliver's Travels*, London: Penguin Popular Classics.

Sykes, G. (1958) *The Society of Captives*, Princeton, NJ: Princeton University Press.

Taylor, I. (1996) 'Fear of Crime, Urban Fortunes and Suburban Social Movements: Some Reflections on Manchester', in *Sociology*, Vol. 30, No. 2, pp. 317–37.

Taylor, I. (1997) 'Crime, Anxiety and Locality: Responding to the Condition of England at the End of the Century', in *Theoretical Criminology*, Vol. 1, No. 1, pp. 53–76.

Tester, K. (2001) *Compassion, Morality and the Media*, Buckingham: Open University Press.

Thomas, T. (2000) *Sex Crime: Sex Offending and Society*, Cullompton: Willan.

Thompson, E. P. (1963) *The Making of the English Working Class*, Harmondsworth: Penguin.

Thompson, E. P. (1977) *Whigs and Hunters: The Origin of the Black Act*. Harmondsworth: Penguin.

Thompson, E. P. (1978) *The Poverty of Theory and Other Essays*, London: Merlin.

Thompson, E. P. (1991) *Customs in Common*, London: Merlin Press.

Thompson, J. (1995) *The Media and Modernity: A Social Theory of the Media*, Cambridge: Polity.

Thompson, K. (1998) *Moral Panics*, London: Routledge.

Thornham, S. and T. Purvis (2005) *Television Drama: Theories and Identities*, Basingstoke: Palgrave Macmillan.

Thornton, S. (1994) 'Moral Panic, the Media and British Rave Culture', in Rose, A. and T. Rose (eds) *Microphone Fiends: Youth Music and Youth Culture*, London: Routledge.

Todorov, T. (1966/2000) 'The Typology of Detective Fiction', in Lodge, D. with N. Wood (eds) *Modern Criticism and Theory*, Harlow: Pearson Education Limited.

Todorov, T. (1973) *The Fantastic: A Structural Approach to a Literary Genre*, Cleveland, OH: Press of Case Western Reserve University.

Trend, D. (2007) *The Myth of Media Violence: A Critical Introduction*, Oxford: Blackwell.

Tuan, Y. (1979) *Landscapes of Fear*, New York: Pantheon Books.

Tuchman, G. (1978) *Making News: A Study in the Social Construction of Reality*, New York: Free Press.

Tunstall, J. (1971) *Journalists at Work*, London: Constable.

Turkle, S. (1988) 'Computational Reticence: Why Women Fear the Intimate Machine', in Kramare, C. (ed.) *Technology and Women's Voices*, London: Routledge and Kegan Paul.

Turley, D. (1986) 'The Feminist Debate on Pornography', in *Socialist Review*, Nos 87–88, May–August.

Turner, B. (1993) 'Outline of a Theory of Human Rights', in *Sociology*, 27(3):489–512.

Turner, G. (1996) *British Cultural Studies*, 2nd edn, London: Routledge.

Turner, G. (2001) *Film as Social Practice*, 3rd edn. London: Routledge.

Turner, J. (2007) 'The Trouble with Boys is They're just too Fickle', in *The Observer*, 4 March, p. 11.

Turner, V. (1974) *Dramas, Fields and Metaphors: Symbolic Action in Human Society*, Ithaca, NY: Cornell University Press.

Tyler, I. (2006) ' "Welcome to Britain": The Cultural Politics of Asylum', in *European Journal of Cultural Studies*, Vol. 9., No. 2, pp. 185–202.

Tyler, T. and F. Cook (1984) 'The Mass Media and Judgements of Risk: Distinguishing Impact on Personal and Societal Level Judgement', in *Journal of Personality and Social Psychology*, Vol. 47, pp. 693–708.

Ungar, S. (2001) 'Moral Panic Versus the Risk Society: the Implications of the Changing Sites of Social Anxiety', in *British Journal of Sociology*, Vol. 52, No. 2, pp. 271–91.

Valier, C. (2001) 'Criminal Detection and the Weight of the Past: Critical Notes on Foucault, Subjectivity and Preventative Control', in *Theoretical Criminology*, Vol. 5, No. 4, pp. 425–43.

Valier, C. and R. Lippens (2004) 'Moving Images, Ethics and Justice', in *Punishment and Society*, Vol. 6, No. 3, pp. 319–33.

van Zoonen, L. (1998) 'One of the Girls?: The Changing Gender of Journalism', in Carter, C., G. Branston and S. Allan (eds) *News, Gender and Power*, London: Routledge.

Vine, I. (1997) 'The Dangerous Psycho-logic of Media "Effects" ', in Barker, M. and J. Petley (eds) *Ill Effects: The Media/Violence Debate*, London: Routledge.

Virilio, P. (1986) *Speed and Politics*, New York: Semiotext(e).

Waddington, P. (1986) 'Mugging as a Moral Panic: A Question of Proportion' in *British Journal of Sociology*, Vol. 32, No. 2, pp. 245–59.

Waiton, S. (2007) *The Politics of Antisocial Behaviour: Amoral Panics*, London: Routledge.

Walklate, S. (1998) 'Excavating the Fear of Crime: Fear, Anxiety or Trust?', in *Theoretical Criminology*, Vol. 2, No. 4, pp. 403–18.

Walklate, S. (2000) 'Equal Opportunities and the Future of Policing', in Leishman, F., B. Loveday and S. Savage (eds) *Core Issues in Policing*, 2nd edn. Harlow: Longman.

Walklate, S. (2007) *Imagining the Victim of Crime*, Maidenhead: Open University Press.

Walklate, S. and K. Evans (1999) *Zero Tolerance or Community Tolerance? Managing Crime in High Crime Areas*, Aldershot: Ashgate.

Walkowitz, J. (1992) *City of Dreadful Delight: Narratives of Sexual Danger in Late Victorian London*, Chicago, IL: University of Chicago Press.

Wall, D. (2007) *Cybercrime: The Transformation of Crime in the Information Age*, Cambridge: Polity.

Watney, S. (1987/1997) *Policing Desire: Pornography, Aids and the Media*, 3rd edn. London: Cassell.

Watson, J. (1924) *Psychology from the Standpoint of a Behaviourist*, Philadelphia, PA: J. B. Linnicott Company.

Watt, I. (1957/72) *The Rise of the Novel*, Harmondsworth: Pelican.

Weeks, J. (1985) *Sexuality and its Discontents: Meanings, Myths and Modern Sexualities*, London: Routledge and Kegan Paul.

Weeks, J. (1989/2006) 'AIDs: The Intellectual Agenda', in Critcher, C. (ed.) *Critical Readings: Moral Panics and the Media*, Buckingham: Open University Press.

White, D. (1950) 'The Gatekeeper: A Case Study in the Selection of the News', in *Journalism Quaterly*, Vol. 27, pp. 383–90.

Wilkins, L. (1964) *Social Deviance: Social Policy, Action and Research*, London: Tavistock.

Wilkinson, I. (2001) *Anxiety in a Risk Society*, London: Routledge.

Wilkinson, I. (2005) *Suffering: A Sociological Introduction*, Cambridge: Polity.

Williams, P. and J. Dickinson (1993) 'Fear of Crime: Read all about it? The Relationship between Newspaper Crime Reporting and Fear of Crime', in *British Journal of Criminology*, Vol. 33, No. 1, pp. 33–56.

Williams, R. (1958/1966) *Culture and Society 1780–1950*, London: Penguin.

Williams, R. (1961) *The Long Revolution*, London: Chatto and Windus.

Williams, R. (1974/90) *Television: Technology and Cultural Form*, London: Routledge.

Williams, R. (1978) 'The Press and Popular Culture: An Historical Perspective', in Boyce, G., J. Curran and P. Wingate (eds) *Newspaper History*, London: Constable.

Williams, R. (1981) *Culture*, London: Fontana.

Williams, R. (1988) *Keywords: A Vocabulary of Culture and Society*, London: Fontana Press.

Wilson, B. (2007) *Decency and Disorder: The Age of Cant 1789–1937*, London: Faber and Faber.

Wilson, E. (1992) 'Feminist Fundamentalism: The Shifting Politics of Sex and Censorship', in Segal, L. and M. McIntosh (eds) *Sex Exposed: Sexuality and the Pornography Debate*, London: Virago Press.

Wilson, J. and G. Kelling (1982) 'Broken Windows', in *Atlantic Monthly*, March, pp. 29–38.

Wolfsfeld, G. (1997) *Media and Political Conflict: News from the Middle East*, Cambridge: Cambridge University Press.

Wolfsfeld, G. (2003) 'The Political Contest Model', in Cottle, S. (ed.) *News, Public Relations and Power*, London: Sage.

Wolfsfeld, G. (2004) *Media and the Path to Peace*, Cambridge: Cambridge University Press.

Wykes, A. (2001) *News, Crime and Culture*, London: Pluto Press.

Yar, M. (2006) *Cybercrime and Society*, London: Sage.

Young, A. (1996) *Imagining Crime: Textual Outlaws and Criminal Conversations*, London: Sage.

Young, J. (1971a) *The Drugtakers*, London: Paladin.

Young, J. (1971b) 'The Role of the Police as Amplifiers of Deviancy, Negotiators of Reality and Translators of Fantasy: Some Consequences of our Present System of Drug Control as seen in Notting Hill', in Cohen, S. (ed.) *Images of Deviance*, Harmondsworth: Penguin.

Young, J. (1973) 'The Myth of the Drug Taker in the Mass Media', in Cohen, S. and Young, J. (eds) (1973) *The Manufacture of News*, London: Constable.

Young, J. (1974) 'Mass Media, Drugs and Deviance', in Rock, P. and M. Mackintosh (eds) *Deviance and Social Control*, London: Tavistock.

Young, J. (1986) 'The Failure of Criminology: The Need for a Radical Realism', in Matthews, R. and J. Young (eds) *Confronting Crime*, London: Sage.

Young, J. (1987) 'The Tasks Facing a Realist Criminology', in *Contemporary Crises*, Vol. 11, pp. 159–83.

Young, J. (1999) *The Exclusive Society*, London: Sage

Young, J. (2007) 'Slipping Away – Moral Panics Each Side of "the Golden Age"', in Downes, D., P. Rock, C. Chinkin, and C. Gearty (eds) *Crime, Social Control and Human Rights: From Moral Panics to States of Denial. Essays in Honour of Stanley Cohen*, Cullompton: Willan.

Zedner, L. (2005) 'Securing Liberty in the Face of Terror: Reflections from Criminal Justice', in *Journal of Law and Society*, Vol. 32, No. 4, pp. 507–33.

Zelizer, B. (2005) 'The Culture of Journalism', in Curran, J. and M. Gurevitch (eds) *Mass Media and Society*, 4th edn. Oxford: Oxford University Press.

Žižek, S. (1992) *Looking Awry: An Introduction to Jacques Lacan through Popular Culture*, Cambridge, MA: MIT Press.

Žižek, S. (1993) *Tarrying with the Negative: Kant, Hegel, and the Critique of Ideology*, Durham, NC: Duke University Press.

Index

A Team, The 128
Abercrombie, Nicholas 12, 26, 29, 73–4, 81, 138
Abu Ghraib prison 147
Adam and Eve 8, *see also* Eve
Adorno, Theodor 29, 142, 183–4, 196n
aesthetics 31–2, 33, 57, 69–71, 95, 104, 125, 127, 138, 183, 194n
aggression 23–4
AIDS 151, 160, 167
Allan, Stuart 100, 142, 150, 159, 194n
Allen, Jessica 66–7
Allen, Richard 59
Alexander, Jeffrey 175–6, 179
Ally McBeal 114
alterity 185
Altheide, David 51
Althusser, Louis 33, 58
AMBER alert 179–80
Amusing Ourselves to Death 11
Anderson, Benedict 81
Anderson, Patricia 101
Andrews, Glen 42
Ang, Ien 68, 74
Angel Heart 62–3
anthropology 33, 53, 63, 72–3, 176
anti-social behaviour 42
anxieties 9, 22, 28, 39–40, 45, 48, 53–6, 75, 109, 154–5, 161, 165, 169–72
apparatus film theory 58–9, 62
Apollo 193n
Archer, Jeffrey 183
Aristotle 120–1, 196n
Arnold, Matthew 31
Ashes to Ashes 194n
As If 186
asylum-seekers 167–168, 186
Attwood, Feona 6
audiences 12
   active 26, 30, 34, 38, 57, 64–75
   ethnography 68–75, 183
   family 11, 67, 68, 74

   girls 25
   passive 21, 26, 34, 183
   spectatorship 58–64, 74
   television 65, 67, 115
   uses and gratifications 25–6, 29

Baccaglini, William 46
Badlands 112
Bahktin, Mikhail 82
bandits 83
Bandura, Albert 24
Banks, Mark 53, 71
Bannister, Jon 49
Barker, Martin 19, 20
Barnaby, Chief Inspector Tom 135
Barnett, Clive 186
Barrett, Andrew 84
Barthes, Roland 33–4, 119, 125–6, 184, 189n
Bates, Norman 112
Baudrillard, Jean 9, 173–4, 196n
Baudry, Jean-Louis 58–9
Bauman, Zygmunt 49, 50, 52, 55, 117, 185
Beck, Ulrich 48–9, 171
Becker, Howard 34, 148, 163
Beetham, Margaret 158
Beggars Opera, The 194n
Bell, Ian 87, 121
Bell, Vikki 153
Benedict, Helen 156, 159
Benjamin, Walter 29, 105–6
Bennett, Tony 32, 126
Benson, Rodney 150
Bentham, Jeremy 98, 105–6
Ben-Yehuda, Nachman 169
Beowulf 190n
Berry, Mike 66
Bertrand, Ina 12, 23, 67
Between the Lines 114, 135–6
Big Brother 117
Bill, The 110, 128, 133–4, 136
Biressi, Anita 87, 103

Birmingham Centre for Contemporary
    Cultural Studies 36, 166–7, 190n
Black, Jeremy 87
Blade Runner 62–3
blame 53
Bloch, Ernst 105
blogging 194n
Blood Simple 114
Bloody Chamber 191n
Blue Lamp, The 193n
Blue Velvet 114
Bogarde, Dirk 193n
Bond, James 124–7
Bondebjerg, Ib 116
Bonnie and Clyde 132
Booker, Christopher 22
Boorstin, Daniel 174–5
Borges, Jorge Luis 196n
Bourdieu, Pierre 148–50
Box, Steven 42
Boyden, Sgt Matthew 136
Boyle, Karen 27, 157, 195n
Boyle, Robert 97
Brand, Dana 105
Brecht, Bertolt 194n
Brewster, Ben 196n
Brookside 152
Brownmiller, Susan 5
Briggs, Asa 10, 29, 80, 81, 85, 86
Brighton Rock 112
Brown, Sheila 23
Brundson, Charlotte 69, 110, 115, 116, 133,
    135, 137, 141
Buckingham, David 20, 68
Buffy the Vampire Slayer 114
Bulger, James, 19, 117, 177–9
Burke, Peter 10, 29, 80, 81, 85
Burnside, Inspector Frank 134
Byron, Lord George Gordon 104, 192n

Cahiers du cinema 58
Cambridge University Public Opinion Project
    191n
Cameron, Deborah 155
Campbell, Alex 43–4
Campbell, Jan 61
Canterbury Tales 190n
Capote, Truman 186
Cape Fear 112
capitalism 29, 33, 95–6, 142–4, 173–4, 196n
carnivalesque 47, 79–83, 114, 191–2n
Car Wars 116
Casualty 110, 152
Carrabine, Eamonn 1, 97, 185, 192n
Carter, Angela   5, 191n–192n
Carter, Cynthia 20, 23, 27, 157, 158
Carver, PC Jim 136
Castel, Robert 52
Caveat for Common Cursitors 84
Cavendish, Gray 137
Cawelti, John 127
celebrity 8, 89–91, 96, 120, 158, 174
censorship 4, 6, 84–6, 100

Cervantes, Miguel de 82–3, 194n
Chandler, Raymond 107–8, 124
Chapman, Jessica 195n
Charters, Werrett Wallace 24
Chaytor, Henry 80
Chesterton, G. K. 106
Chibnall, Steve 85, 89, 91, 102, 148, 192n
child abduction 66, 177–8, 179–80
child abuse 64, 66, 135, 150–5
Child's Play 3 179
Childwatch 152
Chiricos, Ted 46
Chodorow, Nancy 61
Chomsky, Noam 37, 142–3
Christie, Agatha 106–7
cinema 11, 58–63, 74, 108, 110–15, 184
Clark, Kate 157
Clark, Stuart 86, 113
Clarke, Alan 130–1, 132–3
Clarke, John 107, 108, 109
class 20, 22, 31–2, 37, 47, 50, 63–4, 65,
    69–71, 88, 91, 95–6, 100, 103, 106–9,
    125, 129, 142–3, 148–50, 155–6, 158,
    169, 183–4, 192n
Clemmer, Donald, 164
Clerici, Christian 44
Clinton, President Bill 26
Cloward, Richard 164
Code 46 63
Coen Brothers 114
Cohen, Albert 164
Cohen, Stanley 1–4, 35–6, 40, 116–17, 151,
    162–6, 169, 172, 182, 187, 190n
Coleman, Cynthia-Lou 45
Coleridge, Samuel 91, 104
Collins, Wilke 193n
Colonel Jack 92
Color Purple, The 185
Columbine High School 19–20, 27
communication 10–11, 29, 30–3, 80–2, 85,
    95–6, 144–5, 166, 173–5, 179
Connell, Ian 20
Connell, DS Maureen
consumption 11, 29, 34, 38, 49–50, 52, 64,
    69, 73–75, 97, 111, 125
Coogan's Bluff 132
Cook, Fay 45
Cops, The 136
Corner, John 69
Cottle, Simon 144, 145, 148, 176–7, 181
Cracker 110, 137
Craib, Ian 191n
Crash 191n
Crawford, Adam 42
Crime Beat 116
crime reporting 80, 83–91, 100–103, 147,
    159–60, 175, 178
crime statistics 41, 101, 190n
Crimewatch UK 115–16
criminology
    academic and popular 120, 138, 186–7
    and the media 1–4, 34–8
    cultural 138

Home Office 35, 41, 162
Left realism and idealism 37, 42–3, 195–6n
National Deviancy Conference 162
social problem construction 6–7, 13, 34–5, 162, 182
Critcher, Chas 155, 162
critical theory 29, 142
Cronenburg, David 114, 191n
Cross, Simon 153, 154
Cryer, Sgt Bob 134
CSI: Crime Scene Investigation 110, 128, 137
Cuklanz, Lisa 156
cultivation analysis 26–8, 38, 40, 45
cultural relativism 57, 69–70
cultural theory 30–4, 36, 57, 182
culturalism 31
culture 12, 31–3, 57, 62–4, 69–74, 79–83, 87, 95, 100–1, 114, 127, 181–4
culture of fear 51–2
culture industry 29, 142, 184
Cumberbatch, Gary 13
Curran, James 69–70, 98, 100

Daily Mail, The 153, 157, 177, 178
Daily Mirror, The 176
Damon, Matt 111
Dando, Jill 117
Dangerfield 110, 137
Danse Macabre 193n
Davis, Lennard 8, 9, 92, 93, 94
Dalziel and Pascoe 109, 135
De Quincey, Thomas 104
Dead Ringers 191n
Dean, Trevor 192n
death 45, 55, 57
de Beauvoir, Simone 185
Debord, Guy 11, 173
deconstruction 145, 185, 189n
Defoe, Daniel 89–90, 92–3
Deleuze, Giles 61
Denzin, Norman 181
Departed, The 111
Derrida, Jacques 127, 145, 185, 189n, 194n
Descartes, René 62, 63, 97
desire 22, 38, 45, 48, 57, 59–61, 63, 75, 82, 91, 116–17, 169–70, 183, 192n
Deutsch, Sarah 137
deviancy amplification 35–6, 164–6
Dialectic of Enlightenment, The 29
Dickens, Charles 105
Dickinson, Julie 2, 46
DiCaprio, Leonardo 111
Diderot, Denis 97, 192n
Dietrich, Marlene 60
Dionysus 81, 193n
Dirty Harry 111, 132
Ditton, Jason 2, 40, 43, 46, 52, 190n
Dixon of Dock Green 110, 130–1, 132, 133–4
Dobash, Russell 115
Don Quixote 82–83
Doob, Anthony 28
Dostoevsky, Fydor 183
Douglas, Mary 53–4,

Doyle, Sir Arthur Conan 103,
Dracula 104, 192n
Dudley, Lord 192n
du Gay, Paul 12
Dupin, Auguste 103–5
Dutroux, Marc 152
du Vall, Claude 90
Duffy, James 2
Durkheim, Émile 35–6, 148, 166, 179, 181
Dworkin, Andrea 5
Dyer, Richard 184

Eagleton, Terry 96, 126
EastEnders 73, 137, 152
Eastwood, Clint 111, 132
Eco, Umberto 120, 124–6, 189n
effects research
behaviourism 23–4, 30, 182
bobo dolls 24
history 8–9, 13, 19–23, 37–8, 82–3
mass communications approaches 23–9
sociological functionalism 25, 182
Eisenstein, Elizabeth 80, 87
Ellis, John 11, 74
Ellroy, James 109
Empson, William 31
encoding/decoding 12, 30–4, 65, 67
Encyclopédie 97
Engels, Frederick 105
English Rogue Described, The 87
Enlightenment 29, 52, 80, 96–8, 101, 104, 142
Enquiry into the Causes of the Late Increase in Robbers 22
Epstein, Edward 146
ER 110
Ericson, Kai 164, 165, 166
Ericson, Richard 2, 37, 141, 146, 157
ethnicity 63–4, 65, 157 *see also* race; racism
Evans, Karen 52
Eve 122
Everyman 152
Executioner's Song, The 186
executions 79, 86–8, 98
Existenz 191n

Face/Off 111
Falklands War 144, 194n
Faller, Lincoln 83, 90
fantasy 21, 56, 193n
Farrall, Stephen 40, 43
fascism 29, 111
Featherstone, Mike 83
fear 22, 28, 38–40, 45, 48, 55, 91, 103, 104, 165–6, 171–2
fear of crime
criminological context 40–4
emotional complexity 39, 42, 182
feminist critiques 43–4, 182
media research 44–6, 67
rational/irrational debates 42–3, 51–2, 53–4
victimisation surveys 40–1, 43
Feeley, Malcolm 179

feminism 4–7, 13, 59–60, 114–15, 151, 155, 185–6 *see also* fear of crime; gender; pornography; post-feminism; power
FHM 159
Fiedler, Leslie 56
Fielding, Henry 22, 92
film noir 108–9
Financial Times 130
Firestone, Shulamith 59
Fishman, Mark 146
Fiske, John 22, 29, 47, 69, 74–5, 127–8, 167
flâneur 105, 107
Fly, The 191n
Folk Devils and Moral Panics: The Creation of the Mods and the Rockers 172, 190n
Ford, John 25
Foucault, Michel 33, 105–6, 158, 190n
Frankenstein 104, 192n
Frankfurt School 28–9, 32, 142, 150, 175
Frazer, Elizabeth 155
Freedman, Jonathan 24
Freud, Sigmund 23, 55, 58–9, 61, 179, 193n
Fromm, Erich 8
Frost, Inspector 'Jack' 109, 135
Fuery, Patrick 114
Full Monty, The 112
Furedi, Frank 51–2
Fyfe, Nick 49

Gadd, David 40
Galileo, Galilei 97
Gans, Herbert 146
Garafalo, James 41
Garbo, Greta 60
Gauntlett, David 24, 27
Gay, John 194n
gender 43, 45, 47, 59–61, 63–64, 65, 67, 68, 74, 103, 105–7, 108–9, 112, 114–15, 128, 134–5, 142, 143, 152–160
genre 58, 60, 62–3, 72, 79, 89, 92, 95, 100–1, 103–18, 120, 127–38
Gentleman's Magazine 94
Gentle Touch, The 134
Gerbner, George 26–8, 38, 40, 45, 189n
Get Carter 111
Gever, Martha 137
Ghosts 136
Giddens, Anthony 48–9
Gieber, Walter 146
Gilbert, Kevin 46
Gilchrist, Elizabeth 43
Gillespie, Marie 71, 191n
Gilroy, Paul 167
Girling, Evi 42, 51, 52
Girard, René 63–4
Gitlin, Todd 10, 188
Gladfelder, Hal 86, 87, 88, 90, 92
Glaister, Dan 148
Glasgow University Media Group 66
Godfather 111
Goffman, Erving 163
Golding, Peter 143, 145–6
Gomme, Ian 45

Good Fellas 111
Goode, Erich 169
Goodey, Jo 43, 190n
Gordon, Margaret 46
Grade, Michael, 190n
Gramsci, Antonio 31, 36–7
Greene, Graham 192n
Greer, Germaine 59
Gregory the Great, Pope 81
Grella, George 107
Griffin, Susan 5
Gross, Larry 26, 40
Guardian, The 153
Guattari, Felix 61
Gulf War 50, 144, 174, 194n
Gulliver's Travels 93
Gunter, Barrie 27
Gurevitch, Michael 147
Gusfield, Joseph 163–4

Habermas, Jürgen 95–6, 144–5, 185, 186, 194n
Hagerman, Amber 179
Hale, Chris 42, 44
Halford, Assistant Chief Constable Alison
Hall, Stuart 1–2, 12, 30–3, 64–5, 146, 166–7, 168–9, 195n
Hallin, Daniel 141
Hamilton, James 143
Hamilton, Thomas 152–3
Hamlet 122
Hammett, Dashiel 124
Hardy, Thomas 183
Harman, Thomas 84
Harrison, Chris 84
Hartley, John 22, 23, 26, 73–5
Hawkes, Terence 126
Head, Richard 87
Heartbeat 110
Heat 111
Heath, Prime Minister Edward 133
Heath, Linda 45, 46
Hebdige, Dick 190n
Hegel, Georg 62, 186
hegemony 31, 36–7, 47, 69, 166–7, 185, 190n
Herriot, James 183
Herman, Edward 37, 142–3
Hermes, Joke 71–2
Herzog, Herta 24
Hier, Sean 162, 172
Hill Street Blues 110, 134
Hind, James Captain 90
Hirsch, Foster 111
Hirsch, Paul 45
History of Sexuality 158
History of the Remarkable Life of John Sheppard, The 89–90
History of Violence, A 114
Hitchcock, Alfred 59–60, 112
Hobsbawm, Eric 83
Hobson, Dorothy 68
Hoggart, Richard 31–2
Hohendahl, Peter 96

Holby Blue 137
Holby City 110
Holland, Patricia 158, 159
Hollway, Wendy 51, 52, 54–5
Hollyoaks 137
Holmes, Sherlock 103–6
Holohan, Siobhan 63–4, 118
Homer, 191n
Homicide 137
Hood, Robin 83
Hooker, Evelyn 163
Hope, Tim 52
Hot Fuzz 112
Hough, Mike 41, 43
Horkheimer, Max 29, 142, 183
Howard, Michael 153
Howe, Adrian 151
Hubbard, Phil 48, 49
Hughes, Michael 45
Hughes, Peter 12, 23, 67
Hunt, Alan 51
Hunt, Chief Inspector Gene 137
Huntley, Ian 195n
Hurd, Geoff 128–30, 131
Hurricane Katrina 187
Hussein, Saddam 147–8
Hustle 137
Hutchings, Peter 106
hyperreality 9

identity 8, 43, 49, 62–4, 65, 71–2, 163, 172, 177, 191n
ideology 30–1, 36–8, 58, 61–5, 69, 142–3, 166–7, 169, 179, 183
Iliad, The 190n
illness 163, 168
Image, The 174
Image-Music-Text 33
In Cold Blood, 186
Index librorum prohibitorum 84, 192n
individualism 58, 80, 91, 105–6, 118
Information Centre About Asylum and Refugees 167–8
Innes, Martin 66
Inspector Morse 135
Internet 1, 6–7, 9, 148, 180, 194n
intertextuality 126–7, 189n
instrumental rationality 29, 196n
Irigaray, Luce 186

Jack the Ripper 102–3
Jacobs, Ronald 175–176, 179
Jameson, Frederick 138
Jancovich, Mark 58, 71
Jefferson, Tony 51, 52, 54–5
Jenkins, Philip 7, 152, 164
Jensen, Klaus 21
Jewkes, Yvonne 72, 162
John, Prince 83
Johnson, Samuel Dr 94, 121
journalism 31, 47, 83, 87, 90, 99, 141, 142–4, 146–50, 156, 159–60, 194n *see also* 'new journalism'

Joyce, James 191n
Juliet Bravo, 110, 134

Kael, Pauline 111
Kanka, Megan 153
Kant, Immanuel 62, 194n
Katz, Elihu 25, 75
Katz, Jack 46–7
Keane, John 117
Kelling, George 42
Kelly, Liz 154
Killias, Martin 44
King, Anna 191n
King, Rodney 147, 176
King Lear 122
King, Rodney 147
King, Stephen 193n
Kittler, Friedrich 173
Kitzinger, Jenny 66, 152, 154, 160
Knelman, Judith 100
Knight, Stephen 104, 193n
Knock, The 136
Kojak 111, 132
Kornhauser, William 28
Krays, The 112
Kristeva, Julie 189n
Kuhn, Annette 109

Lacan, Jacques 33, 58–9, 62–3, 191n
Lacey, Nick 110, 130
L.A. Confidential 109, 111
Lake, Peter 85
Langbein, John 88
late modernity 48–9, 64
Lasswell, Harold 29
Lauer, Josh 50
Law, Alex 52
Law and Order 137
Lawler, Steph 154
Lawrence, Regina 147
Lawrence, Stephen 63–4, 176–7, 186
Lazarsfield, Paul 24–5
Leavis, F.R. 31–2
Leavis, Q.D. 31–2
Lecter, Dr Hannibal 113
Lee, Murray 40
Lee, Spike 187
Leishman, Frank 117, 131, 134, 137
Leitch, Thomas 108
Lemert, Edwin, 163
Leonne, Serge 132
Leps, Marie-Christine 81, 98, 102
Lester, Marilyn 146
Lévinas, Emmanuel 185
Levinson, Paul 173
Lévi-Strauss, Claude 33, 45, 80, 123
Liebes, Tamar 73, 75
Life on Mars 137
Lincoln, Yvonna 181
Linebaugh, Peter 85, 87, 88
linguistics 33–4, 122
Lippens, Ronnie 118
Liquid Fear 55

Liska, Allen 46
Lister, Martin 173
literacy 81, 100
literary theory 30–4, 58, 61, 63, 82–3, 121–7
Livingstone, Sonia 23, 66–7, 71
Lloyd's Weekly Newspaper 101
Loaded 159
Loader, Ian 51
Lombroso, Cesare 103
London 22, 84, 87, 89, 90, 98, 102–3, 132–3, 176, 192n, 193n
Lock, Stock, and Two Smoking Barrells 114
Long Good Friday, The 112
Longhurst, Brian 11, 12, 29, 74, 81, 181
Los Angeles Times 184
Lotz, Amanda 71
Lull, James 68
Lupton, Deborah 42–3, 53, 55
Lury, Karen 110
Lynch, David 114

Macbeth 122
Mace, Jane 74
MacDonald, Glenn 28
MacDonald, Michael 173
MacKinnon, Catherine 5
Magnum Force 132
Mailer, Norman 186
Making of the English Working Class 32
Mancini, Paolo 141
Mandel, Ernest 8, 107
Manguel, Alberto 192n
Manning, Paul 147
Manufacture of the News: Deviance, Social Problems and the Mass Media 2–4
Marcuse, Herbert 29
Marlière, Philippe 149
Marlowe, Philip 108
Marnie 59–60
Marple, Miss
Martin, Kingsley 102
Maruna, Shadd 191n
Mason, Paul 117, 131, 134, 137
mass society 25, 28
Mathiesen, Thomas 116–17
Matthews, Julian 146
Matza, David 164
Mawby, Rob 135
Maxfield, Michael 42, 45, 48
Maxim 159
Mayfair 4
Mayhew, Henry 105
Mayhew, Patrick 2, 41
Mayne, Judith 61
McCall, Andrew 83
McCracken, Scott 104
McGuigan, Jim 69–70
McIntosh, Mary 84, 162
McKeon, Michael 87, 93, 94
McLaughlin, Eugene 191n, 193n
McLuhan, Marshall 35–6, 148, 163, 172–3

McNeish, Wallace 52
McRobbie, Angela 35, 114, 118, 152, 170–1, 185, 190n, 193n
mean world syndrome 27, 40
meaning 12, 13, 21, 26, 30, 33–4, 52, 57, 61, 65, 69–75, 122, 125–7, 142, 145, 168, 169–70, 189n
media research
    commercial laissez-faire model 3, 14, 182
    mass manipulative model 3, 14, 182
    methods 13, 21, 26–7, 29, 45–6, 65, 66–7, 71–5, 146–7, 167–8, 182, 191n
media technologies 10–12, 68–9, 71, 72, 87, 100, 147–8, 155–7, 171
Memento 63
Memoires of Monsieur Du Vall 90
memory 62–63, 66, 177, 178
Merrin, Will 175
Merton, Robert 24–5, 194n
Messent, Peter 109
Metz, Christian 58–9
Meyers, Marion 156–7
Miliband, Ralph 142
Miller, David 21, 66
Millett, Kate 59
Milner, Claire 6
Milton, John 91
Minority Report 63
Mirren, Helen 114
modernity 52, 116, 125, 149, 165
Modleski, Tania 60
Moll Flanders 8, 92–93
Molotch, Harvey 146
Monk, Claire 112
Montesquieu, Baron de La Brède et de 97
Moonstone, The 193n
moral indignation 35, 164–5, 170
moral panic
    classic theory 35–6, 162–8
    cultural boundaries 54, 165–6
    criticisms 37–8, 168–72
    mediatized public crises 175–80
    postmodern media spectacles 172–5
Moretti, Franco 104, 106, 192n
Morgan, Michael 27
Morgan, Robin 4
Morley, David 65, 66, 68, 71, 141
Morphology of the Folk Tale 122–3
Morris, Meagan 69
Morrison, Blake 177–8, 186
Morse, Inspector 109–10
Mullholland Drive 114
Mulvey, Laura 58–61
'Murder Considered as One of the Fine Arts, On' 104
'Murders in the Rue Morgue, The' 103–6
Murdoch, Graham 24, 143, 145–6
Murdoch, Rupert 158–9
myth 8, 33, 83, 91, 102, 105, 123, 125, 128–30, 155
Mythologies 33

narrative 33, 59, 62, 73, 80, 86–92, 94–5, 101–3, 107–9, 113, 119–20, 122–8, 130, 135, 169, 175–7
Nashe, Thomas 87
Nationwide 65, 73, 141
Nava, Mica 152
Neale, Steve 60
Nelson, William 91
Neveu, Erik 150
'new journalism' 14, 101–3, 158
Newgate prison 8, 88, 89–90, 92, 93
News of the World 101, 153–4
news production
  cultural conflict 37
  'hard' and 'soft' divide 143–4, 148, 150, 158, 174
  processes 3, 14, 36–7, 67–8, 141–50, 165
  reporting of crime statistics 41
  spatial organization of 146–7
Newsnight 144
newsworthiness 36, 148
Newton, Sir Isaac 97
Nightingale, Virginia 25, 30, 34
Nixon, President Richard 133
Norris, Christopher 174
North Briton 98
Northcliffe, Lord Alfred 101, 102
Northern Ireland, 66, 144, 195n
Norton, Rictor 89
Notorious 60
novel
  detective 123–4, 193n
  rise of 91–5,
  reading 72, 73–4
Nuts 195n
NYPD Blue 130, 137

obscene images 5, 22, 174
Observer, The 153
Odyssey 122, 191n
O'Donnell, Ian 6
Oedipus Tyrannos 122
Ohlin, Lloyd 164
Old Bailey 88
O'Keefe, Garrett 46
O'Mahony, David 42
Once Upon a Time in the West 132
oral tradition 79–83, 85
Order of Things, The 33
Ordinary of Newgate, The 88
Outsiders 163
O'Toole, Laurence 6
Othello 122
Oz obscenity trial 3–4

paedophilia 7, 152–5, 195n
Palmer, Gareth 115, 116
Pamela 92
Pandora 8
Panopticon 105–6, 116–17
Panorama 152
Pantazis, Christina 40
Paranoid Parenting 51

parenting 50–51, 64, 66, 165, 179
Park, Robert 195n
Parris, Matthew 155
Patterson, Chris 147
Payne, Sarah 153–4
Pearson, Geoffrey 20, 22
Peckinpah, Sam 132
Penn, Arthur 132
Penthouse 4
Perlmutter, David 120, 129–30, 193n
Petley, Julian 20
Petraitis, John 45
Philo, Greg 21, 66
Picard, Liza 22, 84, 85
Picard, Raymond 126
picaresque 86–7, 92
Playboy 4
Plato 21, 186
Pliny 196n
pleasure 47, 56, 57, 59–60, 69, 72, 75, 121, 138
Plummer, Ken 119–20
Poe, Edgar Allen 103–105, 107
Police Camera Action 116
police procedural 109–11, 113, 120, 128–38
policing 98, 105–7, 120, 129–130, 133, 156, 176–7, 192n
Policing the Crisis: Mugging, the State and Law Order 36–7, 166–7, 168–70, 195n
Polidori, John 192n
polysemy 34, 65
pornography
  child 6–7
  feminist debates 4–6
  industry 4, 6, 9
Postman, Neil 11
postmodern 9, 52, 70, 114, 124, 173–5, 184, 193n
post-feminism 114–15
post-structuralism 34, 52, 189n
Potter, Lynda Lee 178
power
  bureaucratic 105–6, 146–7
  charismatic 192n
  patriarchal 47, 58–9, 60–61, 186
  pluralist perspectives on 3, 25, 30, 37–8, 70, 182
  Marxist perspectives on 30–1, 37–8, 145–6, 166–7, 183
  state 80, 98, 144
  textual 21, 65, 69, 183
Pribram, Deirdre 61
press
  freedom 98
  indoctrination 85
  local and regional 2, 46, 154, 155–7
  ownership 142–4
  radical 100
  regulation 84, 94, 100, 149
  sexualization of 158–60
  see also crime reporting; journalism; news production
Prime Suspect 114, 134–5

Prometheus 8, 52, 122
propaganda 24–5, 28, 81, 85, 142–4
Propp, Vladimir 122–3, 125
pseudo-events 174–5
Psycho 112
psychoanalysis
    and moral panic theory 170
    criticisms of 55, 61
    defence mechanisms 54
    Lacanian 58–60, 62–3
    mirror phase 58–9, 191n
    object relations 61
Freudian 23, 55, 58, 61
public sphere 11, 80, 95–8, 115–16, 144–5,
    161, 186
Pulp Fiction 112, 114
Purvis, Tony 75, 114–15, 128

Quinn, Katie 42

race 103, 159, 166–8, 171, 177, 178, 192n,
    193n
racism 64, 134–5, 167–8, 176–7, 195n
Radway, Janice 72
Rafter, Nicole 120–1, 138, 187
Rantzen, Esther 152
Raphael, Chad 141
Raw and the Cooked, The 123
Rawlings, Phillip 88, 89, 120, 186
realism
    generic codes of 128
    grotesque 82–3
    in novels 121, 184
realist
    forms of representation 27, 72, 94, 130,
        184
    see also criminology
reality
    and the real 62–3, 169–70, 181–2, 191n
    and hyperreality 9, 174–5
    distortion 2–4, 36, 40, 123
Reality Television 8, 99, 115–17, 136, 141,
    184
Rear Window 59
Redmond, Siobhan 114
Regan, Jack 132, 134, 135
Reid-Nash, Kathleen 46
Reiner, Robert   2, 23, 37, 66–7, 110
Reisman, David 28
religion 80–2, 83, 86, 87, 92, 97, 103, 165,
    166, 193n
Repulsion 112
resistance 47, 60, 69–70
Reservoir Dogs 112
Reynolds' Newspaper 101
Richards, I. A. 31
Richardson, Samuel 92
Rinconete and Cortadilo 194n
Rise of the Novel 91
risk 53–54, 103, 183
risk society 39, 48–9, 162, 171–2
rituals 79, 81–2, 88, 107, 123, 175, 177
Robertson, Geoffrey 98

Robinson Crusoe 92
Rock, Paul 146
Rockford Files 132
Rogers, Pat 90
Romantic movement 92, 101, 104, 127, 192n
Root, Jane 74
Rosengren, Karl 21
Ross, Dorothea 24
Ross, Karen 25, 34
Ross, Sheila 24
Rousseau, Jean-Jacques 97
Roxana 92
Ruddock, Andy 21, 26
Ruggiero, Vincenzo 120, 194n
Ryall, Tom 127

Sacco, Vincent 45
Saussure, Ferdinand de 33
Savage Mind, The 123
Sayer, Andrew 70, 183
Sayers, Dorothy 106
scapegoat mechanisms 63–4, 167, 171
Schechter, Harold 56
Scheff, Thomas 163
Schlesinger, Philip 37, 44, 141, 144, 146,
    190n
Schubart, Rikke 179
Schudson, Michael 141, 146
Schur, Edwin 163
Schmid, David 120
Scraton, Phil 148
Screen 58, 59, 61
Scrutiny 31
Seaton, Jean 24, 25, 141
security 28, 48–51, 67, 71, 117, 180
Segal, Lynne 5
Seiter, Ellen 71
semiotics 33–34, 69, 165, 173–4, 182, 183
Sennett, Richard 48
September 11 2001 39, 49, 117, 143, 171,
    174
Seu, Bruna 118
Se7en 113
sex
    construction of crime news 2, 151–60, 167
    and violence 2, 5, 19, 22, 31, 102–3, 115,
        150–8, 192n
Sex and the City 114
Sex Crime in the News 151
Sexed Crime in the News 151
sexuality 5–6, 59, 88–9, 109, 112, 114, 124,
        158–60, 165, 168, 169, 191n, 192n
sexualisation 8, 103, 148, 151–60, 195n
Shaaber, Matthias 85
Shakespeare, William 22, 91, 121, 122, 172,
    190n
Shallow Grave 114
Shamela 92
Shapland, Joanna 48
Sharpe, James 88
Shelley, Mary 192n
Shelley, Percy 91, 104
Shepherd, Leslie 83

Sheppard, Jack 89–90
Shields, Rob 83
Shortest Way with the Dissenters, The 90
Siegel, Don 132
Sigel, Lisa 4
Signorelli, Nancy 27
Silence of the Lambs 113
Silent Witness 110, 137
Silverman, Jon 154
Silverstone, Roger 67–8, 74, 179, 183
Sim, Joe 196n
Simon, Jonathan 179–80
Simpson, Philip 113
Sindall, Rob 101
Skidmore, Paula 66, 159
Skogan, Wesley 42, 45, 48
Smith, PC 'Smiffy' 136
Smith, Susan 2, 48
soap opera 68, 73–4, 127–8, 137
social constructionism 7, 13
Sociology
    of deviance 13, 30, 34–7, 163–4, 166
    of news production 146
    University of Chicago 195n
Sontag, Susan 118, 194n
Soothill, Keith 151, 155–6
Soper, Kate 183
Sophocles 122
Sopranos, The 111–12
Spacey, Kevin 113
Sparks, Richard 1, 28, 35, 42, 43, 45, 51, 52,
    53, 110, 130, 133, 169,
spectacle 11, 79, 96, 173
Spectator 96
Spellbound 60
Spillane, Mickey 125
Spooks 136, 137
sports utility vehicle 50
Stallybrass, Peter 82, 97
Stanko, Elizabeth 13, 43, 182
Starsky and Hutch 112, 132, 134
status 25, 69, 87, 92, 107–8, 126, 164, 165
Stedman Jones, Gareth 102
Stello, Cindy 71
stereotyping 34, 36, 43, 148
Stevenson, Nick 117
Stevenson, Robert Louis 103, 193n
Stoker, Bram 192n
Stones, Rob 118
storytelling 21, 80–3, 119–20, 122–7, 192n
Strange Case of Dr Jekyll and Mr Hyde, The
    103, 193n
structuralism 32–4, 123, 125–6, 128,
    189n–190n
Structural Anthropology 123
structure of feeling 32
Studlar, Gaylyn 60
subcultures 88, 164–7, 164–7
subjectivity 47, 58–62, 72, 105, 180, 191n
Sun, The 144, 157, 159, 176, 179
Sunday Express, The 153
Superman 125
Surette, Ray 24

Suspicion 60
surveillance 26, 49, 105–6, 116–17
Sutcliffe, Peter 156
Sutton, Robbie 43
Sweeney, The 110, 128–9, 132–4, 135
Swift, Jonathan 93
Sydney, Sir Phillip 125
Sykes, Gresham 164
synoptic 116–17

taboo 56
Tale of Gamelyn 83
Tarantino, Quentin 112
Tatler 96
Taylor, Damilola 117
Taylor, Ian 50–51, 52, 162
technological determinism 11
television 11, 26–8, 30, 45, 65, 67, 68–9,
    73–5, 110, 114–18, 127–38, 143–4,
    149–50, 173, 180
Tennison, DI Jane 114, 134–5
terrorism 39, 117, 143, 171
Tester, Keith 118
Thatcher, Prime Minister Margaret 167,
    194n, 195n
Thatcherism 112, 195n
Thaw, John 132, 135
Thomas, Terry 153
Thompson, E. P. 32, 189n-90n, 192n
Thompson, John 9
Thompson, Kenneth 162, 172, 178
Thompson, Robert 178
Thornham, Sue 75, 114–15, 128
Thornton, Sarah 170–1
Threepenny Opera, The 194n
Times, The 152, 155, 176
Titus Andronicus 190n
Todorov, Tzvetan 123–4, 125, 127
Tom Jones 92
Trainspotting 112
Trend, David 56
Tristes Tropiques 123
transgression 8, 82, 91–2, 113, 114, 122, 157
Tuan, Yi-Fu 56
Tuchman, Gaye 146
Tulloch, John 42–3, 53, 55
Tumber, Howard 37, 141, 144, 146, 190n
Tunstall, Jeremy 146
Turley, Donna 6
Turner, Bryan 118
Turner, Graeme 12, 61, 67, 184
Turner, Janice 195n
Turner, Victor 176
Turpin, Dick 90
Tyburn 88, 89
Tyler, Imogen 167, 186
Tyler, DI Sam 137
Tyler, Tom 45

Ulysses 191n
Understanding Media 172–3
Unfortunate Traveller, The 87
Ungar, Sheldon 162, 172

urban change 37, 42, 48, 69, 95–6, 98, 105–6
urban fortress living 49
urbanism 48–53
urbanization 35
Uses of Literacy, The 31

Vagg, Jon 48
Valier, Claire 41, 118
Van Zoonen, Liesbet 142, 159, 160
Venables, Jon 178
Vertigo 59–60
victims and victimisation
    anger 46, 190n
    'ideal' 157
    news stories 2, 155
    on television 26
    see also fear of crime
video 51, 68, 73–4, 147, 178, 194n, 195n
Videodrome 191n
Vietnam war 194n
Vincent, 135
Vine, Ian 24
violence
    against women 13, 43, 182, 192n, 196n
    cinematic 114, 132, 194n
    construction of crime news 2, 165, 176
    mediated 21
    on television 23, 26–7, 131–2, 134, 189n
    profiles 26
    sexual 43, 151, 155–8, 195n
    video 9, 19–20,179
    See also sex and violence
Virgin or Vamp: How the Press Covers Sex Crimes 156
Virilio, Paul 173, 180
Visions of Social Control 190n
Voltaire, 97, 192n

Waddington, Peter 37, 169
Waiton, Stuart 172
Waking the Dead 110, 137
Walby, Sylvia 151, 155–6
Walklate, Sandra 13, 41, 43, 51, 52, 55, 56, 134, 182
Walkowitz, Judith 101, 102, 103, 105, 156
Wall, David 6
Walpole, Sir Robert 94
Watergate 176
Watney, Simon 5, 168, 169–70
Watson, John 23–4
Watt, Ian 91

Wayward Puritans 166
Weaver, Kay 20, 23, 27, 157
Weeks, Jeffrey 160, 168
Wells, Holly 195n
West, Fred 152, 195n
West, Rosemary 152, 195n
When the Levee Broke 187
White, Allon 82, 97
White, David 146
Whiting, Roy 153
Wild at Heart 114
Wild Bunch, The 132
Wilkes, John 98
Wilkins, Leslie 35, 164
Wilkinson, Iain 54, 55, 118
Williams, Paul 2, 46
Williams, Raymond 32, 100, 101, 150, 173, 184
Wilson, Ben 192n
Wilson, David 154
Wilson, Elizabeth 5
Wilson, James 42
Wire in the Blood 110, 137
witchcraft 85–6, 154, 164
Wolfsfeld, Gadi 145
Woman with her Throat Cut 190n
Woodward, Louise 63–4
Woollacott, Janet 126
Wordsworth, William 91, 104
World in Action 152
Wycliffe, DS Charles 135
Wykes, Maggie 195n

X-Files, The 136

Yar, Majid 4
Young, Alison 1, 106
Young, Jock 2–4, 35–7, 40, 42, 162–6, 169, 172, 182, 195–6n
youth
    crime 22, 34, 166–7, 178
    cultures 170
    idealized images 20
    see also subcultures

Z-Cars 128–9, 130, 132, 133–4, 136
Zedner, Lucia 117
Zelizer, Barbie 142
Zeus 8
Žižek, Slavoj 62–63
Zodiac 113
Zoo 195n